RETAIL PET SUPPLY MANUAL

NELSON MILLER

Edited by PAUL A. SETZER

Designed by
RICHARD BROCKMAN

 Harcourt Brace Jovanovich
New York

ISBN 0-15-003246-3

Dedicated to my loving wife, Aggie, whose encouragement and patience was invaluable; to my children, Gregory, Taffy, Clifford and Christopher, who have kept our home a veritable pet shop through the years and have made this book a necessity.

My special thanks to Ole Bjornstad of Cappet Corporation, Alexandria, Virginia, one of the great pet supply distributors in America.

Acknowledgement: The author and publisher would like to thank Raymond Ungemach, Pet/Mark, St. Louis, Missouri, for his valuable contribution of materials for the chapters on "the second store" and "personnel."

contents

advertising sponsor messages

Advertisements in the following Sponsor Section
have helped make this RETAIL MANUAL
possible. It is an initial reference to the kinds of
products, pets and services available to you!

We're Pet Shop People!

We're pet shop people—we know you—we know your problems and how important every dollar is. Because we know you, we know your needs. That's why Longlife makes every effort to offer a long line of pet products… everything from fish food to flea and tick killing collars. A whole range of pet products is available from us…to you! Yes, we're pet shop people.

LONGLIFE ®

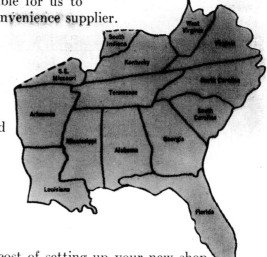

Distinction.

Oster PET PRODUCTS
put the 'life' in a dog's life
...and profits in yours!

OSTER SMALL ANIMAL GROOMING

NEW All Color Coat Brightener Shampoo Special non-bleaching formula conditions coats, adds sparkle and sheen, rinses thoroughly. Gallon.

NEW White Coat Shampoo keeps white dogs truly white, highlights any coat color. Non-bleaching, conditioning. 12 oz. and gallon.

Protein Shampoo Protein additives strengthen coats. Heightens colors, adds sheen. 12 oz. and gallon.

Cream Rinse Special "no snarl" formula removes tangles, makes coat easy to brush. 12 oz. and gallon.

Coat and Skin Conditioner Moisturizer and conditioner in easy-to-use aerosol spray revitalizes coats. 11½ oz. aerosol can.

Model A-5 Detachable Blade Small Animal Grooming Clipper

Model 123 Pet Groomer Clipper Kit

Model 269 Professional Cage and Table Dryer

Model 113 Lucky-Dog Clipper

Here's a great—and growing—name in grooming products to help pets look and feel their best, while helping *you* build bigger sales and added profits through repeat business. Take a name famous for top quality for decades…add carefully formulated, thoroughly tested products that really deliver all they promise…package them in attractive designs that tell and sell busy shoppers—and you have an unbeatable line of "pet approved" profit winners. Including a full line of shampoos pH balanced for the alkaline-acid ratio that provides best grooming and conditioning yet won't remove protein or weaken hair. See your Oster pet supply distributor now!

PRODUCTS SUPERMARKET

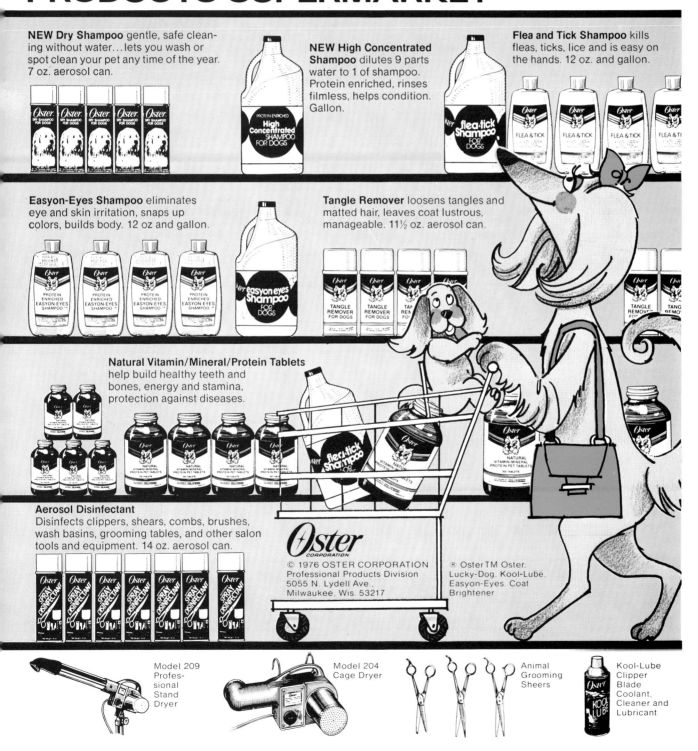

NEW Dry Shampoo gentle, safe cleaning without water…lets you wash or spot clean your pet any time of the year. 7 oz. aerosol can.

NEW High Concentrated Shampoo dilutes 9 parts water to 1 of shampoo. Protein enriched, rinses filmless, helps condition. Gallon.

Flea and Tick Shampoo kills fleas, ticks, lice and is easy on the hands. 12 oz. and gallon.

Easyon-Eyes Shampoo eliminates eye and skin irritation, snaps up colors, builds body. 12 oz and gallon.

Tangle Remover loosens tangles and matted hair, leaves coat lustrous, manageable. 11½ oz. aerosol can.

Natural Vitamin/Mineral/Protein Tablets help build healthy teeth and bones, energy and stamina, protection against diseases.

Aerosol Disinfectant
Disinfects clippers, shears, combs, brushes, wash basins, grooming tables, and other salon tools and equipment. 14 oz. aerosol can.

Oster
CORPORATION

© 1976 OSTER CORPORATION
Professional Products Division
5055 N. Lydell Ave.,
Milwaukee, Wis. 53217

® Oster TM Oster.
Lucky-Dog. Kool-Lube.
Easyon-Eyes. Coat
Brightener

Model 209 Professional Stand Dryer

Model 204 Cage Dryer

Animal Grooming Sheers

Kool-Lube Clipper Blade Coolant, Cleaner and Lubricant

6 Month Flea Protection!

FLEA FREE 30

Flea Free 30 is the aerosol flea killer that gives dogs up to one month protection with each application and, for the average dog, up to 6 applications per can. It kills fleas quickly from head to tail and can be used on bedding for a thorough job.

Flea Free 30 is available in distinctive packaging... an improved design for dynamic consumer shelf appeal. Don't delay . . . Order Today.

PULVEX

PULVEX DIVISION - Burroughs Wellcome Co.
Research Triangle Park, N.C. 27709

17

There's more than one live arrival guarantee in this business.

But none like ours.

When you order fish from Fine Fish Farms, Inc., you must be satisfied with your shipment when it arrives or you get new fish. It's as simple as that.

That means dead fish and the air freight on them will be credited toward your next order. Or if you prefer, your money will be refunded.

It means all the fish you receive from Fine Fish Farms, Inc. are the best obtainable within the size and price range you've ordered.

We can give you a guarantee like this when the other guys

can't for one reason and one reason only. Our conditioning program.

Every import that you buy from Fine Fish Farms, Inc. has been conditioned in our

holding facilities for seven full days, minimum.

So they get a chance to become accustomed to changes in water temperature, hardness and pH. So the injured, weak or diseased fish show up at our place instead of yours.

Conditioned fish. Guaranteed fish by Fine Fish Farms, Inc. They'll take a lot of the livestock losses off your hands.

Write on your letterhead for a complete price list. Or just call 800-327-7104. Florida dealers call collect 305-625-0457.

GUARANTEED FISH FROM FINE FISH FARMS, INC.

Breeders, Importers, Suppliers of Fine Tropical Fish
3475 NW 187th Street, Miami, Florida 33054

Profit-Making Lines. Co-op Advertising. Sales Aids.

Fish, dogs, cats, hamsters, gerbils, birds. We make fine foods, accessories, and just about everything else for all kinds of pets. And with the famous Geisler name on these products, you've got sure-fire sales makers.

In addition, Geisler has a unique, traffic-building co-op advertising program. It shows you how to promote your store and backs you up with the ads and merchandising ideas you need to increase sales...increase profits.

So whether you're already running a well established aquarium or pet shop — or just setting one up — or expanding one — Geisler can help you to do better.

In fact, we'll gladly show you how. Free. Just write or phone Geisler at 800-228-9031 and we'll give you ideas and useful techniques for more and faster sales with one of the best-selling, highest profit lines in the industry.

Geisler
FOR THE LOVE OF YOUR PET

A ConAgra Company

3902 LEAVENWORTH ST., OMAHA, NEB. 68105
30 VALINTINO ROAD, FAIRFIELD, N.J. 07006

THE GEISLER HOT LINE: for immediate assistance or service call us, toll free, at (800) 228-9031.

We've got you covered.

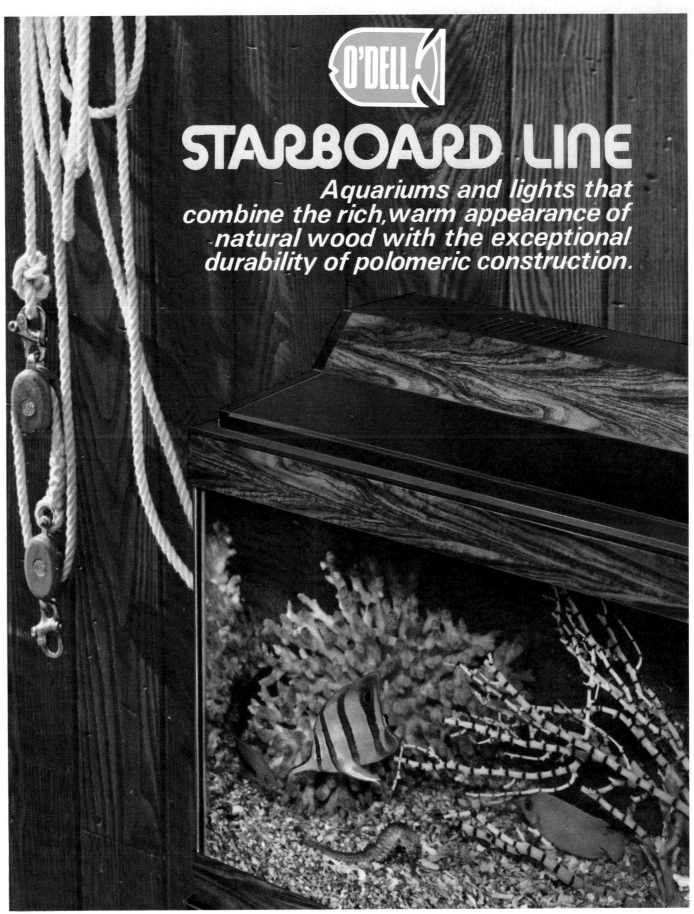

STARBOARD LINE

Aquariums and lights that combine the rich, warm appearance of natural wood with the exceptional durability of polomeric construction.

Distinctive in styling and beauty, Starboard Line by O'Dell opens a wide, new concept in aquariums and lights . . . all with wood-grain finish . . . in an exciting range of sizes and styles, from 5½ to 135 gallons.

O'DELL MANUFACTURING INC.
Saginaw, Michigan • Canton, Georgia

Lambert Kay™
Manufacturers of Quality Pet Care Products.

NUTRITIONAL SUPPLEMENTS

Linatone® Food Supplements for Skin & Coat - for Dogs, Cats, Hamsters, Birds.

Theralin® Vitamin-Mineral Supplements in Powder and Tablet Form for Puppies, Dogs and Cats.

Theralin® Puppy Liquid Vitamins (water soluble)

Avitron® Liquid Vitamin Supplement for birds, cats, hamsters, gerbils, guinea pigs, mice, rats and monkeys. Also - Calcium/Phosphorus Powder, Cal-D-Trons® calcium/phosphorus tablets, pure Norwegian Cod Liver Oil, Stim-U-Wate® High Calorie Food Supplement and Wheat Germ Oil.

TWINCO® PRODUCTS

For grooming: Dog Rake, Combs, Stripper Comb, Slicker Brushes and Nail Trimmer.

Collars & Leads: High Quality American made brass and steel chain collars and leads. Nickel and chrome plated.

GROOMING AIDS

No Tangle® Detangler, Pro-Groom® Coat Conditioner, Tangle Free® Rinse, Pet Duet® Cologne and De-Scent™ aerosol deodorant.

SHAMPOO FOR PETS

Medi-Cleen® Medicated Shampoo, Zenox® Flea & Tick Shampoo, Snowy-Coat® for white coats, Dark Coat for dark coats, Premium® Shampoo, Terri-Coat®, Pro-Coat® Tearless Shampoo for Dogs and Cats, Herbal Essence, Wheat Germ Shampoo and aerosol Foam Shampoo for Dogs.

FLEA & TICK CONTROL PRODUCTS

Victory® and Victory® 120 Flea Collars for Dogs and Cats, Flea & Tick Dip, Lawn & Kennel Dust, Kennel Insecticide Concentrate, Flea Shield® aerosol spray for Dogs and Cats, Flea & Tick Powder for Dogs and Cats, Indoor Foggers and Zenox® Flea & Tick Shampoo.

TRAINING AIDS

Boundary® Indoor/Outdoor Dog & Cat Repellent aerosol.

Good Boy™ Housebreaking Aid

CAT FAMILY PRODUCTS

Femalt® Hairball Remedy, Linatone® Food Supplement for Skin & Coat, Theralin® Cat Tablets, Pro-Coat® Cat Shampoo, Victory® and Victory® 120 Flea Collars, Flea Shield® for Cats and Concentrated Flea & Tick Powder for Cats.

HEALTH AIDS

Avimycin™ antibiotic tablets for Birds.

Chlorophyll Tablets for pet odors.

Cortisynth®, First Aid Skin Cream for Dogs and Cats.

Ear-Rite® Ear Cleaning Formulation.

Eye-Brite® Eye Wash (sterile) for Dogs and Cats.

Femalt® Hairball Remedy for Cats.

Happy Breath® Dog Dental Spray Powder.

Tranquapet® Calmative for Dogs.

Pet Pectillin®. Aids in treatment of diarrhea in dogs, cats & birds.

Worming Tablets for Puppies, Dogs and Cats.
Worming Capsules for Puppies, Dogs and Cats.

Available Through Pet Supply Wholesalers.

Lambert Kay, Div. of Carter-Wallace, Inc., Cranbury, NJ 08512

13

FULL LINE LIVESTOCK SUPPLIER

TROPICAL FISH

GUPPIES
COMMON GUPPIES
FANCY GUPPIES
GOLD FLAMED GUPPIES
VEILTAIL GUPPIES
DELTA VEILTAIL GUPPIES
COBRA VEILTAIL GUPPIES
MULTI-COLORED GUPPIES
SUPER DELUXE DELTA GUPPIES

MOLLIES
ALBINO MOLLIES
ALBINO LYRETAIL MOLLIES
BLACK MOLLIES
BLACK LYRETAIL MOLLIES
GREEN SAILFIN MOLLIES
MARBLE MOLLIES
SPHENOPS MOLLIES

SWORDTAILS
PAINTED SWORDS
BLACK SWORDTAILS
BRICK SWORDTAILS
BRICK TUXEDO SWORDTAILS
BRICK WAG SWORDTAILS
GOLD SWORDTAILS
GOLD TUXEDO SWORDTAILS
GOLD WAG SWORDTAILS
GREEN SWORDTAILS
HI FIN SWORDTAILS
LYRETAIL SWORDTAILS
RED TUXEDO SWORDTAILS
RED VELVET SWORDTAILS
RED WAG SWORDTAILS

PLATIES
BLACK PLATY
BLUE PLATY
GOLD CRESCENT PLATY
GOLD WAG PLATY
HI FIN PLATY
MARIGOLD VARIATUS
MARIGOLD WAG VARIATUS
PAINTED PLATY
RED PLATY
RED TUXEDO PLATY
RED WAG PLATY
SUNSET VARIATUS
MARIGOLD TUXEDO VARIATUS

BARBS
ALBINO TIGER BARB
BLACK RUBY BARB
CHERRY BARB
CLOWN BARB
GOLD BARB
ROSY BARB
TIGER BARB

DANIOS
GIANT DANIOS
LEOPARD DANIOS
PEARL-GOLD DANIOS
ZEBRA DANIOS

PANCHEX
GOLD AUSTRAL PANCHEX
CHOCOLATE PANCHEX

BUBBLE NEST BUILDERS
ALBINO PARADISE
RED PARADISE
BETTAS MALE LARGE
BETTAS MALE SHOW
BETTAS FEMALE
BLUE GOURAMI
DWARF GOURAMI
GOLDEN GOURAMI
GREEN KISSING GOURAMI
KISSING GOURAMI
OPALINE GOURAMI
PEARL GOURAMI

TETRAS (TANK RAISED)
AUSTRALIAN RAINBOWS
BLACK TETRA
BLACK PHANTOM TETRA
BLIND CAVES
BLOODFIN
GLASS FISH
GLOW LITE
HI FIN BLACK TETRA
JUMBO NEONS
EMPEROR TETRA
LEMON TETRA
PENGUINS
RED MINOR SERPAE
WHITE CLOUDS

GOLDFISH

CICHLIDS
BLACK ANGEL
BLACK LACE VEIL ANGEL
BLACK VEIL ANGEL
SILVER ANGEL SMALL
SILVER ANGEL MEDIUM
SILVER VEIL ANGEL
MARBLE ANGEL
MARBLE VEIL ANGEL
GOLD VEIL ANGEL
BLUSHING VEIL ANGEL
ZEBRA ANGEL
PINK CONVICTS
FIREMOUTH MEEKI
JACK DEMPSEY
JEWEL FISH
KRIBENSIS
OSCAR
RED OSCAR
TIGER OSCAR

FAR EAST IMPORTS
ALBINO AENEUS CATS
ALGAE EATERS
BLACK NEONS
BLACK SHARKS
BOTIA REDTAIL
BUMBLE BEES
CLOWN LOACH
FIRE EEL
KUHLII LOACH, GIANT
LEOPARD PUFFERS
MONODACTYLUS
PHANTOM GLASS CATS
RASBORA HET.
RED FIN SHARK
REDTAIL BLACK SHARK
SCATS GREEN
SCATS RED
TINFOIL BARBS
SCISSORTAIL RASBORA
SPINEY EEL

SOUTH AMERICAN IMPORT
ABRAMITES
ANOSTOMUS ANOSTOMUS
BANJO CATS
BLACK GHOST KNIFE
BLEEDING HEART TETRA
BUMBLE BEE CAT (PACAMU)
CARDINAL TETRA JUMBO
CARDINAL TETRA
CORYDORA AENEUS
CORYDORA AGASIZZI
CORYDORA ARCUATUS
CORYDORA ELEGAN
CORYDORA GOLD AENEUS
CORYDORA GREEN
CORYDORA JULII
CORYDORA MELANISTUS
CORYDORA METAE
CORYDORA PUNCTATUS
DISCUS BLUE SMALL
DISCUS BLUE MEDIUM
DISCUS BLUE LARGE
DISCUS GREEN SMALL
DISCUSS RED SMALL
DISCUS RED MEDIUM
DISCUS RED LARGE
GOLD TETRA
HEADSTANDERS
HEAD & TAIL LITE
HATCHET MARBLE
HATCHET SILVER
LEPORINUS FASCIATUS
METYNNIS SMALL
METYNNIS MEDIUM
METYNNIS LARGE
METYNNIS EXTRA LARGE
RED HOOK METYNNIS
NEON TETRA
OTOCINCLUS
PENCIL FISH AURATUS
PENCIL FISH TRIFASCIATUS
PIMELODELLA ANGELICAS
PLECOSTOMUS
PORTHOLE CATS
RAFLES CATS
RAMERIZI
RED PHANTOM TETRA
SHOVELNOSE

AQUATIC PLANTS

SPINOS (TALKING CATS)
TRANSPARENT KNIFE
WILD ANGEL LARGE
WILD ANGEL JUMBO
STINGRAYS

AFRICAN IMPORTS
BUTTERFLIES
ELEPHANT LONG NOSE
ELEPHANT ROUND NOSE
UPSIDEDOWN CATS
KNIFE FISH
REED (ROPE) FISH

AFRICAN CICHLIDS
PSEUDO. AURATUS
PSEUDO. TROPHEOPS
PSEUDO. ZEBRA
PSEUDO. TREWAUASAE
PSEUDO. ELONGATUS
TRITON TIGER

GOLDFISH
BLACK MOORS—SMALL
BLACK MOORS—MEDIUM
BLACK MOORS—LARGE
CALICOES—SMALL
CALICOES—MEDIUM
CALICOES—LARGE
COMMON COMETS—SMALL
COMMON COMETS—MEDIUM
COMMON COMETS—LARGE
RED FANTAIL—SMALL
RED FANTAIL—MEDIUM
RED FANTAIL—LARGE
SHUBUNKINS—SMALL
SHUBUNKINS—MEDIUM
SHUBUNKINS—LARGE
POOLFISH 5"-6"

FANCY GOLDFISH
SMALL BUBBLE EYES
SMALL CELESTIAL
SMALL LIONHEAD
SMALL ORANDA
SMALL REDCAP

MISCELLANEOUS
AFR. UNDERWATER FROGS
ALBINO MYSTERY SNAILS
MYSTERY SNAILS
RED BELLY NEWTS
WATER NEWTS
FLOUNDERS

AQUATIC PLANTS
AMAZON
AMBULIA
ANACHARIS
BANANA PLANTS
BOCOPA
BRAZILIAN SWORD
CABOMBA
WAFFLE SWORD
CHAIN SWORD
CONTORTION VAL.
CORKSCREW VAL.
CREEPING CHARLIE
CRISPUM
CRYPT BECKETTI
CRYPT CORDATA
CRYPT HAERTILIANA
CRYPT WILLISI
DWARF SAG
FOXTAIL
GIANT SAG
JUNGLE VAL.
HORNWORT
PHILODENDRON
HYGROPHILIA
ITALIAN VAL.
PARROT FEATHERS
RED LUDWIGIA
SANDRIANA
SPATTERDOCK
SUBULATTA SAG.
TEMPLE PLANT
UNDERWATER PALM
VIOLETS
WATER LILLIES
WATER SPRITE
WATER WISTERIA
PURPLE CRINKLE
PRINCESS PINE

MARINES

ANGELS (SMALL-MED.)
BLACK
FRENCH
BLUE
QUEEN
PIGMY
ROCK BEAUTY

BASSLETS
HARLEQUIN
LANTERN
ROYAL GRAMMA

BUTTERFLYS
BANDED
FOUR EYE
PAINTED

DAMSELS
BEAU GREGORY
BLACK AND WHITE
CARDINAL, RED
JEWELFISH
ORANGE-YELLOW
SGT. MAJOR

DRUMS
HI HAT
JACKNIFE
PORKFISH

EELS
CHAIN MORAY

GOBYS
NEON

GROUPERS
BROWN
RED HIND
SOAPFISH

HAMLETS
BANDED
BLUE
BUTTER
RED SPOTTED HAWK

HOGFISH
CUBAN
SPANISH

JAWFISH
DUSKY
PEARLY

PARROTFISH
PAINTED

REEF FISH
BLUE
PINK LADY

SQUIRRELFISH
BLACK BAR
RED
STRIPED

TANGS
BLUE
SURGEON
YELLOW

TRIGGERFISH
QUEEN

WRASSES
BLUE HEAD ADULT
BLUE HEAD JUVENILE
NEON
SLIPPERY DICK

MISC. VARIETIES
BEANFISH
COMMON BLENNY
COWFISH
FILEFISH
FLA. BATFISH
FLOUNDER
MOLLY MILLER
OCTOPUS DW.
OCTOPUS LG.
PIPEFISH
PORCUPINE
RAYS
RED LIP BLENNEY
SCOOTER BLENNEY
SCORPION
SHARP NOSE PUFFER
SPADEFISH
SPINYBOX
TRUNKFISH
BLUE VELVET

SEAHORSES
DWARF
GIANT SM.
GIANT LG.

SHRIMP
BANDED
CANDY
MANTIS
PEPPERMINT
PISTOL

ANEMONE ETC.
CONYLACTUS
REEF TYPE
ROCK MAT
FLAME SCALLOPS
FEATHER DUSTERS

CRABS
ARROW
HERMIT
HERMIT LG.
HERMIT RED LEG
HORSESHOE
ASSORTED

SNAILS
CROWN
ASSORTED (MARINE)
TULIP
FLAMINGO TONGUE

STARFISH
BRITTLE
BRITTLE RED
OCEAN
REG. SM.
REG. MED.
REG. LG.
SERPENT

URCHINS
LONG SPINE
PENCIL
PIN CUSHION
SHORT, BLACK SPINE
SHORT, GOLD SPINE

LIVE PLANTS
BERMANS SHAVING BR.
XaMAS TREE
GREEN FANS

PACIFIC VARIETIES

ANGELS
BICOLOR
BLUE FACE
CORAL BEAUTY
HALF BLACK
KORAN
LEMON PEEL
MESOLEUCOUS
SIX BANDED

BATFISH
ORBICULARIS

BUTTERFLYS
ASS'T MEDIUM
AURIGA
COPPERBAND
CORALCOLA
FALCULA
LEMON
LINNEOLATUS
LONGNOSE
LUNULA
MELANOTUS
OCTO-FASCIATUS
ONE SPOT
PEBBLED
PLEBIUS
SADDLEBACK
HENIOCHUS, BL. & W

LIONFISH
DWARF
PEACOCK
RADIATA

CLOWNFISH
BLACK AND WHITE
MAROON
PERCULA
PINK SKUNK
SADDLEBACK
SEBAE BR. & W.
TOMATO

DAMSELS
APOGON
BLUE DEVEL
BLUE FIN
DOMINO
FIJI DEVIL

GREEN CHROMIS
2-3-4 STRIPE
Y.T. BLUE DEVIL

TANGS
BLUE (HEPATUS)
LIPSTICK (NASO)
SAILFIN
YELLOW

TRIGGERS
BURSA
HUMU HUMU

WRASSES
CLEANER
CORIS GAIMARD
CORIS, YELLOW

MISC. SPECIES
CORAL CATFISH
CORAL HOGFISH
FANTAIL FILEFISH
MANDARIN
PANTHERFISH
SWEETLIPS, SPOTTED
SWEETLIPS, STRIPED
ZEBRA GOBY
CLOWN ANEMONE
ASST. ANEMONE LG.

SMALL BIRDS

PARAKEETS
BABY PARAKEETS
BABY MALE KEETS
BABY BLUE MALE KEETS
ALBINO KEETS
LUTINO KEETS
HARLEQUIN KEETS
YELLOW FACE BLUE KEETS
BOBBI PARAKEETS
BREEDER PARAKEETS

COCKATIELS & LOVEBIRDS
COCKATIELS, UNSEXED
COCKATIELS, MALE
COCKATIELS, PIED
COCKATIELS, ALBINO
PEACH FACE LOVEBIRDS
PIED PEACH FACE LOVEBIRDS

DOVES
WHITE DOVES
RINGNECK DOVES
DIAMOND DOVES
ZEBRA DIAMOND DOVES

FINCHES
GRAY ZEBRA FINCHES
WHITE HOODED NUNS
GOLD BREASTED WAXBILLS
RED EARED WAXBILLS
ORANGE CHEEKED WAXBILLS
CUTTHROATS

CANARIES

PARROT-TYPE BIRDS
PANAMAS
BLUE CROWNS
YELLOW NAPES
ORANGE CHEEKED
WHITE CROWNS
MACAWS, ASST.
DOUBLE YELLOW-HEADS
MEX. RED HEAD
SPECTACLES
LILAC CROWNS
HALF-MOONS
BLUE FRONTS
GIANT MEALIES
MINIATURE MACAWS
SUN CONURES
BROWN THROATED CONURES
BLAC KHEADED CAIQUE

SMALL ANIMALS
GERBILS
TEDDY BEAR HAMSTERS
GUINEA PIGS, SHORT HAIR
GUINEA PIGS, ABBYSINIAN
GOLDEN HAMSTERS
FANCY HAMSTERS
WHITE MICE
COLORED MICE

REPTILES
RED BELLY NEWTS
SPOTTED WATER NEWTS
GIANT CALIF. NEWTS
BABY CAIMAN
WESTERN PAINTED TURTLES
GARTER SNAKES

FREE FISH SENT ON ORDERS OVER $100.00 • BI-MONTHLY SPECIALS

"Serving the Pet Industry for 18 years."

Phone: (305) 592-3780 • Daily 8:00 AM-5:00 PM
GATORS OF MIAMI, INC.
5500 N.W. 74th Avenue, Miami, Florida 33166

master charge
BANKAMERICARD

24

Tetra Test

pH Test Kits (Fresh Water), pH Test Kits (Marine),
General Hardness Test Kit, Complete Hardness Test Kit,
Nitrite Test Kits, & Aqualab

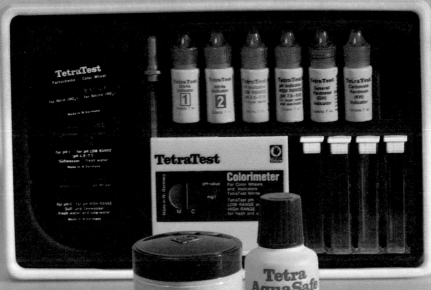

Staple food, Staple tablets
Squid flakes, Krill flakes
Ruby ColorPride, Marin Staple
Growth food, Conditioning food
Algae flakes, Guppy food
Goldfish food, Baby fish food
Brine Shrimp Treat, TetraMenu
FD Menu & SML Mix

AquaSafe,
Blackwater Extract,
FloraPride, TetraAlgmin,
Tetra FishSafe, Tetra ContraIck,
Tetra FungiStop &
Tetra MarinOomed

Tetra Staple & Special Foods

Tetra Health Aides & Water Conditioners

The complete prescription-Tetra Products

Tetra Sales. (U.S.A.), 360 Forbes Blvd., Mansfield. Ma 02048. Canadian Representative: Rolf C. Hagen, Ltd., Montreal, Que.

Quality • Profit
Exclusively
For Pet Shops

ZODIAC

12200 Denton Drive
Dallas, Texas 75234

WE WANTED YOU TO KNOW!

Valley Pet Supply has recently moved to a new 10,-000 square foot warehouse.

We now have five air conditioned trucks to serve our Northern California customers and to expedite air shipments to our many customers throughout the United States and Canada.

Our knowledgeable sales staff has been trained not only to sell products but to supply our customers with the necessary background information to make their pet departments a profitable operation.

In our new facility hamsters, mice, and guinea pigs are raised under strict laboratory conditions in specially controlled breeding rooms. This helps to prevent disease in the several thousand animals that are produced weekly and assures the highest quality available for our customers.

A new quarantined bird room has been added to hold a larger inventory of parrots, finches, macaws, and parakeets to provide our customers with a large selection of birds throughout the year.

Yes we have supplies too! Valley is now distributing Metaframe, Eight In One, St. Aubury, Oasis, and Nelson Products, along with packaged foods, cages and crockery dishes.

SEND FOR FREE PRICE LIST!

VALLEY PET SUPPLY
1200 Zephyr Ave.   Hayward, CA 94544
Area Code 415   Telephone 489-3311

The old idea of making money starts with new ideas.

Therma-Flow Heater

Plant-Air

Magna-Scraper

3-D and 2-D Aquarium Backgrounds

Pet Dinette and Heavyweight Pet Dish

Flowing Water-Fall

That's why successful pet shops and departments all over the country feature the Penn-Plax line. They count on Penn-Plax for new ideas, new thinking, new products. Things you can't get anywhere else. Like our action aerating aquarium ornaments. Or our 3-D and 2-D aquarium backgrounds, Sea Horse and Work Horse pumps, Hi-Intensity Aqua-Plants, Aquari-Lux, Color-Lux, and Clear-Lux bulbs. And our Lok-Tite Gang Valves that show you at a glance which valve is on or off.

Even our Heavyweight dog dishes and our Top-Cat Litter-Pans and Litter-Liners are special.

In fact, everything about the Penn-Plax line is special.

Specially the way it moves off your shelf.

Penn-Plax Plastics, Inc.
720 Stewart Avenue, Garden City, N.Y. 11530

© MCMLXXVI Penn-Plax Plastics, Inc.

29

introduction

Owning and operating a pet shop is more than a business, more than just a means of earning a living. It is a way of life different from that of any other retail business because it is built around creatures that require care, constant attention and love. Other retail concerns need only a good knowledge of product and business management. The pet shop owner needs these but also has to have an understanding, an affinity, for the animals under his charge. Make no mistake in this: any person interested in the retail pet business must consider very carefully the important area of animal care. A new litter of pups will need special attention 7 days a week. The compressor for the fish tank set-up never quits during the day; it only breaks down at 4 A.M., greeting you with a crisis the minute you walk in the shop the next morning.

Pet shop people are a breed unto themselves. They find rewards far greater than money. In no other business can you place a puppy into the arms of a small boy and watch his face glow with love. No other business catches the joy a young couple shares when they set up their first aquarium. Discouraging, messy, time-consuming the business is, but the love and joy you have the opportunity to bring to others outweighs the extra work you will have to put in to make your shop a monetary success.

It is assumed, because you are reading this book, that you are in or seriously hope to join the pet industry. The monetary returns are excellent for a well-run operation and the personal rewards can not be exceeded. But there are a few "tricks" to success and this is what this book is all about. So with this in mind, let's roll up our sleeves and begin.

chapter 1

Why the Full-line Pet Shop?

People will always be attracted to the retail pet business just as they are attracted to any other businesses—simply as a source of income. But most individuals find their way into the business because they are hobbyists or fanciers. They become shop owners later, mostly out of necessity. The tales are myriad about men who started with one 10 gallon tank of guppies in the basement and kept adding until the place looked like a public aquarium. When the tanks finally moved up into the bedrooms, the wifely ultimatum would be given: get rid of this mess, open a shop, or goodbye! Many opened the shop and were successful. Many failed. A few, we guess, were divorced. The same story, but with a different pet, the parrakeet, was repeated many times during the late 1950's when these attractive birds were the rage and thousands of people were breeding them. Finally, bird shops were opened in self-defense. The stories could go on and on...and one would probably apply to you. It is doubtful, indeed, that you have, or will approach the subject of opening a retail pet outlet with a cold business eye, having determined that this is your cup of tea because you have made detailed studies on the economic advantages of retailing pets. Actually, this type of approach is valid and may well produce better businessmen. But this type of individual is still the exception in the pet retailing world.

When the words "retail pet outlet" are used, they usually imply a complete pet line, a total retail service encompassing all aspects and items that are associated with the word "pet." But as the song goes, "it ain't necessarily so." Each segment of the industry identified with a specific group of livestock has been able to survive without the support of the other areas. In many cases, this specialization in an already specialized field has been as successful as it is astonishing. And because of this extreme specialization, a great number of people have entered the industry, spreading the world of pets further and at a faster rate this last decade than thought possible.

THE AQUARIUM SHOP

The aquarium area of the industry has spawned the greatest number of specialists, and no segment of the field has seen as dynamic a growth as has this area. The illustration at the beginning of this chapter mentioned the man with the one tank who kept adding and adding until, in self-defense, he opened a shop—an aquarium specialty operation. Many such outlets eventually expand their inventory to include dog, cat, bird and small animal sections, but just as many continue to be solely aquarium devotees, even claiming their specialty shop should not be counted as in the pet field because fish, they maintain, really aren't pets.

This type of operation has many advantages. First, the capital outlay is not as great, generally, as the full-line shop. Nor does the aquarium shop require the investment of the shop specializing in dogs and dog supplies. But it does, by comparison, take a larger dollar outlay than a bird shop. Second, an aquarium shop operator finds less stringent zoning regulations for a particular location than does the man who plans to stock dogs, cats and other carnivorous animals. Third, the aquarium shop owner can, if necessary, more easily afford to locate in an out-of-the-way area. Fish hobbyists are wandering folk. They'll drive all over town, even to other cities, seeking certain species to add to their tank. Since they will travel these long distances, your chances in a lower rent district are better than with the other segments of the business—with the possible exception of the dog grooming area which tends to build up a definite clientele of loyal customers. Fourth, and so often all-important, hours for the aquarium shop proprietor are conducive to a second job. A young couple starting out might be happy with the first 3 advantages listed above but could well be stymied if working hours would prohibit the husband from continuing, at least part-time, his first job until the store is firmly established. But a shop should not need this type of beginning. It is never recommended. The best situation would be the availability of enough capital so the store could be furbished completely—a going business established as of grand opening day. But since this is not always the case, it is possible to start with limited capital and limited time.

Aquarium shops generally stay open evenings. This is prime selling time and it means your store can open later in the day, say from noon until 8:30 or 9:00 P.M. The owner who works at another job can take over the shop duties after the supper hour if he is willing to work that long and hard a day. It is being done and more so in the fish business than in any other part of the pet field. Again, it is not the best solution and can be expected to generate frayed nerves and thin bodies, but it has proven successful for many people. This type of arrangement must be considered temporary until the business has begun to bloom. But it can be done.

AQUARIUM LEASING/FISH BREEDING

A sector of the fish business sometimes associated with a retail outlet, but not always so, is the aquarium display or aquarium leasing service. This type of operation is usually centered in the larger cities where large numbers of doctors, dentists, lawyers and other professionals can be sold on aquarium set-ups for their waiting rooms and are willing to pay for the initial set-up plus a weekly or monthly fee for the servicing of the tanks. A venture such as this normally requires little start-up capital as long as the clients are willing to pay outright for the tanks and accessories. Where a customer prefers a lease arrangement, your money is tied up in equipment and this can become critical if you grow too quickly.

The problem in some areas is to gain a rapport with the local aquarium supply distributor in order to obtain the necessary equipment at wholesale prices. The aquarium service business is viewed as a quasi-retail operation and does not automatically entitle you to buy at wholesale prices. It would be wise to check with your distributor before becoming too involved in such a venture. On the plus side, however, is the low capital outlay. Also, it is a part-time operation to start with and gives the owner the flexibility and security of a second job. Such a service business is often the first step toward owning a retail outlet and a good many people have followed this path. And once in the retail business, it can serve quite nicely as a buffer during slack seasons, acting as supporting income to an established retail aquarium operation. Of course, once coupled with a retail program, there is no question as to legitimacy to the supply distributor.

As a business within the retail framework of the pet field, tropical fish breeding is

FIGURE 1 *The aquarium specialty shop, apart from the full-line pet store, is the most common retail outlet in the pet industry.*

FIGURE 2 *The dog shop seems to have lost some of its popularity in the past few years.*

insignificant. Many retail outlets breed their own special fish, but by and large, it is for their own retail consumption and very rarely becomes significant in terms of direct sales to the consumer. Fish breeding is really a specialty in itself and is more a form of manufacturing. People who have entered the retail aquarium field from the hobbyist ranks and have breeding experience usually continue for a time, but as they develop a successful retail trade, they tend to drop the breeding, leaving it to those who can do it more profitably and in larger quantities. There are only so many hours in a day and it is far wiser to concentrate on the retail end.

THE DOG SHOP

Until recently, specialization in the sale of puppies and their accessories was largely confined to kennels and, to a more limited degree, veterinarians who might have a kennel on the side. The first step was to own a kennel; the supplies usually appeared later as demand grew. Once the accessory sales took on a significant role, the kennel owner would develop his facilities to the point where he was in the retail pet supply business as a dog specialist. Now this concept has been more fully developed by the advent of retail stores located in heavily shopped shopping centers and catering exclusively to a dog-owning clientele.

Initial cash outlay for this type of store is greater than for the aquarium shop of comparable size for here the concentration is on the puppy, an exceptionally high dollar item. Accessories are needed to round out the sale of the puppy, but the emphasis is on the sale of the dog. In contrast, the fish customer is apt to return week after week in search of some new gadget in addition to new and different fish. Fish is truly a hobby. But the dog shop must depend on the sale of the puppy and the sale of accessories at the same time to provide the bulk of its business. Obviously, supplies are continually sold in the dog shop, but to no greater or lesser degree than the full-line pet shop.

In the specialized dog shop the number of animals kept on hand at one time varies, but the tendency is to display a large selection, from 30 to 75 puppies, in a wide variety of breeds. This is, of course, a far cry from the dog shop of yesterday that kept 5 or 6 puppies around, and then not always on full display. In the section concerning the aquarium shop it was noted that often the fish operation will expand into a full-line shop. For some reason this is not true of the dog shop. The addition of fish tanks, birds or

FIGURE 3 *Common in the 1950's, the bird shop is very rare although most full-line shops have a bird department.*

small animals seldom creeps into the dog shop's inventory. This does not reflect a weakness in the fish operation or a strength in the dog shop concept. It is simply a characteristic that has no easy explanation.

The dog shop operator has an advantage over the other outlet operators in the field in that he sells a high ticket item. Most puppies that are in good condition go for well over $100, some reaching $400 and $500. There are exceptions naturally. Many dog shops sell puppies under $100 but $50 seems to be the lowest. But bear in mind that these high retail prices depend upon an affluent society, a good urban population concentration and steady advertising. Sales of these high ticket items also depend on the availability of a charge account system that will allow the average wage earner to make a $200 purchase on a time-payment plan with easy monthly terms. This business also requires a thorough knowledge of dog care. You might blunder into the aquarium field and lose a tank or 2. Such a loss could be handled. But lose 4 or 5 expensive poodles and the picture changes

quite dramatically. To sum up, in the dog shop you are working with a high dollar item that gives a good return and high volume but at a high risk.

THE GROOMING PARLOR

While not considered a pet shop in the classical sense, grooming shops have become important enough in the last few years to become accepted as another specialized retail area of the pet industry. This kind of operation can be tied directly to a dog shop or full-line store (taking up a back room) or it can be a separate entity, having its own location, decor and advertising program. Regardless of its location, basic grooming shop equipment includes grooming tables, holding cages, dryers, clippers, other hair-working accessories and a bath tub or other suitably large container with hot and cold running water. An old bath tub is the most frequently used. Placed on a base waist high, it performs adequately. If the grooming shop is part of a larger pet operation, the equipment and decor can be kept to a minimum in terms of investment.

The grooming shop that is an independent business is a full-time operation. As such, it requires a fair amount of capital—from $2,000 to $5,000—to set up and operates on a strict profit and loss basis. Decors in this type of shop vary, but the tendency has been to the more and more elaborate. This is because the grooming business has grown very rapidly in the past 10 years, mainly because of the popularity of the poodle. And a poodle, bless him, needs constant grooming. The more Madame wants to fuss with her little Fifi, the more attention the shop must give to image. So poodle salons have developed a rococo visage worthy of any beauty parlor, built primarily on the premise that what is good for Madame is good for Fifi.

The great majority of grooming salons have added a few dog accessory products as the demand required, having entered the retail field through the service door, so to speak; others increase their accessory lines to the point where they eventually become small dog shops with a large grooming operation. But, by and large, the supplies remain a sideline, a plus part of the business that helps cover overhead expense. Because grooming shops are normally smaller than any other type of pet shop and grooming equipment the only major investment to be considered, initial capital outlay is less than that of the dog shop or the aquarium store. Location for a grooming parlor is also not of prime importance. A clientele is generated by good work. Every grooming shop has its list of regular customers and because of this, a business shopping center is not necessarily the best location. One can afford to put a grooming operation in a lower rent area without having to suffer the pangs of profit hunger due to loss of traffic.

THE BIRD SHOP

Back in the 1950's when the parrakeet reigned supreme, bird shops sprang up like magic and distributors counted profits by the number of bird cages and bird toys they sold. It was a great business for a while. But now the bird store business is a weak shadow of its former self. Certainly there are still a few of these specialized shops around but they are no longer a factor in the industry. Those that have existed as separate operations are either taking in other items to supplement their sales or are closing their doors.

Bird stores, like grooming shops, are small and generally require a small outlay of capital.

No recommendation or condemnation can be given a bird shop. Remember that the pet industry will always consist of people who love animals and are attracted to this form of business because, hopefully, they can care for pets and make a fair living at the same time. So it would be foolish to turn thumbs-down on a bird shop; there is always that rare individual who can take such an operation and make a success of it. Caution, however, must be the rule. The popularity of the small bird has waned significantly. Prices are high and the danger of more government regulations restricting bird sales because of disease must be kept in mind.

THE "FULL-LINE" OUTLET

The full-line pet shop is the best type of operation for constant, year round profit. Stop for a moment and assume that in any given area of the country and with any type of customer profile, 100 percent represents the total amount of available pet business for you. You can't have it all, of course, if there is competition. But you should expect to tap a certain portion of the total. Assume further that you have an aquarium specialty operation. With only fish and accessories you can expect to get approximately 40 percent of the sales you would have obtained if you had a full-line shop. Assume you tire of fish and open, instead, a dog shop, stocked only with puppies, kittens and accessories. Now you would tap about 40 percent of the total portion of dollars possible if you had a full-line shop. Combine the dog, cat and aquarium shops and you would have approximately 80 percent of the total dollar potential. Add small animals (hamsters, gerbils, guinea pigs, mice, an occasional rabbit) and gain another 10 percent; put in birds and a grooming department and you would be tapping the total pet business available to you in your location.

Of course, these are ficticious figures in that with a specialized operation you would tend to generate more of the specialized sales potential because you would tend to have more selection, more expertise in, say, fish than the full-line shop operator. So, the figures would become distorted to a certain degree, but the fact remains that with a full-line shop you have a bigger total dollar potential to work within.

The remainder of this book will be devoted to developing theories and specifics within the framework of the full-line shop. But the specialty operator can still benefit as we will cover the individual departments within the full-line shop. So, if your interests lie in a specialized operation, simply apply the points brought out in that specific chapter.

chapter 2
How Much Money Do You Need?

There are 3 ingredients necessary for success in any business: sufficient capital, good management and knowledge of products. At the beginning of this book, one more ingredient was added to the pet shop picture—the love of animals. The need for knowledge was just noted. But a pet shop operator does not have to necessarily fail for lack of knowledge. Or conversely, he does not succeed because he has a great amount of knowledge. The success (or failure) of your business will rest, most often, on how much (or how little) capital you intend to put up and how successful a manager you are from that point on.

"How much cash do I need?" is the constant question that every potential pet shop proprietor asks, for this is something he must know before he can commit himself to a lease, to fixtures, to merchandise. The answer, "All you can get your hands on," doesn't say much. You need to have more specific responses because your bank or a friend or the Small Business Administration will want an exact and detailed estimate of what you will require.

"All you can get your hands on" is certainly not good enough. By the same token, it is difficult, indeed, to tie down an absolute figure for any store unless you have, on paper, some idea of what kind of decor you're shooting for. As an illustration, are you going to use inexpensive pegboard on the walls at 16¢ a sq. ft. or will you use a quality grade such as Marlite at 60¢ a sq. ft.? Do you intend to use paneling in the store? Will you use pre-finished luan mahogany at about 17¢ a sq. ft. or will you install one of the finer non-staining durable panelings that run 26¢ per sq. ft.? Or would you prefer a fancier fine-grain wood paneling such as pecan, pecky cypress or elm at 47¢ a sq. ft.? At each step of the way you can pick, high or low. So these things must be thought out ahead of time. Materials must be picked so they will do the job and suit your pocketbook at the same time.

THE $20 RULE

A rule of thumb in today's market. . .and keep in mind that this is a guide rather than a hard and unalterable figure. . .is that $20 per sq. ft. will put you in business. That $20 includes tanks and cages, stock room partitions, dividers and cages for the bird and grooming rooms. It means gondolas and wall units on the retail floor, the cash register and the sign out front. It means your advance rent and utility deposits, your initial stock, both dry and live. It also means your grand opening and initial advertising. Planning a complete pet shop 25′ wide by 75′ deep? It should cost around $37,000. If you want just an aquarium shop instead of a full-line store, the cost would run down around $15 a sq. ft.; for a grooming shop, considerably less.

Can you begin any one of these at a lower figure? Absolutely! It becomes a matter of shaving on the depth of your stock and the quality of your decor. The figure of $20 is not an arbitrary one; it is based on costs for some of the finest shops in the country located in some of the busiest shopping centers and can be taken as an average guide for anyone contemplating a start in the pet business. But with forethought, it can be lowered.

Labor is one important factor that keeps the square foot figure mounting. The more work you can do and are willing to do in the store pre-opening, the lower your square foot costs can be. Are you willing to paint? To build the rack for the aquariums? Can you put up the bird room or the partition between retail and stock areas? The $20 per sq. ft. rule to open is where you do the directing and someone else does the work. We have seen beautiful shops go in at $14 to $16 that were "stick built" by the owners themselves. But remember, there are many talents among us; it is not mandatory that you be a master carpenter or painter. It only helps.

Once this figure of $20 per sq. ft. has been established as a norm, the next step is to prepare plans and come up with a typical opening inventory which will be discussed at greater length later. This must be done for you to talk intelligently to banker or friend or mother-in-law about borrowing money.

There are 3 sources of investment money that you might tap. The first is completely separate from the second and third. . .which are closely related. This first approach is a loan from a friend. That thought is quickly forgotten and we pass on to number 2. Most people going into business cannot turn to a friend. They are nice to have but not too many are floating around with available money. Besides, once they do let you borrow they have a tendency to cease being friends. So the number 2 source is your bank. This is an obvious place and should you see your banker, go armed with all the facts. What do you intend to do? How do you intend to do it? Where will you do it? How much are you willing to put into the business in time and finances? It is also important that you know what kind of collateral you can put up against the borrowed money.

Finally, for number 3, should your local friendly bank cease to be as friendly as you would like, there is the Small Business Administration which will (A) guarantee a loan through your bank or (B) will advance funds on a participation basis with the bank or will, if necessary, (C) make a direct loan to you from federal funds. SBA will require just about the same preparation as your bank but could be more agreeable and could lend up to half of your total costs.

SBA REQUIREMENTS

From SBA's leaflet OPI-18, the following are requirements for a new business in order to qualify for a loan.

1. Describe in detail the type of business you wish to establish.

2. Describe your experience and management capabilities. (They want to know at the very outset what you know about pets and supplies.)

3. Prepare an estimate of how much you or others have to invest in the business and how much you will need to borrow. (Like any bank, SBA wants you to share the burden of responsibility by carrying a portion of the initial indebtedness.)

4. Prepare a current financial statement (balance sheet) listing all personal assets and liabilities.

5. Prepare a detailed projection of earnings for the first year your business will operate. (Once you know how much stock you will maintain by drawing up your opening inventory of both dry goods and livestock, you can then project the gross profit by estimating turns of inventory for the year and subtracting all projected expenses.)

6. List collateral to be offered as security for the loan, indicating your estimate of the present market value of each item. (There is no difference here between SBA and a private lending agency.)

A CHECK-LIST FOR PROSPECTIVE PET SHOP OWNERS

Money Source———————————————

Location of the Shop———————————————

Estimated Required   **Actual**

Size of Store——————————————— ———————————————

Cost of any Renovations necessary——————————— ———————————————

Cost of Gondolas, Counters, Fixtures—————————— ———————————————

Cost of Cash Register———————————————— ———————————————

Cost of Tropical Fish Set-Up—————————————— ———————————————

Cost of In-Store Kennels——————————————— ———————————————

Cost of In-Store Aviary Set-Up————————————— ———————————————

Cost of Exterior Signs——————————————— ———————————————

Cost of Interior Signs——————————————— ———————————————

Utility Deposits——————————————— ———————————————

Advance Rent Costs——————————————— ———————————————

Initial Advertising Cost——————————————— ———————————————

Attorney's Fees——————————————— ———————————————

Total Cost for Setting up Store ready to
receive initial inventory——————————————— ———————————————

(1) Total———————————————

Total Initial Dry Merchandise————————————— ———————————————

Total Initial Live Merchandise————————————— ———————————————

Cost of Give-Aways for Grand Opening———————— ———————————————

Total Cost of Saleable and Give-Away———————— ———————————————

Merchandise for Opening——————————————— ———————————————

(2) Total———————————————

Complete Cost to Opening Day————————————— ———————————————

(3) Total———————————————

Reserve Cash for Contingencies————————————— ———————————————

(4) Grand Total———————————————

FIGURE 4 *Use this sheet or one similar as an initial planning tool.*

7. Take the above material to your bank. Ask for a direct bank loan and if declined, ask the bank to guarantee the loan under the SBA's Loan Guaranty Plan or to participate with the SBA in a loan. If the bank is interested in an SBA guarantee or participation, ask the banker to contact them for discussion of your application. In most cases of a guarantee of a participation loan, the SBA will deal directly with the bank.

8. If a guarantee or a participation loan is not available, visit the nearest SBA office.

Again, it is important to understand that any lending agency will want to know your capabilities in the pet field. If they are putting out good money to back your venture, they want to be assured in some way over and above securities that you will have a fair chance of success. So the more preparation you make to provide your banker or SBA with complete and detailed information as to what and where and how you will spend their money and, most important, how you expect to pay it back later, the better chance you will have of obtaining a good loan at fair terms. This would include having a location picked, plans for the interior of the store drawn up, a model inventory set up and projected inventory turns, gross profit, expenses and net profit for a 12 month period. This will take some study and preparation but it is as important to you as to the lending agency because only by doing the digging necessary to come up with such figures will you be cognizant of the complete spectrum of business problems to be encountered once the operation is, in fact, rolling along.

RETURN ON INVESTMENT

Since the topic of capital is so important, it would be natural to want to know what one could expect to make with this money. And so at this point, some explanation of projected profits is in order. The money you spend to set up the store, i.e., fixtures, lighting, wall finishes, grooming room, types of outdoor and indoor signs, opening inventory. . .all of these are variable from one store to the next and it is impossible to pin down anything but an average as a guide. But the profit picture is something else again. Many of the manufacturers of pet items today suggest the price you should pay through your distributor. Many even suggest the retail price of their items. As labor costs rise and the quantity of help decreases, it becomes more and more important to help the retailer with his product. Thus, manufacturers, by suggesting retail prices, save you valuable labor and at the same time tend to stabilize the retail price across the country. Most pet shops will follow the suggested retail guidelines set up by manufacturer or distributor. The end result, with some variance, is that the majority of pet shops find themselves channeled into a certain profit alley. Of course, there are often local competitive conditions existing which send prices down and thus change the profit picture markedly, but this so called "price warfare" seems to be predominant in the aquarium business. This text is not designed to give you a profit picture where discounting exists to any great degree. This is another area, important but complex, which is not to be dealt with at this point. The desire here is to come up with a profit analysis that is based on following the manufacturer's suggested retails or higher.

Profit on most of the dry goods in a pet shop will run between 45 and 50 percent of the selling price, with the majority of items running around 45 percent. To give you some examples: Fish foods run 50 percent. Fish remedies run the same. Aquarium accessories, dog accessories and dog and cat remedies run from 40 to 45 percent. Leather and chain goods run from 50 to 55 percent. ("Chain goods" is a term used to describe in its broadest sense choke chains, chain leads and tie-out chains for dogs). Bird cages and small animal cages run from 40 to 45 percent. Books run from 45 to 50 percent. Usually, an item that is highly advertised and has gained brand identity nationally will have a slightly lower profit than non-advertised, just-coming-along items that the public is not mindful of today. Overall, the gross profit on dry goods throughout the store should run from 45 to 48 percent.

Livestock is another matter. The situation is much more lucrative in your livestock department but losses can often bring you down close to drygoods in ultimate profit. Your ability as a livestock keeper comes into play and your profit picture varies in direct relation to the care and knowledge you display toward pets. Profit on livestock runs 50 to 75 percent but since losses will occur more often than with drygoods (by the term losses for dry goods we mean items broken or stolen), the gross profit can drop considerably. Boiled down, you can make money if you know your livestock and keep it alive and in a healthy condition; get careless and it will cost you money.

For tropical fish and goldfish the norm is to triple your money. A 20¢ tetra should bring 59¢. Small animals that are common at most any pet shop will bring 50 percent. Expensive kittens and puppies will return 60 percent. Reptiles, like fish, should return 66 to 75 percent. In many cases, it is a matter of what the traffic will bear. Outstanding specimens will always bring more money and it is up to the wise manager to price his livestock accordingly. If you have the only reptile selection in the area, then obviously you should price your snakes to show 4 times their cost. By the same token, if all the shops and syndicates in the area are selling hamsters at $1.99, then your price must be $1.99.

PROFIT FROM SELLING PRICE

For this discussion, and in the future, profit percentages refer to the percent of profit you make from the selling price. . .not what profit you add to the initial cost of the item. Example: A man buys an item for 60¢ and decides to make 40 percent by adding 40 percent of the 60¢ cost to the item. Forty percent of 60¢ is 24¢ and he sells the item for 84¢. He has made a profit of 40 percent based on his cost. Now another shop owner desires to make 40 percent on the selling price, so he sells the same item for $1.00. At that retail price, 40 percent belongs to him as profit. In the former case, the store owner only realized 28 percent profit; the latter case brought a true 40 percent.

Many manufacturers have regular merchandise "deals" in which they offer an extra 5 or 10 percent. This might be their way of introducing a new item and they open the market by giving you an extra discount through your distributor. Or it may be a method of jumping the gun on their competition. An extra discount could be offered for early orders, such as sweaters or wild bird feeders or wild bird seed or bird houses. . .any item can gain by giving a little extra to tie-up your business before competition gets in. Usually there is a minimum order involved to make you buy in quantity. In that way many manufacturers can lock up a store for an entire season.

There is nothing wrong with this providing these are items that you know you can sell and assuming you have the cash to tie-up in this extra inventory. Many manufacturers also offer a regular quantity discount passed on through the distributor to you. These are not special promotion or seasonal discounts. These are standard discounts for quantity buying. Retailers who are aware of these conditions and try to tailor their buying to obtain the extra percentages involved can raise their gross profit picture 2 to 4 percent.

Another, but more risky method of milking more profit, is that of buying up odd lots of discontinued merchandise from the distributor. This takes keen knowledge on your part and is something you shouldn't attempt until you have been in the business a while, until you have developed a sense of what's hot and what isn't. Many distributors find themselves with odd lot quantities of salable merchandise from time to time and are only too happy to move it out at a reduced price. Another percentage point or 2

can be gained in this manner. Close rapport with your distributor is necessary so that he will call you whenever he has merchandise he wishes to move out quickly.

TAKE HOME 20 PERCENT

Talking percentages can be all well and good but the question you would like answered now is how much money you can expect to make with such and such an investment? It's a good question and a difficult one to answer because, truthfully, there are so many variables that it is difficult to come with an answer that satisfies all situations. However, there can be and there is an average that can be used as a firm guideline. Once this is established you can take off from there, the sky the limit.

Assume now that the man who opened a store 25 x 60 ft. used as his average cost $18 per sq. ft. (He was able to do much of the work himself and thus cut $2 per sq. ft. from the $20 rule.) The entire store cost him in the neighborhood of $27,000. Out of that, $14,400 was merchandise that could be sold at his cost. (The difference, $12,600, is what went into remodeling, fixtures, register, utility deposits, rent advance, phone, etc.) Working on a 40 percent profit, this man should be able to turn his $14,400 into gross sales of $24,000.

That would be his total sales if he turned his complete inventory over once. But a pet shop should turn its inventory at a minimum of 6 times each year. Thus 6 turns x $24,000 shows a gross sales figure of $144,000 for the year. At 40 percent profit on that gross, he would have $57,600 before expenses. As mentioned, 6 turns a year is on the low side. With good, sound and frequent promoting and advertising, this could be increased to 7 or 7½ turns a year. At 7½ turns annually, the gross sales for a shop with an inventory of $14,400 at cost would be $180,000, with $72,000 being profit.

The amount of livestock stocked and sold is a very important factor in the dictation of turns per year. Tropical fish could easily turn 30 times. Small animals, puppies, kittens could turn 20 to 25 times in a year; birds less frequently. You can see that the more tropical fish and animals you sell, the more you pick up the slower turning dry goods. A busy tropical fish shop could easily move up from 7 to 8 turns per year to 10 turns simply by increasing the sales of the livestock. Thus, the assessment of 7 to 7½ turns is a modest one if you assume that some livestock will be sold.

All very well and good, but how much can you make for yourself? What kind of a return before taxes should you expect at the end of the year? Again, there are many variables to bear in mind.

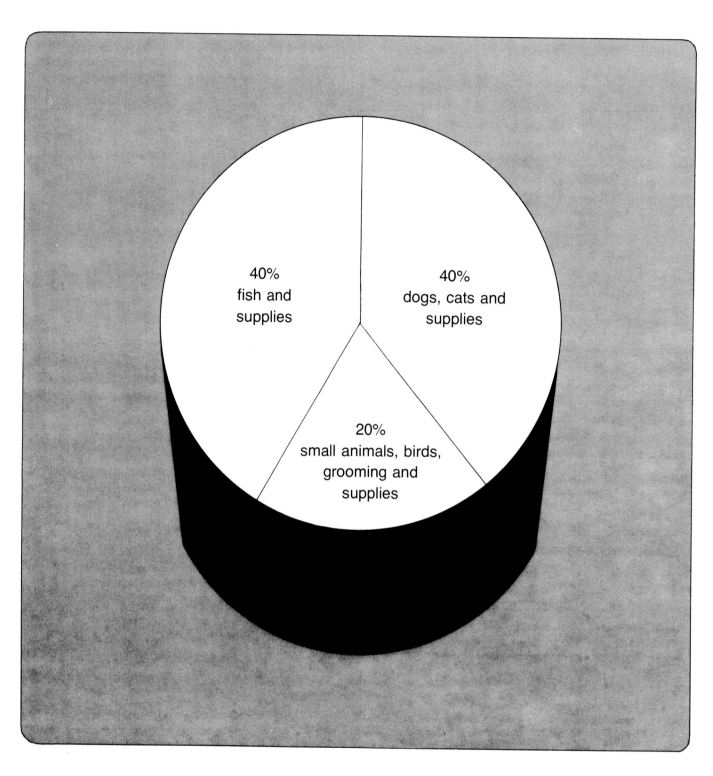

FIGURE 5A *Sales in a full-line shop are pretty stable and national averages for these operations have been developed.*

It is always an easy thing to toss figures around and never very difficult to make this whole affair the most lucrative business in the world. Of necessity, figures will be averages, but the figures given in this text are from known pet shop operations and thus are reliable as far as these specific shops are concerned. Whether you can meet or beat these figures is another matter. So, to answer the question of what you can make for yourself, there are 2 ways to approach the question in order to come out with an intelligent and honest answer.

If you are investing money in this type of business and are not going to work at it. . .i.e., this is simply a capital outlay and whether the manager of the store sells pets or peanuts makes no difference to you so long as he makes money, then your return should most certainly be 12 percent. If it does not return 12 percent, it is a poor investment and your money should be elsewhere considering the risk involved. On the other hand, if this is a family-owned and family-run business with husband and wife working together or at least with the wife working part-time and even one of the teen-age children working a few hours each week, then your net return should be between 18 and 20 percent. This means, quite simply, that you should expect to take home as a family salary (which would include cash put aside for future business expansion) about 18 to 20 percent of your gross volume.

THE BOOKKEEPING SYSTEM

Now it's time to discuss your future bookkeeping system because your careful attention to the details of keeping a correct set of books will give you the true answer to the question of whether you make or lose money. An accurate set of account books is the camera that will give you the profit picture. And whatever system you use, it will really be a detailed exposition of your cash register tapes. We'll discuss at length later the various types of cash registers to consider but it is important at this point that you understand the progression of sales (or disbursements) from cash register to bookkeeping system and finally to the hands of your accountant.

There are still shops in operation today. . .and not limited to the pet business by any means. . . that have what is known as a cash drawer. They have no cash register, per se, and determine the day's business by counting the money in the drawer and checking this total out against handwritten sales slips. This laborious, antiquated method has worked for many operators for many years and they have no intention of changing. But for the modern, high

volume store where 4 or 5 clerks are making sales simultaneously, attempting to do business and control business by the cash drawer method is outright insanity. Suffice to say that a respectable cash register is a necessity in business today.

As mentioned earlier, an accounting system cannot wait until the store is open. Proper bookkeeping must begin before you sign a lease and it is because of this that you should be aware of the ramifications of methods currently in use: By the word 'method' is meant any system that you can buy or put together which will tell you, month in and month out, which way your business is going. This can be done with a simple ledger divided into sections to show sales, purchases, expenses, deductions, payroll, accounts payable and (on occasion) accounts receivable. Or you can use separate account books available at most good stationery stores that will give you more space covering each necessary subject to be entered. Separate account books should prove more accurate than one simple ledger book unless the ledger book is large and can be refilled with extra pages as required.

COMMERCIAL LEDGERS

Probably the simplest and most satisfactory would be to purchase one of the bookkeeping systems on the market. Here everything needed is incorporated in one looseleaf book. The Wilson-Jones "All Facts Bookkeeping System," Ideal's Bookkeeping System (No. 5021 for merchants) or Dome's Simplified Bookkeeping and S.E. & M. Vernon Complete Ledger, are just a few of the good systems available. With such a system, whether one named here or any other, be sure to look for the following sections to be included:

1. Facsimile pages throughout the book to guide you in making entries.
2. A sales and cash receipts section with quarterly summaries.
3. Pages for purchases with quarterly summaries.
4. A section on the distribution of expenses and deductions.
5. A section devoted to monthly summaries of the business and a statement of income.
6. A good system should also include pages for bank deposits, cash record and special accounts (such as the proprietor's account), insurance account, fixture account, record of notes and loans, inventory, etc.
7. There should also be a payroll section with summary plus a section on accounts payable for your suppliers and, heaven forbid, a section on accounts receivable.

FIGURE 5C *The grooming shop is the least expensive to set up in terms of fixtures and location and can deliver satisfactory profit if the quality of work is good and consistent.*

FIGURE 5B *The full-line shop requires the most capital but also returns the most consistent profit.*

Regardless of how simple or how complicated you wish to become with any method you choose, it is good business to have an accountant standing by who can help steer you in the right accounting direction.

In the beginning you might get by with using his services once each quarter to help with estimated taxes and to prepare a summary of how your business is doing. As the business grows and your time becomes more valuable, you might desire to use an accountant once each month to go over your books and prepare a summary. Certainly a monthly summary is desired to keep you on top of the business. Your dependence on an accountant is directly related to your interest and knowledge of bookkeeping and your desire to know what is happening in your operation.

There are pet shop operators, and successful ones at that, who accumulate paid invoices, sales tapes from their registers, payroll check stubs and all the other paperwork concurrent with running a business. This not-so-neat pile is presented in toto to the accountant once each month. This sort of thing is the stuff of which heart attacks are born. If you cannot afford a full-time accountant (and the majority cannot in the beginning), then look into one of the complete bookkeeping systems mentioned earlier and make your own entries. Pass this system on to your accountant once each month or once every quarter and he will be happy to come up with a statement of the entire operation. Don't lose sight of the fact that your bookkeeping, no matter how basic or how sophisticated, must begin with the first penny spent and must continue faithfully as long as the business is in operation.

BUSINESS DEDUCTIONS

Any accountant should be able to fill you in on what business deductions you are allowed. And if this is your first venture into business, you should be aware of the many tax advantages that can accrue for the pet shop owner if he has the foresight to study his tax situation. Some examples are given below but certainly each operation will have tax advantages not open to others. Those listed here are intended as guidelines, not final and firm rules.

1. Depreciation on store fixtures. All equipment used in your store such as gondolas, registers, show cases, stock tanks, cages used for holding birds and animals, equipment used for cleaning, grooming equipment, air compressors, etc., fall into the category of fixtures and equipment and can be depreciated. On this type of equipment there is also an extra

first year depreciation which you should be aware of when you discuss your taxes with the accountant. Note: There are 3 methods of computing depreciation: Straight line, declining balance and sum of the years-digits method. It is not the intention to detail these 3 avenues here but you should discuss them with your accountant and decide at the outset which method will offer you the greatest tax relief for the longest period of time.

2. Depreciation on leasehold improvements. Here again, you can recover the cost of any improvement you have constructed on leased property by either depreciation or amortization. Do not assume that such improvements pass on to your landlord with no recovery open to you should you vacate. Depreciation or amortization is certainly to be considered a recovery and your accountant should assist you in setting up the machinery to do this. A few leasehold improvements that can be depreciated or amortized are things like a partition to hide your stock room, a slop sink you install to wash cages and kennels, permanent carpeting, permanent wall paneling, a pool with fountain in the floor, a partition to close off the front display window.

3. Depreciation and expense allowances on cars and vans used for your business. The many ramifications of automobile and van deductible expenses and allowable depreciation are too numerous to approach here but actual expenses or a U.S. Treasury allowance is deductible and depreciation under certain conditions is also allowable.

4. Expense allowances for overnight trips or extended stays in connection with your business, which also includes partial allowance where business and pleasures are combined.

5. Actual expenses deductible or a Treasury allowance applicable when driving to look over and compare competitive prices.

6. Actual expenses deductible or a Treasury allowance granted when delivering items to customers or picking up merchandise from your distributor.

This subject of taxes, deductions, expenses and depreciation is an extensive one. Since this book is not intended to discuss every tax law, it would be well for you to check the various depreciations and other deductions open to you by writing to the U.S. Government Printing Office, Washington, D.C. 20402 and asking for their publication called: Depreciation Guidelines and Rules, IRS Publication 456. There are any number of comprehensive income tax manuals printed that can offer you a wealth of information on all facets of your tax situation. J. K. Lasser's "Your Income Tax" (Simon & Schuster) is just one of the easy-to-read-and-digest publications available at a nominal and deductible cost.

chapter 3
The Importance of The Right Location!

Twenty years ago it would have been almost impossible to find a pet shop in a shopping center. But then, 20 years ago there were only a few shopping centers and none as we know them today. It has only been in the last 10 years that we have witnessed pet shop growth in the larger centers, centers which, by and large, tend to locate in the single family suburban areas clustered on the periphery of every major American city. Of course, the definition of "shopping center" could connote any group of 2 or more retail businesses banded together in one central location; that definition, as you can well imagine, would cover a lot of territory.

The great shopping centers have evolved from small lines of shops along main thoroughfares which offer little or no parking facilities. These centers are still in business. In fact, they are still being built but they no longer attract either high rent or high traffic. Eventually, the shopping center became larger, had space for more stores offering a greater variety of services and ample parking. Because of the very size of such a center, proximity to the "heart" of town was usually out of the question. These centers were placed on main metropolitan arteries and were designed by their very size to contain the buying public in that one area and inhibit as much as possible their movement downtown. This type of center is still being built and has become a true American institution. Any town large enough to have a mayor is large enough to have its shopping center; and some that do not have mayors still have their shopping centers.

Now, of course, the designs have changed. The cities have felt the pinch to their downtown vitals. The retail businessmen in the heart of the metropolis see business slipping away to the encircling shopping centers and they have been making great efforts to develop and encourage new business and new customers down on "Main St." So the outlying malls have come up with a new twist, a new advantage, another attraction to keep the customers from leaving their suburbs. They have created the enclosed mall. Sometimes square, often rectangular, and even oval, they are nothing more than completely covered shopping centers whose retail shops all face on a common, covered promenade, heated in winter and air-conditioned in summer, decorated with tropical plants and coin-collecting fountains and generally following a decor theme that repeats throughout the entire center. It is a glorified version of the country market where merchants congregated and set up stalls to sell their wares. There are as many arguments for these large suburban centers as there are against them and it is not the intention here to set your mind in either direction. But it would be well to discuss the pros and cons of the various location concepts and let you be the judge.

THE IDEAL LOCATION

If anyone were to ask you what you desire as an ideal location you would most probably respond: "Maximum traffic in a high-income area and minimum rent." That's utopia, and friend, you can never set your mind at ease. That ideal has been and never will be found. You will have to settle for something less and this something less, whatever and wherever it might be, is what you can afford or more accurately, what you think you can afford. And in that statement, you see, this whole matter of location boils down to the degree of capability on your part and the law of supply and demand on the part of real estate.

When you rent a location in a shopping center you are paying for real estate by the square foot. No matter how the lease reads or what the agent tells you, it comes back, eventually, to a square foot figure. And this amount that you pay is relative to the success of the entire shopping center. The more prosperous the center proves to be, or even how prosperous the developers can make the merchants think it is going to be before they start construction, the more rent they can ask. A prosperous, busy center normally has no trouble keeping filled. Space demand is greater than space supply. It might make you grit your teeth if you have a certain mall in mind for a pet shop and learn that there isn't a thing available and nothing is available in the forseeable future, but it makes the real estate agent happy indeed.

Let's look over this business of locations from what we might consider a 'prime' spot down to locations that could be called down-right risky. A prime pet shop site can be measured by its location in the community. Is it located along a main artery in or out of town? Traffic should flow past the shopping area all day, not just at peak morning and evening hours. In talking of a shopping center, it should be what we call a regional and not a neighborhood center. Does it have a variety of retail shops? Developers like to give their centers a flavor of downtownishness. By this we mean they know that the more services they can offer, the more attractive will be the area for business. A large department store, drug store, ladies ready-to-wear, haberdashery, shoe shop, book and music shop, barber, cleaning establishment, variety store, liquor store, etc., are all necessary to the ultimate success of the center. And this is why more and more centers want to include the pet shop. Pets and pet supplies are big business. As one of the top hobbies in the country, it is just good business for a developer to see to it that his customers have a pet shop available. So, in summary, a prime location would include an area or center with as many different types of retail outlets as possible.

Is there ample parking? Can cars get in and out of the area easily? Most locations we would call "prime" must, under today's urban zoning, have ample parking but the question of getting in and out of that parking area and onto the main thoroughfare is something else again. People will have a tendency to shy away from a center that is difficult to get in and out of and where frustrating traffic snarls develop during peak hours.

Is the shopping center an enclosed mall type? This may not be a deciding factor in accepting or rejecting a site but certainly the enclosed mall has more appeal. Shopping is much more relaxed and leisurely. For a pet shop, the enclosed mall is ideal. With controlled temperatures in the promenade at all times, cold winter drafts rushing in every time the front door opens is a thing of the past. For the full-line pet shop or for that shop that wishes to specialize in dogs and dog accessories, the large shopping center is an assurance of necessary traffic. And traffic, especially what we call "walk-in" traffic, is paramount for steady high volume. Keep in mind that few people come shopping for the express purpose of visiting your shop, that few have decided before leaving home exactly what they want, what size, what color, what price. The majority of buyers come into your store simply because they are walking by and see the puppies in the window or the monkey begging from his cage near the check-out counter.

You see this immediately brings up a discussion on window display but we'll save that

FIGURE 6B *Location for an aquarium shop is not as critical as a regular clientele tends to build.*

FIGURE 6A *Most new full-line shops are located in shopping centers. The rents are high but so is the traffic.*

FIGURE 6C *Shops in a re-vitalized downtown area can be as successful as center locations.*

one for later. For now keep in mind that walk-in traffic is necessary for high volume and there can be no doubt that the large shopping center complex is in business to provide just this traffic. You'll pay for the privilege, to be sure, but there is nothing wrong with that if it increases profits.

When discussing the location for an aquarium or grooming shop, we are talking about a parrakeet of a different color. Earlier, when we spoke about opening a specialty shop, we noted that people will tend to drive many miles to visit an aquarium shop; and we said that a dog grooming salon can be in an out-of-the way area because it depends on a steady repeat clientele for its income. This is true. But there is nothing in the book that says that you cannot open an aquarium shop in a large shopping center.

Heavy traffic flow with impulse buying customers is tantamount to high volume. A dog grooming salon will obviously do a better business where people walk by constantly and are subject to the desire to have their pet well groomed and sweet smelling. But what we are saying is that the shopping center complex is not necessary for good volume and good profits. There is a point of diminishing return when the increase in volume over a less expensive location is not enough to justify the increase in wages for more help and the higher rent.

DETERMINATION OF RENT

What are we actually talking about when we start comparing "high-traffic" location costs with "off-Main St." spots? We said before that when you rent any location you are paying for real estate by the square foot. In fact, you will usually pay all the landlord can extract. In this respect, his rents are set by competitive locations, by the desirability of the shopping center or shopping area and by the very quality of the space in demand.

For a shopping center, rent is usually discussed in terms of so much per square foot. For an off-street location, rent would probably not be discussed in footage but rather in terms of a flat amount. You could say it amounts to the same thing eventually but there is a significant difference in the way you bargain. When you discuss rent with an agent handling a shopping center, you discuss increase or decrease in terms of so much per square foot. You debate round figures when you discuss rent with the agent for a smaller, older building.

Let's put down some figures to get an idea of comparable costs for a shopping center location. You can pay anywhere from $3 per square foot to $10 per square foot depending on the size and popularity of the center. The age of such a center is not as significant as you might think. Many centers 10, 12, and 15 years old are still pulling in customers, still renting to capacity and still demanding premium rents. The big secret is how many people a center can pull in, week after week. That's the crap game played by developers. If they win, you pay the premium rent, obtain the volume; if they (the developers) do not guess quite right, then you have a not-so-choice location at a lower rent.

We spoke of a square foot rent when dealing

with shopping centers. On top of that figure there is usually a little add-on percentage. Five to 8 percent seems to be the going rate. On the surface this seems like a little extra bonus for the landlord, but what he is saying is this: "We'll rent you 1,500 square feet for $6 per square feet per annum. This means you will pay the shopping center $9,000 in rent for the year. We'll be content with that $9,000 until you have reached a sales volume of $150,000. Once you exceed that figure, we will no longer be content with our $9,000. From that point on we would like to have an average percentage of 6 on all sales above $150,000. In effect, you will be paying us 6 percent of your volume as long as you hit sales of $150,000 or better."

Now this dialogue is not intended to show you the fairness of this type of rental system. But it does show that you will be paying a substantially higher percentage on volume should your gross drop below $150,000 as the landlord has no intention of giving you a refund.

If you hit $90,000 the first year and your rent is $9,000, you are paying 10 percent of your sales in rent. When you reach $125,000 you are paying 7.2 percent and when you hit $150,000 the percentage is down to 6. By asking for a 6 percent overage on all sales over $150,000, the landlord insures that your percentage for rent never gets below 6 percent, that he gets in on your action and your good fortune. Fair or not, this is business, and in particular, the shopping center business.

On top of the cost per footage for rental and the percentage over a minimum volume, there will probably be a fee for promoting the shopping center. If the mall is to draw maximum traffic, there has to be some radio, newspaper and TV advertising. Each shop, therefore, will kick in a stipulated sum to the general advertising kitty. There could also be a fee for keeping the mall clean, shoveling snow, picking up trash. There could be a protection fee for maintaining a security patrol. These are all possible added costs and you should investigate and consider each before you sign a lease. And you should compare with other centers in the area. Never forget that every percentage or part of a percentage off the gross is that much less for you in the final net.

Today, the newer centers are adding one more rule. In some areas, mall managers are writing into the lease a proviso that allows the manager or an assistant to check the figure in your register known as the non-resetable consecutive total. In a word, your register keeps a running total of all sales that you cannot alter. This total is absolute proof of what you're doing and it will indicate to you and to the shopping center management your store's volume at all times. It is just their way of insuring that 6 percent for sales over a minimum volume.

A FINAL CHECK-LIST

When we talk about rents for locations other than shopping centers, it is possible to cover a complete range of figures. Actually, it becomes impractical and of little value to make flying guesses at rental costs without knowing what kind of a location and in what condition the premises are in. You might find a store 25' by 60' in a small country town for $75 a month. That same store in a low income section of a large city would cost $120 to $150 per month. The same space relocated among a small group of stores along a main thoroughfare in the suburbs could easily go for $2.50 to $3.50 per

So, you can see it is of little value to set a criterion on rent because there are so many variables that must be taken into account. When you find a spot that you feel has merit, spend time watching traffic patterns in and around the shopping area. Is there a dry cleaning establishment nearby? Or a laundromat? Is there a quick service food market near the location? You need the traffic created by these retail establishments.

Whether you go into a mall or a less glamorous location, there are a few questions you must ask before you sign any lease.

1. Unless you are buying out an existing pet shop, there will never be a location made to order for your operation. There will have to be alterations. So your first questions is: Who pays for the alterations? Naturally you'll want the landlord to do it all if you can push him that far. In the newer malls the policy seems to be that the developer provides the 4 walls and the roof and you do everything else. They don't want to know your problems. You fix it up in any way you desire so long as you pay for it. In smaller centers or in solitary locations you will have a better chance to dicker. Many times landlords are completely agreeable to making all renovations at their expense if you'll sign a long-term lease, long enough to allow them to recoup the costs of renovation.

2. Who pays for the air conditioning unit? And the water and the heat and the light?

3. What kind of a lease does the landlord want? Is he looking for a 5 year lease with a renewal option and a review of the rent with the possibility of increasing after 5 years? If this is your first venture into business, it might be well to negotiate a short-term lease, one that runs 2 or 3 years with an option to renew at the end of that time if all goes well. There's nothing wrong with this if the landlord is willing and you're not too sure of yourself. However, in the newer, more glamorous malls, agents will talk nothing less than 5 years. They don't have to. At this point, you must have the faith, determination and conviction that this shopping center is the one for you and you're there to stay.

chapter 4

What Should Your Shop Look Like?

Looking at a hypothetical situation for a moment, you have found a vacancy in Prosperity Mall. Not exactly dead center in the shopping area but, nevertheless, close to a very popular department store. You have spent 2 Saturday afternoons and 2 whole weekdays clocking the traffic flow and you have noticed that not only is the "cars-in-per-hour" figure better than at 2 other possible centers, but there seems to be a nice stream of traffic into the department store. The agent wants $4.50 a sq. ft. and 5 percent over $135,000. You pay the utilities. The air conditioner is part of the center and is thus built-in. That's part of the rent. Same for the heat. The agent says the developer will put up one partition which must not be any longer than the width of the store. He'll also install a slop sink in your storage area. Any other alterations will be up to you. There is also a flat $45 per month charge for shopping center advertising and snow removal. This fee is to be paid 3 months in advance at the time you sign the lease. You will also have to put up 2 full month's rent as surety advance. The store is 25 ft. wide by 60 ft. deep.

Before you sign the lease you must determine whether this shop is the right size and the right shape for your particular operation. So you must come up with a layout to give you some rough idea what alterations or additions will cost. And you need to come up with this layout and estimate as quickly as possible because the agent will not give you more than 2 weeks. He obviously wants to rent the store as quickly as possible and you know he can do just that quite easily. How then to draw up plans that will be both functional and aesthetically pleasing in that space of time?

Luckily, most developers today lay out stores 20, 25 or 30 ft. wide and from 40 to 75 ft. in depth. The average is 25 ft. wide by 60 ft. deep. Obviously you can find many variations to this but 25 ft. wide seems to be a common width and 50 to 75 ft. deep a common length. Thus, at the outset you will be working with a dignified rectangle.

Whatever the size or shape store you intend to rent, 3 universal requirements must be met in order to open the most primitive of operations. The first is a retail space for livestock. The second is a retail space for dry goods. The third is the storage area. Add to this if you wish. You can put in a 4th requirement, that of grooming area. Or a 5th . . . that of boarding pens. Or a 6th of breeding pens. But no matter how elaborate you become, you must start with the 3 fundamentals. Now you can juggle these around anyway you wish to come up with any workable combination that pleases you.

Figure 7 shows the retail space for dry goods at the front of the store with retail space for livestock down both walls and across the back, separating the total retail area from the overstock area. Figure 8 shows a plan where the livestock area forms a partition lengthwise the store behind which is the storage area. Figure 9, on the other hand, shows the livestock area situated in a large rectangle in the middle of the dry goods retail area with the storage room decreased but still along the back of the store. There is a fourth situation, a variance of Figure 7. As shown in Figure 10, the overstock room is maintained but the livestock retail area becomes somewhat separated from the dry goods retail area. This is departmentalization on a grand scale. Obviously, any of these plans will be workable in a rectangular store. If the store is square, plans in Figures 7 and 10 would not be workable. And if the store is in a shape like Figure 11, then you must come up with a specific floor plan to suit that shape as there is no pat layout for such a situation.

LAYOUT COMPARISONS

With variations, the layout in Figure 7 is used quite often because it is economical and adaptable to just about any rectangle. In this particular illustration livestock forms the partition between the back stock room and the retail area. Livestock also comes up both walls. An alternate to this plan could be to have livestock form the partition as shown but then come up only one side wall. Or another variation would be to have the livestock all on one wall and not form any part of the stock room partition. Any of these variations can work. It becomes a matter of taste and the extent to which you are going

into livestock. The good points of this layout are that it is economical to construct. All livestock cages and fish tanks go against a wall. The only partition that is needed is the one between stock room and retail area. It is flexible. As business grows, the stock room partition can be pushed back to give more retail space. The only disagreeable feature with this plan is that all cleaning of the livestock area must be done from the front. This could be bothersome if the store were crowded and cleaning of cages or tanks became necessary.

The layout in Figure 8 is a good one in that the livestock department forms the dividing line between the dry goods area and stock room. All livestock can be cared for from the rear, eliminating unsightly cleaning equipment on the retail floor. However, this plan allows little for dry goods expansion. Once constructed, there would be little more an owner could do to increase his retail space. It also offers the objection of needing more than one person in the store at any given time. A store utilizing this design with only one sales person would be quite vulnerable to theft were that one person in the stock room tending livestock. Because of the extra partition needed, this layout is considerably more expensive to build than that shown in Figure 7. However, from a convenience standpoint and from an aesthetic angle, this scheme is far superior.

Figure 9 shows another layout that is pretty well locked-in once it is constructed. Other than reducing the stock room area, which is already quite small, there is little room for retail expansion. This layout is used frequently because it puts all the livestock in one spot, making the livestock easy to work on and easy for the customer to view as he makes one large circle around the complete pet area. With the appropriate dry goods positioned across from each variety of livestock, this plan offers a close tie-in between live animals and their necessary supplies. However, it also offers the disadvantage of requiring plumbing in the middle of the store for the livestock or else the burdensome problem of carrying dirty food and water dishes back and forth to the stock room for cleaning. It also has the same bad feature as Figure 8 in that the livestock corral is a perfect sight barrier. Keeping a close watch on merchandise and checking on customers who might need service could become quite frustrating for a clerk.

Figure 10, as we mentioned before, is an alternative to Figure 7. By bringing the ends of the livestock area out into the room, a semi-private area is thus formed. The extent to which you would separate livestock from dry goods would be determined by how far into the room you bring the partitions.

It isn't often that we find stores with unusual

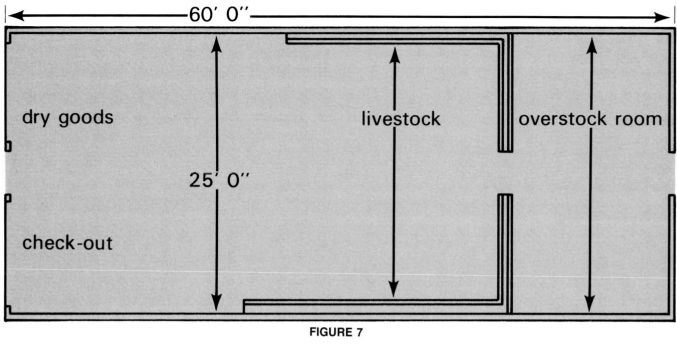

FIGURE 7

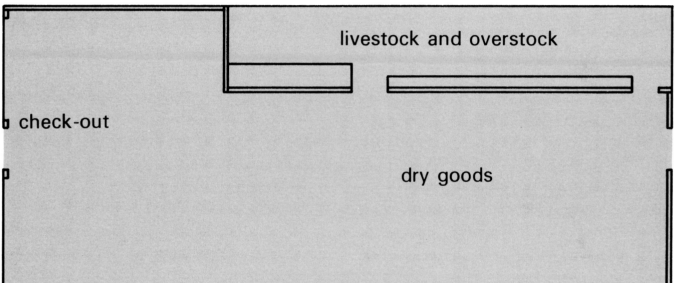

FIGURE 8

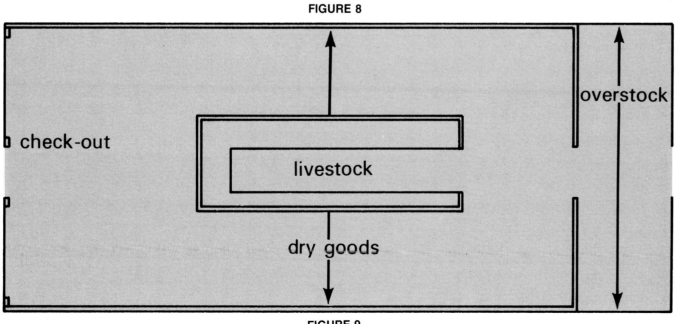

FIGURE 9

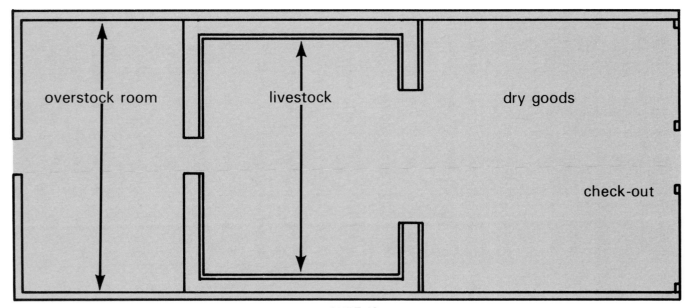

FIGURE 10

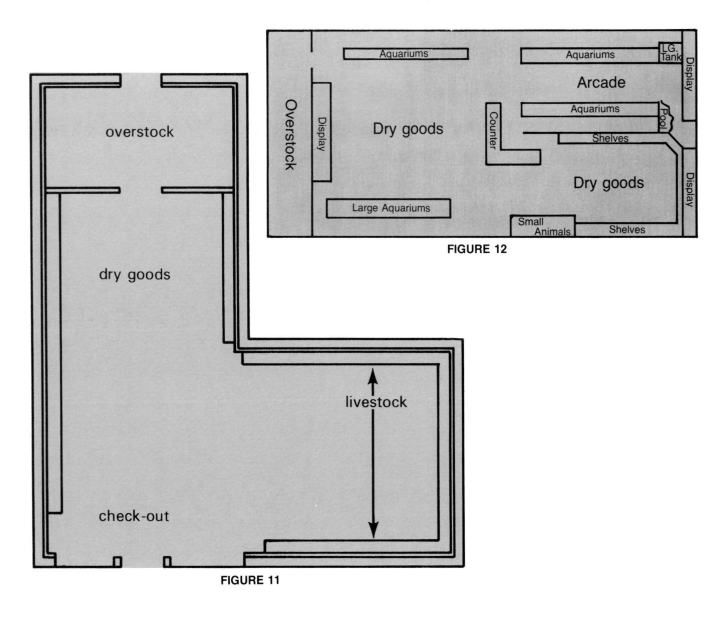

FIGURE 12

FIGURE 11

58

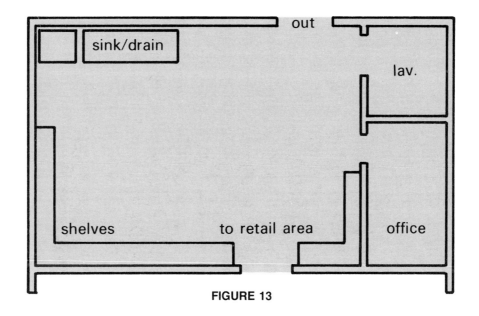

sink/drain

out

lav.

shelves

to retail area

office

FIGURE 13

dimensions such as the one shown in Figure 11; this layout is given as one possibility when anything other than the rectangular occurs. This situation sometimes develops where more room is needed and expansion takes place into an adjoining store.

The rather unique design shown in Figure 12 is the creation of Bob Via who operates several complete pet shops in the Washington, D.C. area. Designed to gain the greatest amount of customer traffic with a minimum of employees, you will note the entrance arcade running between two rows of aquariums. This arcade acts as a colorful funnel; once through it, you become captive to the displays of dry goods and other livestock in the store. By situating the check-out counter at the mouth of the funnel, complete surveillance of every corner of the store can be maintained. Normally, two people can operate a store of this size under the plan shown. Note that there is a working area in back of each row of aquariums to facilitate cleaning and maintenance.

THE STOCK ROOM

Notice that the stock rooms shown in Figures 7, 8 and 10 run about 300 sq. ft. or 20 percent of the total store space. Figure 9 has only 200 sq. ft. in the stock room but makes up the 300 by having 100 sq. ft. in the livestock rectangle.

Remember that all of the figures given above, although valid, will be determined finally by your proximity to a good wholesaler. The size of your stock room is directly proportional to the distance to your distributor. Where you to obtain deliveries of supplies weekly or, if you are lucky, twice-weekly, a large stock room will be superfluous. If your store is to be hundreds of

miles from the closest wholesaler, and you can only obtain supplies by commercial truck, bus, parcel post or air freight, then your backup stock room will have to be larger to keep supplies flowing steadily to the front retail area.

A stock room has definite needs. In Figure 13 we see a lavatory. Two would be more convenient but one seems to be the rule. You should plan a space for your desk. An office here will be out of the way of retail traffic. The size of the lavatory is not too critical but your office should be large enough to hold a small desk and chair, a file cabinet or 2 and possibly a chair for any salesman calling on you. The stock room will have a door to the outside through which all supplies enter and all trash leaves. There should be a slop sink room with a fairly substantial drainboard for washing crocks, dishes, cages and especially tanks. If you are using the plan in Figure 9 you might wish a sink in the livestock corral up front as well as one back in the stock room, but the feeling is that whichever plan you use, a sink with a large drainboard should be in the stock room. Last, but by no means least important, there should be ample wall space for rows of inexpensive wood or metal shelves to hold back-up merchandise for the store.

Now let's see what these layouts might look like when put together in isometric form. Figure 14 shows the layout in Figure 7 but with slight variations. The stock room is in the back of the store. The fish tanks come up one wall, the remaining livestock up the opposite wall. Dry goods in this design are in the middle of the store, right up to the check-out counter. The main difference here is the treatment of the livestock area. Instead of keeping puppies, birds and small animals and exotic animals up against the wall and allowing the public to move up close to the cages, rooms were built to shield

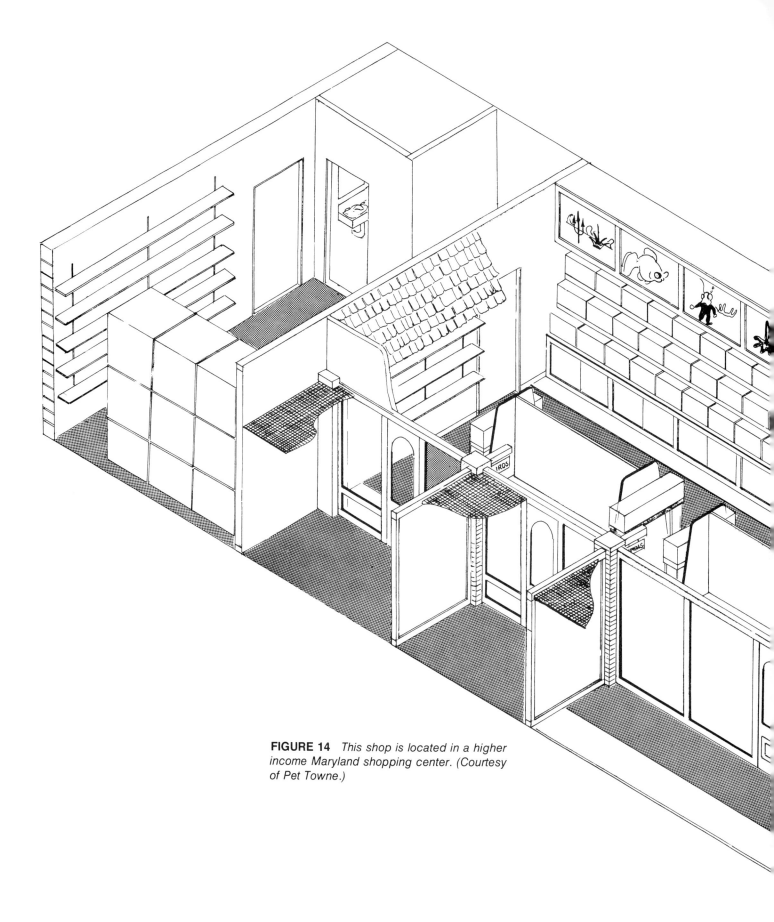

FIGURE 14 *This shop is located in a higher income Maryland shopping center. (Courtesy of Pet Towne.)*

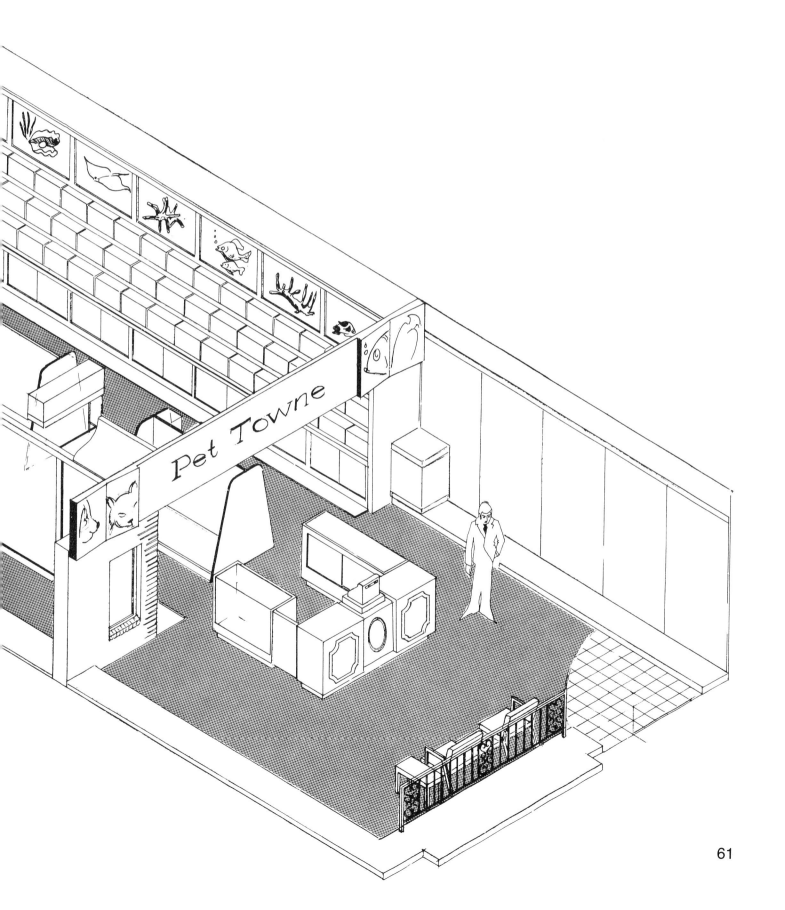

Pet Towne

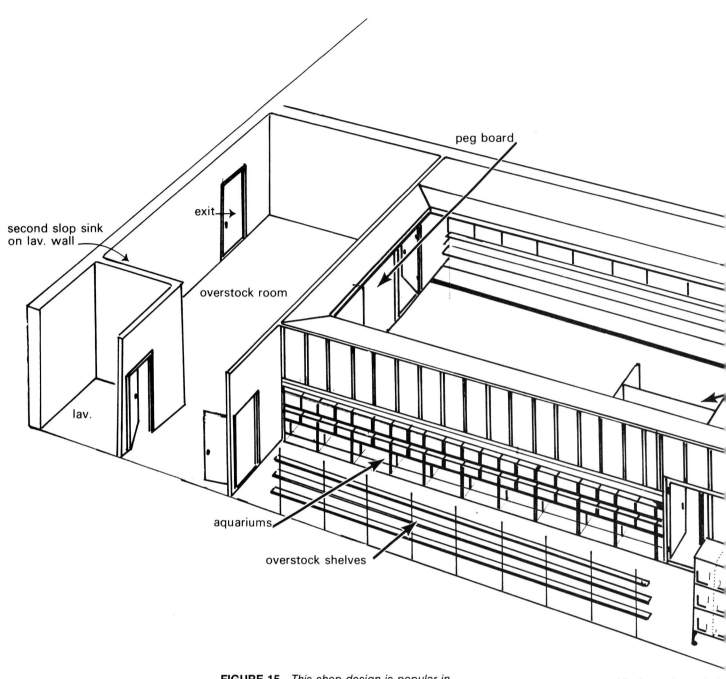

second slop sink
on lav. wall

exit

peg board

overstock room

lav.

aquariums

overstock shelves

FIGURE 15 *This shop design is popular in the south Atlantic states area.*

movable kennels, aviaries

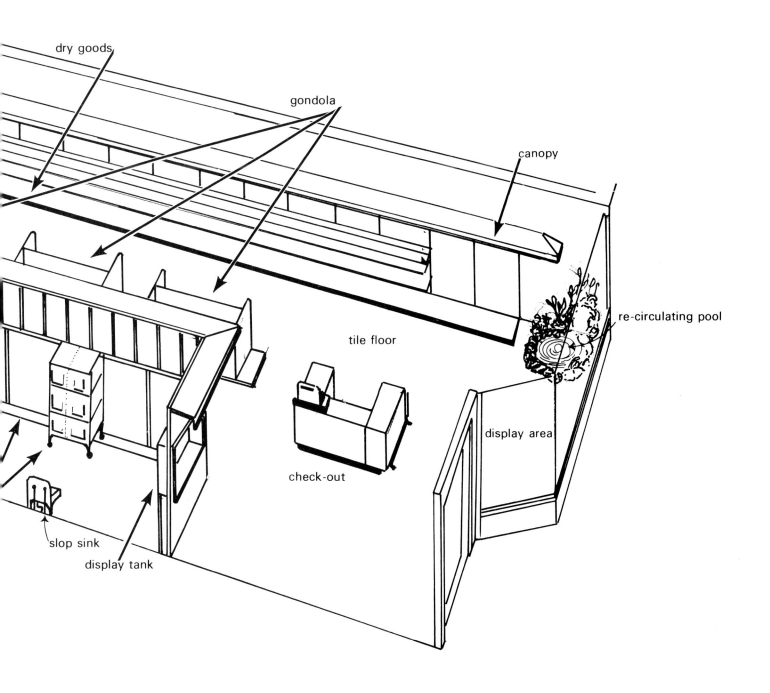

dry goods

gondola

canopy

re-circulating pool

tile floor

display area

check-out

slop sink

display tank

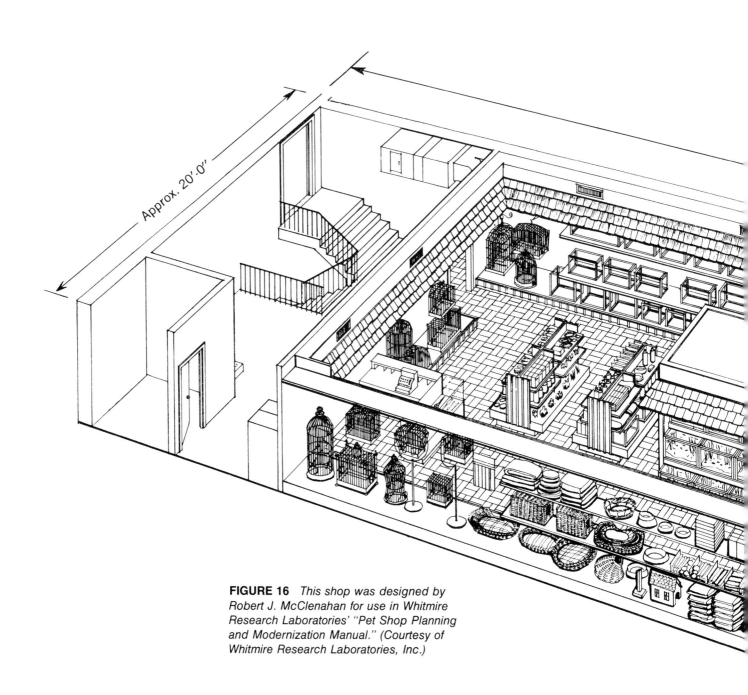

Approx. 20'-0"

FIGURE 16 *This shop was designed by Robert J. McClenahan for use in Whitmire Research Laboratories' "Pet Shop Planning and Modernization Manual." (Courtesy of Whitmire Research Laboratories, Inc.)*

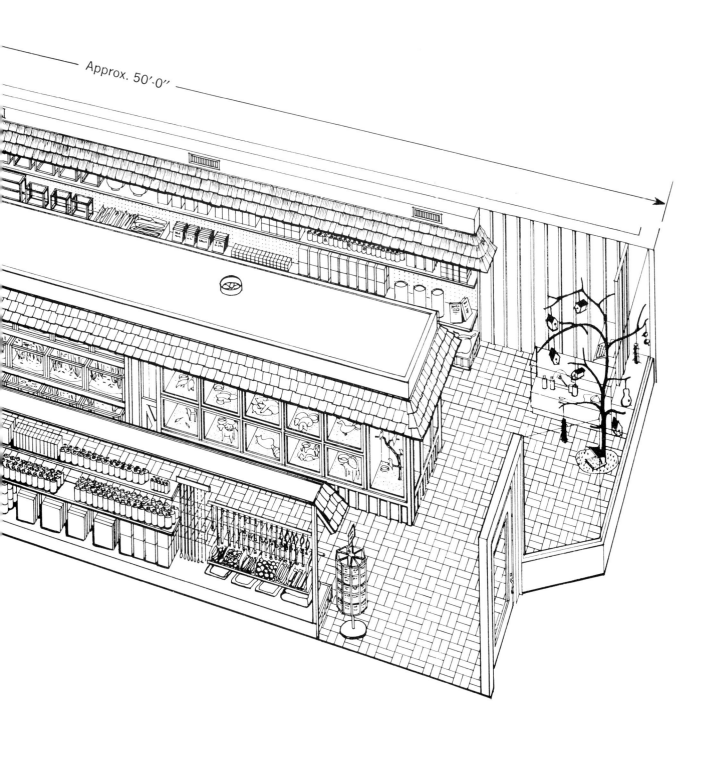

Approx. 50'-0"

livestock from customers as well as to shield the customers from noise, dirt and odor.

The aquariums are in a step-up formation, all to be worked from the front. There can always be a dispute between dealers as to whether tanks should be worked from front or back. One advantage to front operation is that you can see exactly what you're doing, what is required. If you are working from the back, aquarium backgrounds or paint or foil on the backs of the tanks inhibit sight and makes cleaning from the rear much more difficult. The other advantage, mentioned earlier, is that you can keep attention divided between the work and the customers. In back of the tanks you would be much less aware of customers coming and going.

Notice the check-out counter and its position in Figure 14. Up front to greet the customers, up front to serve the customers, up front to watch the customers. The 2 glass show cases do double duty as check-out counters and display centers, holding poodle collars, expensive aquarium pumps and dog clippers. Kennels and cages would be stacked against the wall (wall not shown) and all work done on them would be from the front but with complete freedom. And because of the individuality of these cubicles, temperature ranges could be varied.

This particular shop has a Spanish decor which you can see carried out in the livestock room doors, in the 4 by 4 jut-out beams holding the display signs for the livestock rooms and in the cedar shingle treatment over the back shelves. The back room is large enough for stock and possibly a future grooming department. In this case, should you desire, these back shelves could be taken down, a window installed and customers could view the dog grooming. In the final construction of this store, by the way, the decorative panels above the fish tanks were omitted and in their place a row of cabinets was built. The owner felt that these cabinets, with the Spanish motif repeated on each door, would be far more sensible than decorative wall panels. The extra cost was worth the extra storage space gained.

Figure 15 is a diagrammatic perspective drawing to show what Figure 8 could look like when set up. As mentioned earlier, all livestock is behind, and actually forms a partition running down one long side of the store. Notice how the kennels or bird cages (2 are shown) can be moved up to the large glass partitions for viewing or can be moved back for cleaning. A certain amount of noise will get through to the customer, but there would be no odor problem as long as the back room is kept reasonably clean. Shelves placed along the near wall (wall not shown) afford ample overstock storage space. A slop sink here and in the back room makes cleaning a snap. The opposite store wall is for display of dry goods. Gondolas, as shown,

may or may not be required depending on the amount of stock you might wish to carry and the width of the particular store. (Keeping in mind that your livestock room would be no less than 8 ft. wide and the shelves on the opposite wall would come out into the room at least 20 in., any store less than 20 ft. wide would prohibit use of a gondola or a series of gondolas.)

As in Figure 14, notice the placement of the check-out counter. It is located close to the front door with a good view of the store interior. A 24 in. canopy has been run completely around the store at about the 7 ft. level. Fluorescent lights have been installed under the facia board to throw light down on the merchandise displayed below. In the front far corner a re-circulating waterfall has been installed to attract outside attention and is used to hold large pool goldfish and outdoor pool plants. Since this particular dealer also sells underwater pumps such a display serves a profitable purpose.

The back room of this particular store is quite large and unless a grooming salon was to be installed later, it would be heavy on overstock room. The fish tanks are set directly over each other, 2 high and are serviced from the rear. A 3 tier arrangement could also be installed but with 3 rows of tanks the problem of the bottom one being too low and the top one too high is ever present. Fish are caught from the front.

Figure 16 is a diagrammatic treatment of Figure 9 where the livestock area is situated in one large structure in the middle of the store. In this drawing by interior designer Robert J. McClenahan for the Whitmire Research Laboratories of St. Louis, Missouri, a canopy is covered with cedar shingles as is the roof of the livestock compound to give an over-all rustic appearance. Two check-out counters will be noted: one at the front on the far side and one at the rear near side. Where a store is large and such a livestock enclosure is contemplated, 2 check-outs could well be imperative.

There are stores in existence now that have used this plan and have built in only one check-out counter in the front. With such a large center-of-the-store structure, blind spots are bound to occur. Having 2 check-outs in operation, the chances of dangerous blind spots can be cut to a minimum. Notice the stairs leading to a back door. In many areas, rear-of-the-store entrances for customers are quite common. The rear check-out counter in this case would not be optional. It would be a necessity. The dealer who owns this store is also fortunate in having a basement with a wide stairway. If he doesn't mind the trips up and down he will have unlimited storage. In fact, a basement is ideal as a fish holding center, a boarding center for birds, cats and even certain breeds of dogs. And, of course, it could be a great grooming area.

The 3 foregoing designs are not intended as a layout panacea for future pet shop dealers. Rather they are possible schemes from which ideas might be extracted. Your pet shop, whatever the money put into it and regardless of its size, should reflect something of your personality. To follow one of these 3 plans without question or change would mark you as unimaginative. Of course, it is true that certain similar conditions should and do exist in every pet shop, but once those conditions are met, your choice of decor, arrangement, mood and color should not be bound by any conventional pattern.

Now, let's look at a few of the objectives one should keep in mind when planning any layout. At the beginning of our discussion on layout we mentioned that any good plan must fulfill 3 requirements: Retail space for livestock, retail space for dry goods and space for storage. Let's pass by the storage space aspect since this has been covered adequately and take a closer look at other retail areas. So, before you pick up a pencil to make sketch number one or before you call an interior designer, consider these few points.

AISLES, GONDOLAS

1. Are you thinking of nice wide aisles? Any aisle should be wide enough to allow 2 people to pass comfortably. In fact, an aisle should be wide enough to allow one person to pass a second person bending down to examine bottom-shelf merchandise.

2. Are you planning to install gondolas that may be too high? In which direction will they run? Most department stores frown on any gondola over 50 in. high. Invariably something is put on the top shelf that increases the height of the gondola and obstructs easy vision across the room. Don't put in gondolas over 50 in. high. If you do, fight the tendency to pile things on the top shelf. Try planning your gondolas to run the length of the store or whichever way affords the easiest viewing from the check-out counter. Try to maintain clear aisles, straight aisles, unobstructed aisles. To do so means that you can service your customers quicker, be more aware of their presence and at the same time keep down the pilferage that always exists in a retail store.

3. Will you try to design your check-out area in line with the traffic flow on its way to the exit? If the designer of the shop in Figure 16 had positioned only one check-out counter in the store and that one at the rear, what a miserable adventure it would be for customer and store owner alike. The object is to keep customers circulating as long as possible in the store.

Displays should stimulate them into buying. Once this has run its course, the check-out counter becomes the final spot for a possible sale.

4. Are you planning an area of changeable display? You should. If you build-in partitions and show cases right up to the front window, there will be little room for that feature display of seasonal or promotional merchandise that you might wish to set up. Leave a hole near the front window for that special something. The special display will also attract attention from the outside.

5. Will you be selective and objective in planning your store lighting? The easiest thing in the world is to instruct the contractor to put row upon row of fluorescent fixtures in the ceiling. Easiest thing for him too. But it makes the whole store look white, cold and so antiseptic. Notice that in Figures 14, 15 and 16, a canopy has been run around most of the store. Under this canopy fluorescent lights are installed to throw soft illumination down on the products and livestock on display.

Fluorescent lights are also placed in the livestock area, either directly in the pens, as in Figures 14 and 16, or hidden in such a way outside the pens that the animals can be seen but the lighting fixtures cannot. See Figure 15. (Fluorescent lighting should be used wherever illumination is required in a confined space such as dog pens, animal and bird pens, etc. Incandescent light gives off too much heat. Some shops like to use table lamps on the show cases for soft, calming light that encourages browsing. High intensity lights around tropical fish displays should be avoided. Let the colorful borealis of reflected light from the aquariums themselves be enough. There is nothing more beautiful or pleasing to the eye than rank on rank of illuminated tanks in a pet shop. Don't ham it up by adding more light.)

6. What kind of a floor are you planning? The most durable, easiest to clean and most expensive is a terrazo floor. Your first cost is your greatest cost but what a cost that is. But then, how beautiful and how permanent. Vinyl asbestos and solid vinyl are also popular. Vinyl asbestos, for a commercial floor, is probably the best bet. It requires more tender care than does terrazo but it is much less expensive. Solid vinyl, while it maintains its lustre with much less work than vinyl asbestos, is softer and is prone to reflect sharp heel prints, tank stand legs and any sharp object that hits it.

A strong trend in the pet industry is carpeting. This has been used quite successfully and the trend seems to be with more and more shops installing such a floor covering. Conventional commercial carpeting and the indoor-outdoor all-synthetic carpets are both being used. With carpeting, the question is not one of cost as it is a matter of taste. Carpeting can make a pet shop look very luxurious but it can be a real pain if a fish tank should break. Carpeting can add that extra touch of elegance that says you have the cleanest, most formal shop in town. But carpeting will stain. It is something to consider when you plan your shop. (Combinations of tile and carpeting have also come into vogue with much success; carpeting at the check-out area and around the gondolas...tile in front of the fish tanks and other livestock areas.)

7. Have you any ideas in mind concerning a ceiling? A suspended ceiling seems to be the most practical. This type of construction appears to be standard in all shopping centers. Most tiles for suspended ceilings have insulating and sound-deadening values that are essential in a shop. Some dealers have used beamed ceilings with startling effect but the accoustical tiles were still placed above the beams to deaden sound. A few have used tongue and groove paneling but this is expensive and has a high echo factor that bounces all sounds back to the floor instead of absorbing them. On this matter of a ceiling, you must realize that if you install a canopy around the perimeter of the store with indirect lighting tucked away in this canopy and if you rely on your aquariums to provide a certain amount of colorful illumination, your ceiling will not become an important point in the decor simply because you will have lowered the ceiling, figuratively, to the canopy level.

8. How about the walls? You can use wood paneling all the way 'round. It's fine, but it stains and could buckle in the high-humidity aquarium section. Good paneling, wood or synthetic, looks beautiful and will improve the decor of any pet shop. If you believe you can get by with some of the less expensive veneers, your wall covering costs can be very low. But should you aim for walnut, cherry or elm the cost can be considerable. Another thought would be hardboard wall panels that look like real wood paneling but are actually wood grains printed or photographed onto a hardboard backing. Here, again, there are different grades but keep in mind that this type of paneling needs no upkeep and unless you hit it quite hard, will hold up very well against normal pet shop traffic.

THE WALLS, A LOUNGE

Most wall areas in a pet shop are covered by kennels or cages, aquariums or shelves. Little open wall space, other than what remains from canopy to ceiling, is in view. So your decision as to the kind of paneling you will have must be made with tongue in cheek; you'll need to decide on one more wall covering anyway. The most versatile material is pegboard and this you will need regardless of what other wall covering you choose. Pegboard, used under the canopy in the open sections, will hold leather goods, dog and cat toys, aquarium accessories, bird toys and miscellaneous items. It can be used to hang shelf cages and other large cages in your bird area. It can be purchased as unpainted hardboard and then painted any color you choose. It is also available pre-painted in wood grain or solid colors with a mar-resisting finish at higher cost. Pegboard can be obtained to match the artificial or real wood panels and wood trim to complete the shop's overall wood tone scheme. Or it can be had in bright colors that will complement and/or contrast to the softer wood tones. You or your designer can decide that. But because of its versatility and ease of installation, pegboard, whatever finish you select, combines looks, durability and merchandising properties possessed by no other wall covering. One suggestion, however! The use of this material should be restricted to 7 ft. or to the height of your canopy, if you use one. Above that line, wood paneling or just pastel painted walls will suffice. There is no need to go to the ceiling with pegboard...at least if you do not intend to use it to display

While we're on this subject of pegboard, every department in your dry goods section has items that lend themselves to both shelf and pegging. Aquarium items such as foods and filters, pumps and remedies all need shelves. But there are many food items, remedy items But there are many food items, remedy items and a host of others that take to pegging. Same with dog and cat items. Most of these items can be placed on shelves, but there are others, such as toys and accessories, that need a nice pegboard. (Leather and chain goods should be on pegboard and this is taken for granted here). Bird food and gravels come in boxes. They can go on shelves. But how to display bird toys and accessories without pegboard? What we are getting at is this: YOU MUST PROVIDE NOW, IN THE DESIGNING STAGE, FOR BOTH PEGBOARD AND SHELF SPACE FOR EVERY DEPARTMENT IN THE STORE. . . IN CLOSE PROXIMITY TO EACH OTHER. Time and time again pet shop owners run into the problem of having items of one department on a shelf or a gondola and then way across the room they are forced to display items from that same department that need hanging on a pegboard.

9. Planning to include a lounge? There are pros and cons to this one and you can lay down your money and take your pick. Some dealers contend a lounge allows dad to sit while mom takes her time looking. It's a point well made. The little ones can be deposited in your small area of sofa and 2 easy chairs and end table

and be left to drip ice cream on the furniture while the folks look at the fish. Frightening? Never. Better to have them in that spot, quiet and gooey, than banging on your tanks, feeding ice-cream to the monkey or pulling feathers.

Then there are dealers who take a different view. They want everyone on their feet, looking and wanting at all times. Their argument against a lounge is that it takes up too much valuable retail space and tends to create disinterest, a left-out attitude, on the part of those sitting.

They feel that the tendency is for mom and dad to want to return to the lounge as quickly as possible, gather up the children and leave. A lounge, whatever the arguments for or against, is something that will certainly add to the decor. The important thing is to decide if the space necessary for the lounge will return to you a fair profit in terms of customer pleasure and satisfaction. As we said a moment ago, the lounge concept comes down to personal choice on your part.

chapter 5
What Kind Of Fixtures Do You Need?

Unlike many other retail businesses, the pet trade is fortunate in that elaborate fixtures for display of stock are not a prerequisite for satisfactory traffic and profit. It is true, as in all retail areas, that taste and decor, neatness and cleanliness, are important, but it is not true that the relation between traffic and sales is, at any time, proportional to the quality of the fixtures used to display merchandise.

On the other side of the coin, amateurish fixtures, make-do gondolas and shelves, mismatched and scratched equipment, can go quite a way toward leaving a bad impression with a customer. That person might not be aware of why he or she is annoyed while visiting your store, but the overall picture of your shop has a definite bearing on his or her mood and desire to stay longer . . . which is, after all, what you are trying to accomplish.

Earlier, when we discussed wall coverings, we recommended pegboard as a versatile and economical wall covering. Obviously, there will be wall areas reserved for a more elaborate material treatment, but pegboard is always excellent behind shelves and for any wall where pegging can be utilized now or hopefully in the future. (An item that can be 'pegged' is any piece of merchandise that is packaged in such a way as to allow it to hang from a hook on a pegboard and be in perfect display; this differs from a 'shelfable' item that will stand by itself on a counter or a shelf.) To discuss pegboard for walls, let's discuss custom made walls as well as manufactured modules.

If you should settle on one type of decor, be it the Jungle motif or the South Sea Island motif or the Spanish motif. . . whatever you might consider your particular cup of tea. . . the

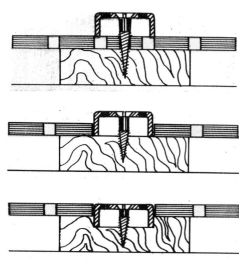

FIGURE 17 *Pegboard and standard installation techniques can be applied to almost every firm's individual display products.*

INSTALLATION OF FURRING STRIPS

For maximum strength under merchandising weight loads, RHC recommends that a wood furring strip (1″ x 3″) be mounted to the existing structural wall so as to provide a strong support to screw-mounted standards.

1. Determine high point of floor (to provide a constant point of reference; (2) determine height of strip above floor (to suit your installation requirements). (3) use plumb line to obtain vertical line; (4) determine height of furring strip; (5) strike a horizontal line; (6) mount furring strips from any constant (such as a corner or door); (7) mount each furring strip on desired On-center dimension, leveling each strip vertically (use level) as you work.

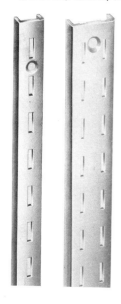

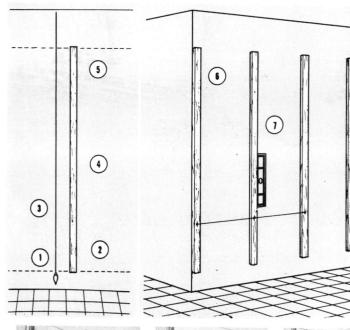

PROCEDURE FOR MOUNTING Spacemaster WALL STANDARDS

1. Center standard, and nail lightly. Drill holes to correspond to holes provided in standards. Secure with screws.

2. Insert one end of 24″, 30″, or 48″ crossbar (determined by on-center spacing of furring strip) into top-most and lowest slots of standard. Insert other end of crossbar into corresponding slots of second standard. Use spirit level on crossbar to achieve horizontal alignment. For running walls repeat step 2 to desired wall length.

3. and 4. For panel installation BEHIND standards, secure ends of panels with screws to furring stip. Secure standards over panels with screws. Attach desired accessories.

5. For panel installation BETWEEN standards, follow step 2, then install pre-cut panels between standards. Use panel retaining clips to secure panels. Attach accessories.

chances are that you will want to 'build-in' your own wall covering. For instance, if you should use a design such as in Figure 16, shown earlier in the book, you would want the canopy built-in to your specifications. Nothing manufactured would be quite as suitable to you as your own design translated into final construction.

Under your canopy. . . or under where the canopy will be. . . and against the masonry wall, you would nail vertical 1″ by 3″ furring strips every 2 ft. on center. This construction would be for double standards and details of this construction plus a picture of the double standard is seen in Figure 17. The double standard is most ideal because it allows for a continuous shelf run whereas the single standard does not. However, for short wall runs, you might desire the single standard. If so, you would then nail in your 1″ by 3″ furring strips 23 13/32″ on center. Once these furring strips are up, the standards (double or single) are nailed or screwed up vertically on these strips. Short lengths of the same 1″ by 3″ material are nailed at the floor, midway up the wall and at the top edge to give support to the pegboard which is cut in panels and nailed flush to the standards.

When completed, the wall will appear as one continuous sheet of pegboard with vertical slotted double or single standards visible at the surface every 2 feet. This is completely versatile. Items can be hung from the pegboard at any point desired. Shelf brackets can be installed and either wood, metal or glass shelves placed at any height to cover whatever portion of the wall necessary. The shelves can be taken down in minutes or more added in an equal time. The panels can be painted along with the standards to make the entire wall one homogeneous unit. It can turn any wall into a very effective display panel. Simple to build, inexpensive in cost, it becomes part of your store, depreciable as a lease-hold item. But bear in mind that this type of construction, although inexpensive, is permanent. If you find that something else would be better suited on that wall, you must tear it down back to the masonry (or wood frame wall). It cannot be moved.

On the other hand, there are prefabricated wall units available that can be mounted against the wall. Such a unit, with accompanying sketches, is seen in Figure 18. Once against the wall, such a unit looks as though it were built in. But for an occasional anchor, it is completely moveable, completely flexible. This type of wall unit is available with canopy as shown in Figure 19 or comes without the canopy and can be made to fit under and become part of a canopy that you would build to your own specifications. The pegboard panels can be had in hardboard

or in stamped metal. The shelves are available in wood (solid) or compressed wood chips (composition board), metal or glass, depending on the manufacturer and your desires. (We'll talk about other shelves a little later on.) An advantage of the pre-fab wall unit is that, buying all fixtures from one manufacturer, you can purchase various accessories that will make the wall unit so much more versatile. At the same time, these accessories can be taken from the wall unit, when the occasion arises, and used on other display gondolas.

GONDOLAS, SHELVES

In most pet shops, wall shelving is not an end-all for displaying stock. It is often necessary to have floor gondolas, such as those pictured in Figure 20. Normal gondola lengths are 4, 8 and 12 feet. Widths are 3, 4 or 5 feet. Height is usually 50 to 54 inches. The length of a gondola depends on the available room, obviously, but the width should be 4 feet. This would give you bottom shelves on both sides of the gondola that are 2 feet wide, just about as wide as you will need. The height should not be over 54 inches to allow you a complete view across the store. A tall gondola means less visual control. Oftentimes, dealers will put an easel display on the top shelf of a gondola which can block out vision, especially for a woman clerk who is only 5′6″ tall. Remember, tall gondolas can make security a problem.

Shelves normally come in 2½, 4 and 5 feet lengths. The lengths you will need will depend on the distance apart you place your standards. (We suggest 2 ft. for a wall installation, which means that you can purchase your shelves in 2½ ft. lengths.) Widths are from 6 to 24 inches in 2 inch increments. For the greatest versatility, you would want a minimum of 4 of these widths: 6, 10, 14 and 18 inches. As we mentioned earlier, materials come in wood, metal and glass as shown in Figure 21.

The various types of brackets to hold these shelves are shown in Figure 22. As you can see, they come straight, adjustable, and in different lengths to match the widths of your shelves. An adjustable bracket is one that can be lowered from horizontal to allow the shelf it holds to slant. With glass or wire retainers on this type of shelf, dump or bulk displays can be made of items such as dog toys, fish foods, bird toys, promotional dog coats and other items that lend themselves to dump merchandising. In Figure 22 are pictured glass binning, wire binning and wire baskets, all designed to make display work easier for you. Each of these items runs the cost of a gondola or wall display up. But over the years, the savings in stocking time

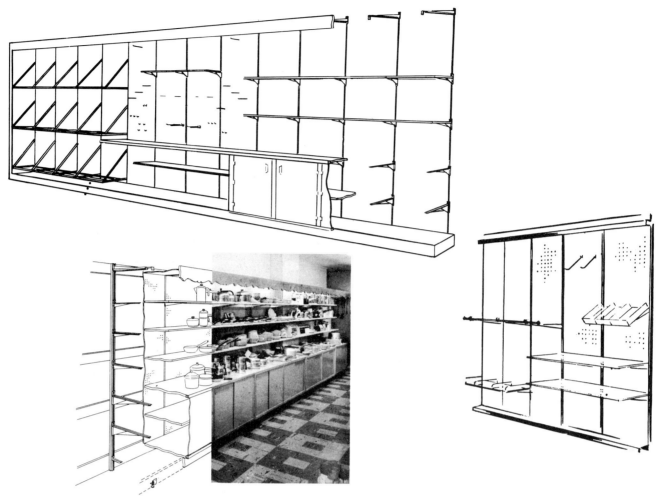

FIGURE 18 *Here are some typical wall unit set-ups, with and without canopy.*

FIGURE 19 *Pre-fabricated canopies are readily available.*

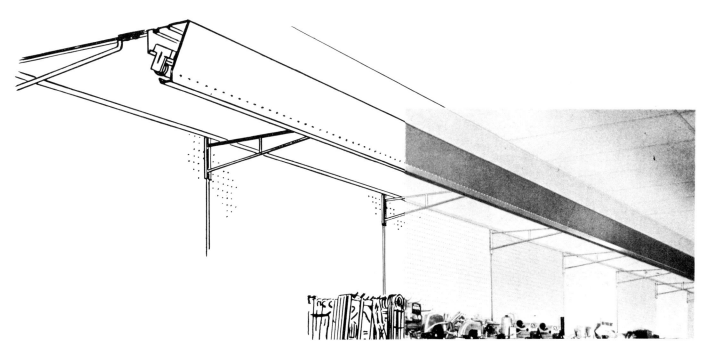

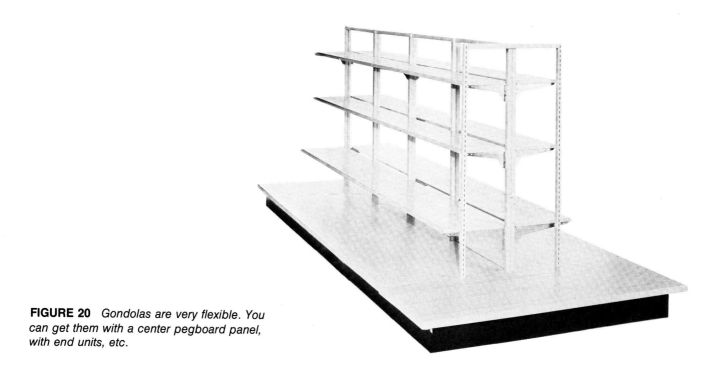

FIGURE 20 *Gondolas are very flexible. You can get them with a center pegboard panel, with end units, etc.*

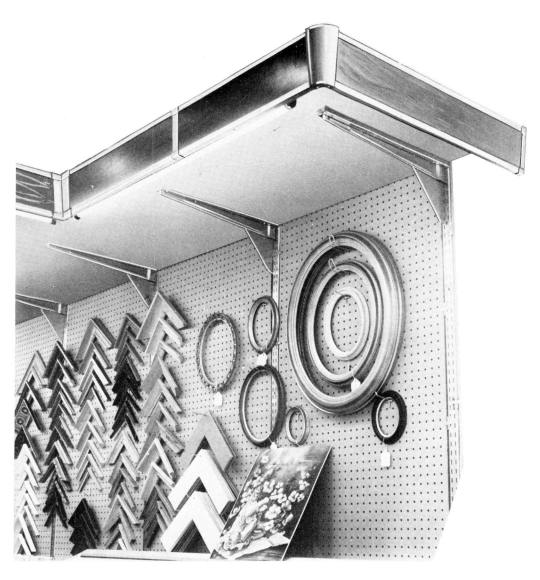

FIGURE 19 *Pre-fabricated canopies are readily available.*

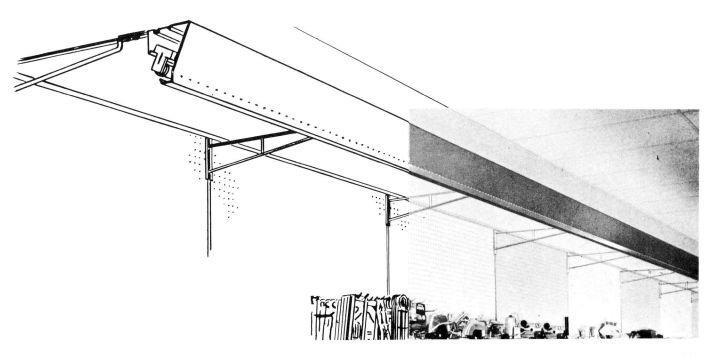

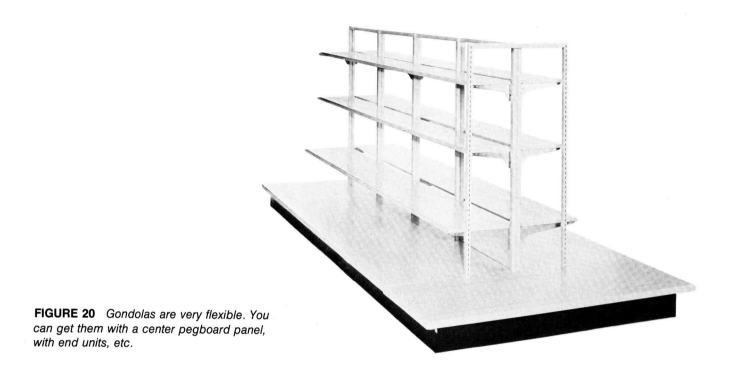

FIGURE 20 *Gondolas are very flexible. You can get them with a center pegboard panel, with end units, etc.*

76

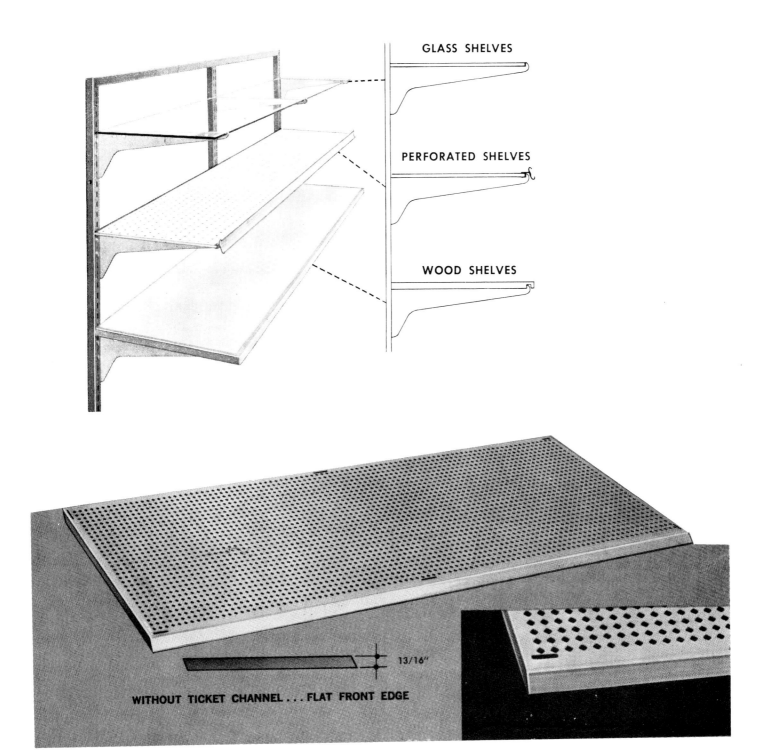

GLASS SHELVES

PERFORATED SHELVES

WOOD SHELVES

13/16"

WITHOUT TICKET CHANNEL . . . FLAT FRONT EDGE

FIGURE 21 *Shelving is also very flexible.*
Here are just a few examples.

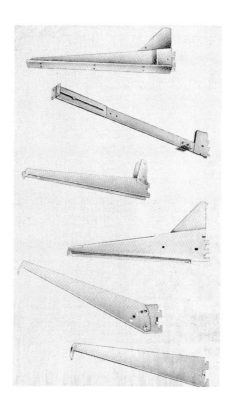

BANDING APPLICATION

DIVIDING APPLICATION

BINNING APPLICATION

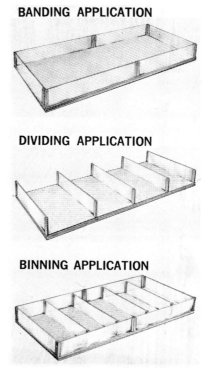

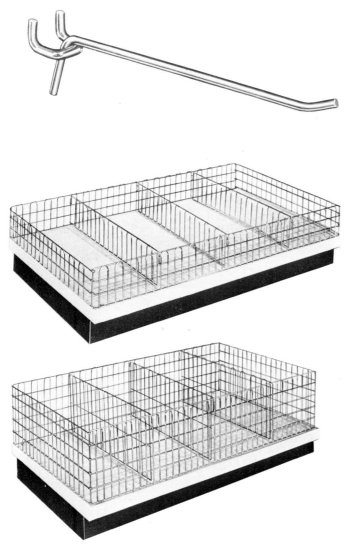

FIGURE 22 *Pegboard components are numerous. Here are some you will need.*

78

and the increased sales because you have the product out for the customer to get to it will more than pay for the initial outlay. None of these things are essential; but they all make for a smoother operation, a neater, more modern shop.

You will need a variety of hooks for pegging items. . .a variety of lengths as well as a variety of hook diameters. Should you display your leather and chain goods on a wall (and we'll discuss that next), you will need hooks 5/32'' in diameter up to 3/16''. In fact, it's smart to buy both of these diameters simply because not all the manufacturers punch the same diameter hole in their poly bags and you thus gain in flexibility by having hooks of 2 different diameters available when stocking starts. Hooks are available in other diameters, but these 2 should suffice for all products. Hooks come 2½, 4, 6, 9 and 12 inches in length and it is just as well to have some of each on hand.

Once you begin to display, you'll be amazed at the various lengths of hooks you will need. Hooks are available straight single, straight double, curved, inclined. You will find that the single straight hook in the lengths we discussed above should do for any and all display work you will come up against. A dozen cat collars will fit on a 9 inch straight hook with a diameter of 5/32''. A dozen 21 and 23 inch heavy collars will fit on a 12 inch hook with a 3/16'' diameter. A dozen fish nets, hung by their handles, will fit quite easily on a 4 inch hook, 5/32'' diameter. However, a dozen of the extra heavy rawhide bones, blister packed on cards, will take at least 2 of the 12 inch straight hooks, 3/16'' diameter, 6 per hook.

HARD-TO-DISPLAY ITEMS

Normally, most merchandise, especially cans and boxes, will fit on your shelves with no problem. But here and there there are lines of merchandise that require special display treatment. Leather and chain goods, books and dog apparel (sweaters, blankets, coats) are 3 such categories. Let's tackle them one at a time.

When we say leather and chain goods we mean collars, leashes, harnesses, choke chains, chain leads, muzzles, tie-out stakes and tie-out chains, training and traffic leads. In short, any and all restraining items for pets that can be worn with the exception of the fancy collars. These will be discussed later and will be displayed elsewhere in the shop.

Leather and chain goods can be displayed in one of 2 ways: on a revolving rack or on a pegboard wall panel. The revolving rack concept (Figure 23) contends that such a rack takes little space on the floor, is accessible completely

from one position and does not take up valuable wall space. For the shop that needs every bit of wall space, the revolving rack might be the best way of displaying these products. But, the revolving rack is easy to 'mess.' Never, never think that your customers will be thoughtful enough to put an item back where they found it. It will never happen. A revolving rack is just a maze of projecting hooks that all look alike. The collar is taken off one hook; the rack revolves slightly and the customer, still not satisfied, puts the collar back on another hook. A revolving rack can be completely jumbled and disheveled in one afternoon of heavy traffic. It must be straightened constantly and for this reason, taking an inventory of such a display is very difficult.

The other method of displaying leather and chain goods is on a pegboard wall. To my way of thinking, this is the most sensible, most convenient and easiest to check. Different collars of different sizes and different qualities can be hung on hooks in neat rows, short hooks for small collars, longer hooks as the sizes and weights graduate to the heavy dog class. Six foot leads would go on hooks at the top of the panel; the 4 foot leads would be further down on the wall. Tie-out chains can be displayed on hooks providing the bags and bag headers are strong enough to support them. (Oftentimes, the weight of the chain in the bag is too great to be supported on a hook and it rips out.) Tie-out stakes can also be hung easily from hooks. So can muzzles. Round collars can be displayed best on hooks if you roll them first, much as they'll appear on the dog's necks. However, do not put the tongue through the buckle but by-pass it and put the tongue through the supporting loop behind the buckle. This is done so that the collar will retain its round shape yet not be marred by the buckle and the eye creasing the leather.

Harnesses, no matter how you hang them, are never as neat looking as you would like. Use 12 inch hooks for harnesses. My suggestion is that you put one size per hook and then not over 6 harnesses on a hook, depending, of course, on the size harness in question. Some of the smaller puppy-kitten harnesses can be displayed 12 to a hook, but 12 would be the limit.

Choke chains hang easily. They can be displayed on hooks according to their weight and length. If you have 3 weights, (or 4), allow a separate section for each and display the different lengths for each weight. Thus, if you stock light, medium and heavy chokes (to cover yourself against all breeds), allow one section of paneling for the light chokes and have a separate hook for 10, 12, 14, 16 and 18 inch sizes . . . all light chains. Then have a section of paneling for medium chokes and a hook for 16,

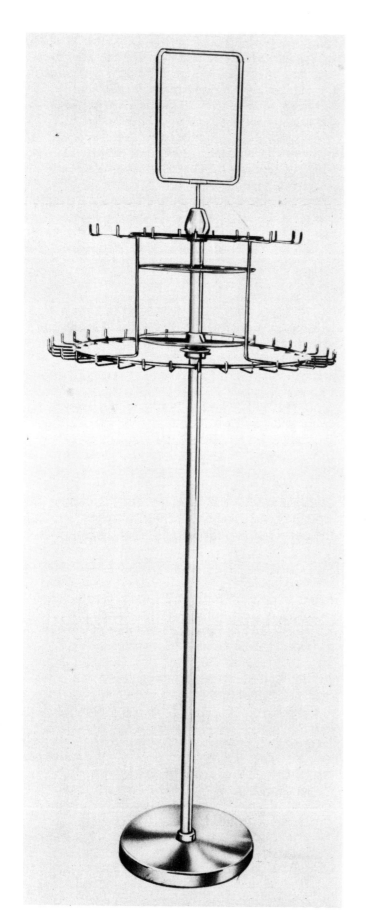
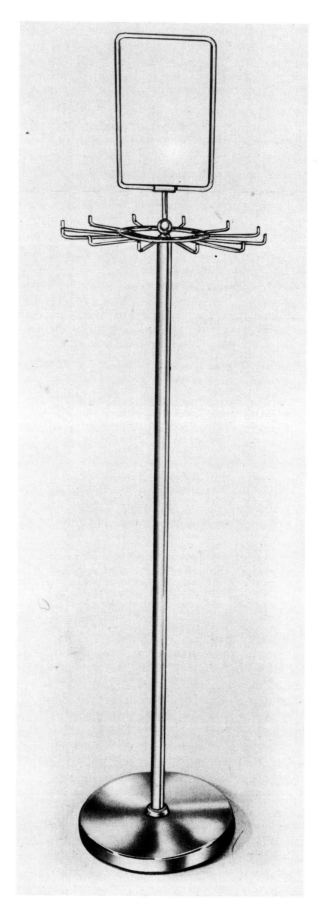

FIGURE 23 *Here are 2 revolving racks
suitable for small, medium and large leather
and chain display.*

18, 20, 22 and 24 inch sizes. Finally, you would have a last section for the heavy chokes and a hook for 16, 18, 20, 22, 24, 26, 28 and 30 inch sizes. Keep all the hooks at the same level on your pegboard and you will be able to tell at a glance the ones that are out of place.

One thing more on choke chains. Many pet shops stock both imported and domestic chokes. Imported ones are less expensive than our domestic chokes but the chrome lasting qualities on the imported ones are not as high. Unless you inspect the rings at the ends of the chokes to locate country of origin, you cannot tell at a glance which are imported and which are American-made. For this reason, it makes good sense to separate on your pegboard the 2 types and to make some kind of a sign to help both your clerks and your customers determine which is which.

Small, pressure sensitive labels and a marking pen make suitable identifying signs. A machine, such as the Dymo, that makes exact plastic one-line labels, will do an excellent job. Other markers, such as the Label-Matic, are discussed later under the chapter on setting up your first inventory. The important thing is to identify both quality and size of the various chokes. Going one step further, this same marking system can be used quite effectively for identifying all leather and chain goods when a pegboard system of display is used. Neat, concise and permanent markers will help your customer. Later on you will find that it will also be of great help to you when making an order or taking inventory.

THE BOOK SECTION

Books can be hung from the wall or gondola pegboard by the same brackets that hold the shelves. A 4-pocket rack is shown in Figure 24. This is suitable for the smallest book department. The 2 and 3 pocket racks are shown because some shops prefer scattering several racks around the shop in the various departments rather than concentrating all the books in one location. Any of these wall racks will display books effectively but keep in mind that they do eat into valuable wall space. In Figures 24B and 24C, gondolas for book display are shown. Both of these racks will hold better than 700 books and are really too large for the average pet shop, but for the larger shop that stresses pet books and keeps a large assortment, one of these gondolas will be the answer.

Figure 24D shows 2 floor revolving racks which take up very little floor space and will hold enough books for the medium to large shop. This revolving rack, however, will not take some

of the larger hardcover books. So, you should provide a small book shelf close by to hold a few of the more expensive hard cover volumes. If all this discussion on racks for books seems a bit confusing, keep in mind that if you have extra wall space, any of the racks in 24A would work. A large floor area with an emphasis on books would necessitate either 24B or 24C. The racks shown in 24D would be for the average shop with a minimum of wall and floor space.

The tried and true method of displaying dog coats, blankets, sweaters and raincoats has been to pile them out on a table, much in the manner of a ladies-ready-to-wear department. In recent years, however, this rather not-so-tidy way of display has given in to a more sophisticated, and certainly neater, system. Look at Figure 25. Here are 5 of many different racks available to suit your needs. The coats or sweaters are hung from young ladies' or girls' skirt hangers, the type with the built-on metal clothes snaps, and then hung on the rack of your choice.

Figures 25A, 25B and 25E are floor racks of different design. Figure 25A has the advantage here because some items for dog wear not suited to hanging can be displayed on the middle glass table. Figure 25C shows how a suitable hangrail can be had to mount on pegboard standards. This can be added to or decreased as needed and can be taken down completely and stored when the apparel season is finished for the year. Figure 25D is the same idea but here the hangrail is mounted on the top of a gondola. This type has the advantage of being able to merchandise tie-in items on the gondola below the hangrail. Example: On one rack you hang raincoats and on the shelf below the rail you display dog boots. Or another: On a rail you display fancy coats and on the shelf beneath you have hair ribbons, hats, perfumes and other specialty items.

Some sweaters and blankets will come to you boxed. This is fine for strict shelf display but, in all honesty, you would rather have the customer come in, pick up the sweater or the coat and get the feel of the material. It will always sell easier in the hand than in the box; so although boxes look neat and are easy to inventory and to keep straight, they will inhibit the sale of apparel in the long run. The hangrails shown in Figure 25 should provide your answer.

THE CHECK-OUT COUNTER

Whether you built it in at layout time or bring in a ready-made fixture, you will need a check-out counter. In Figures 26A, 26B and 26C we show typical components of a check-out counter. Figures 26A and 26C could be used

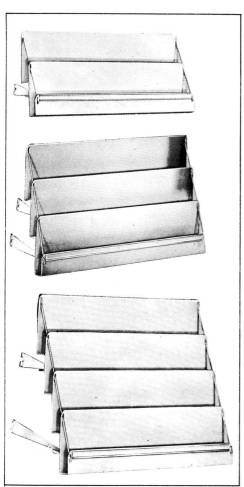

FIGURE 24A

FIGURE 24 *Books can be displayed in a number of ways. They can be shown from wall pockets on pegboard (Figure 24A) or from book gondolas (Figures 24B and 24C). Or, you can have your choice of floor racks available from pet book publishers (Figure 24D).*

FIGURE 24B   **FIGURE 24C**

FIGURE 24D

FIGURE 25A

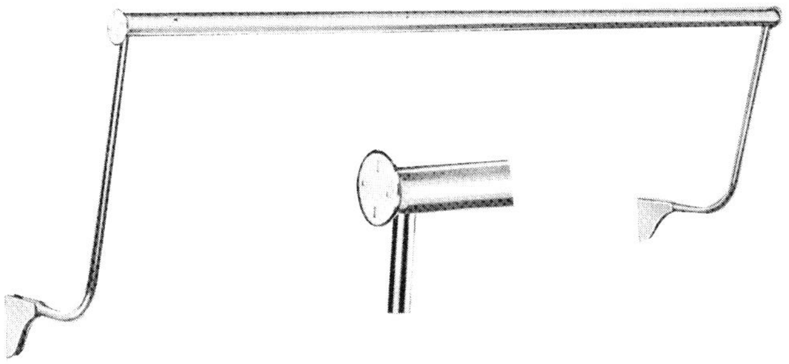

FIGURE 25C

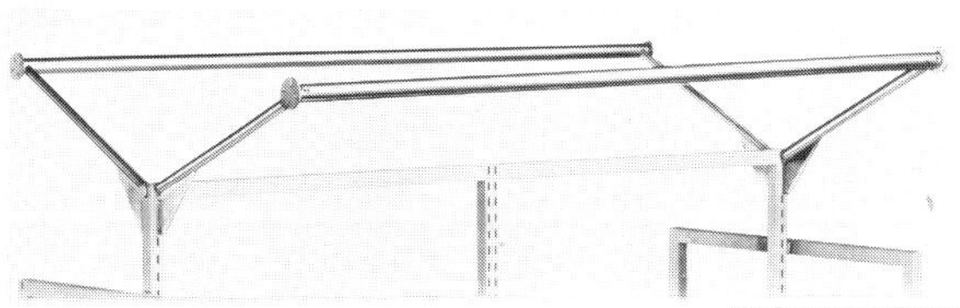

FIGURE 25D

FIGURE 25E

FIGURE 25 *Two examples of floor racks are shown in Figures 25A and 25B. A hangrail for use on wall standards is shown in Figure 25C. A hangrail mounted on top of a gondola is illustrated in Figure 25D and a double floor rack in Figure 25E.*

FIGURE 25B

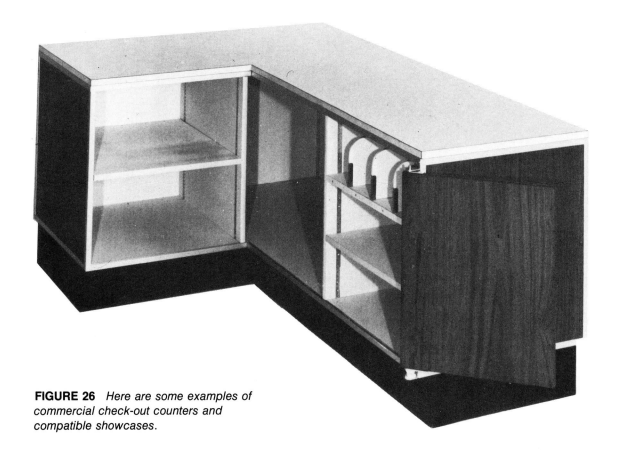

FIGURE 26 *Here are some examples of commercial check-out counters and compatible showcases.*

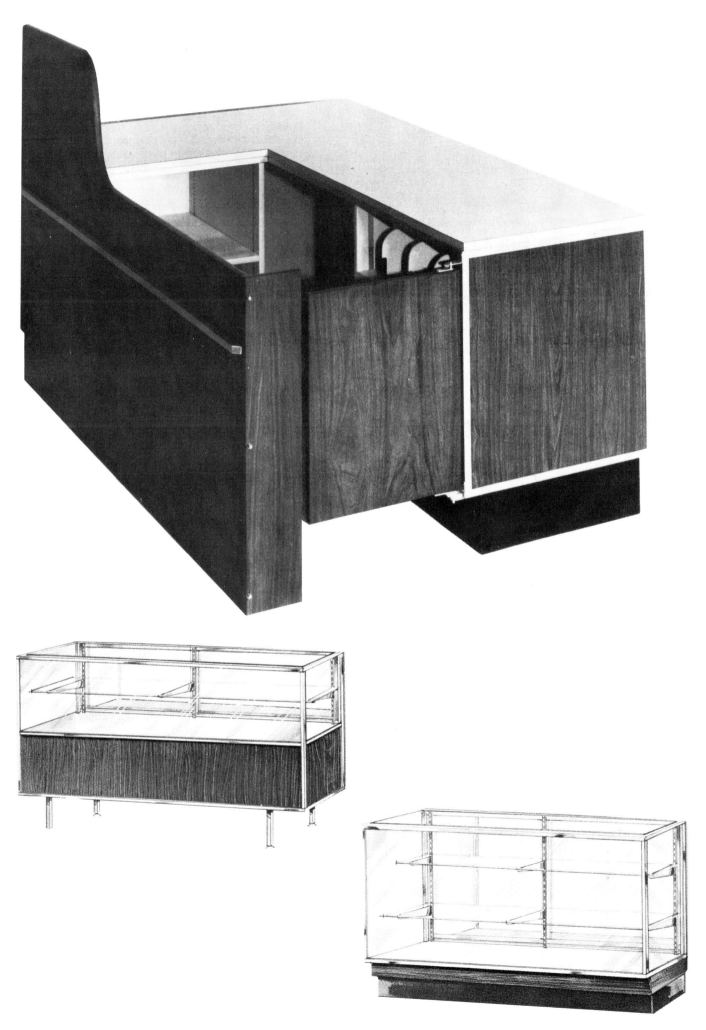

alone. There is plenty of room on the counter for a register and room under the counter to store bags, tape, suppliers' catalogs, etc. Figure 26B might be a little on the small size and should either be tied-in to the counter shown in 26A or possibly it could be joined to one of the showcase counters shown in 26D and 26E.

Back in the leather and chain goods discussion we mentioned that fancy collars are displayed differently, usually layed flat on a dark background material (such as velvet) under light and usually in a glass showcase. This allows the customer to see but not always touch. It displays the collars to their glistening best, keeps them clean and sparkling and guarantees the upmost security against pilferage. This is mentioned because so often it is possible to use a glass showcase in conjunction with another counter to form a satisfactory check-out area. A "U" shaped check-out section could be easily put together by using the glass showcase (26D) as the base of the "U" and 2 counters as 26B to come up both sides to form the 2 arms of the "U." Not only does the showcase function as part of the check-out system but it becomes a very desirable display area, especially for high dollar items that need maximum security. And while we are on the topic of security, let's look at security cases.

There are many items in the pet shop which should, by virtue of their size and cost, be kept in special locations, preferably one that is visible to the public but locked. As we just mentioned, a glass showcase in part of the check-out complex works fine so long as there is a lock on the doors of that showcase. Not only are poodle collars usually found in such a case, but clipper blades, clippers themselves, expensive grooming items, expensive pumps and fancy pet jewelry are frequently added.

In Figure 27 you see a typical security case. Two shelf as well as 4 shelf cases are also available to fit any need, any desired area. They can be either mounted on pegboard or placed right on the shelf. The lock gives them the necessary protection. Not an absolute item for store use, it merits mentioning because so often glass showcases are crowded with poodle collars while the dog clippers are left out on some obscure shelf, quite out of sight. . . or so you think until you find that all you have on the shelf is the empty clipper box. Unfortunately, theft is one small negative side to the retail business and a factor that is with us whether we like it or not. None of us do, but you learn to live with it and keep pilferage to a minimum. For general pet supplies throughout the store, good visibility is mandatory; for the small and expensive items, the security case is the answer.

Metal sign holders, normally found in large department stores, have come into use in the pet industry in recent years. In Figure 28 we show quite a few sizes and shapes of metal sign holders that can be used in a pet shop. As the need for better design and quality of layout has increased, the retail pet business has come to the realization that good signing is part of the overall decor. Metal sign holders add professionalism to the displays, make it easier for the customer to locate items, help feature a promotion and act as silent salesmen in many ways. They should be considered if only as feature points for the various departments, i.e., one for fish foods, one for filters, one for tanks, dog remedies, bird feeds, etc. Fifteen such signs strategically located throughout the store would allow customers to locate desired merchandise quickly and without bothering you.

Panel signs, made of 3 dimensional letters, can be made up to suit any decor. With this type of signing, panels are constructed for only the main section of the shop, such as Tropical Fish, Dog and Cat, Bird and Small Animals. The letters used should be in agreement with the decor pattern you set. If, for example, your store is to have a circus air, then the letters you use would be a type known as P.T. Barnum. If your decor followed the South Sea Island motif, then your letters might be of a type known as keynote; if you should prefer an oriental or jungle motif, your letters might follow the type Verona. But there should always be a design relationship between the sections of your shop. Of course, this search for detail goes right down to the kind of colors of the signs you use throughout the store. Figure 29 shows styles of panel signs that are available.

CASH REGISTERS

It is not our intention here to go into the various cash registers available on the market today. That would be a treatise unto itself. However, the cash register is a very important member of the bookkeeping section of your business and there are a few points we would like to make in behalf of registers.

There still exists today the feeling that somehow a shop can be run successfully without a register. And this is quite true. There are hundreds of very profitable operations going on at this very minute where every transaction is written out on a sales slip and every bit of cash goes into what is simply known as a "cash drawer." But this method is slow and does not allow you the opportunity to check out the success or failure of any one department in the store without going back and separating items on each and every sales slip at the end of the day. Can you imagine what it would be like trying to come up with a total of, let's say,

FIGURE 27 *Every shop needs at least one security case. They come in various shelf sizes and, of course, with locks.*

FIGURE 28 *In-store signs are tools for creating sales. Too many retailers don't invest the few extra dollars needed to get the professional look.*

PET SHOP

TROPICAL FISH

|←6″→|

|6″|

DOG SUPPLIES

FIGURE 29 *Panel signs and type are available from fixture stores or art supply outlets.*

AB
ABCDEFGHIJKLMNOPQRS TUVWXYZ&1234567890

Style: Microbold (Upper Case)

Height	Average Width	Thickness
4″	5″	½″
6″	7¾″	¾″
8″	10″	¾″
10″	12½″	¾″

ABC
ABCDEFGHIJKLMNOPQRSTUVWXYZ& 1234567890

Style: Helvetica (Upper Case)

Height	Average Width	Thickness
3″	2½″	½″
4″	3¼″	½″
5″	4″	¾″
6″	5″	¾″
8″	6½″	¾″
10″	8¼″	¾″

abc
abcdefghijklmnopqrstuvwxyz 1234567890

Style: Helvetica (Lower Case)

Height	Average Width	Thickness
4″	3″	½″
6″	4″	¾″
8″	5¾″	¾″
10″	7″	¾″

ABC
ABCDEFGHIJKLMNOPQRSTUVWX YZ1234567890

Style: Baskerville (Upper Case)

Height	Average Width	Thickness
3″	3″	½″
4″	4¼″	½″
6″	6¼″	¾″
8″	8½″	¾″
10″	10½″	¾″

abc
abcdefghijklmnopqrstuvwxyz&1234567890

Style: El Boldo (Lower Case)

Height	Average Width	Thickness
4″	3″	½″
5½″	3¾″	½″
8″	5¾″	¾″

89

livestock sold each day for a week by the sales slip method in a busy shop? Every slip would need inspection and the livestock transactions written down and totalled every evening. The cash drawer is fine if you are not interested in the various departments of your store. It is also a very dangerous system where there are more than the owners working the store. And face it, your desire is not to run the business by yourself indefinitely.

With expansion and growth will come more assistance, more employees, and it is at this point that the need for a register becomes immediately evident. It would be wise, at the beginning, when such a machine would be part of the initial investment package, to consider a register. We are not speaking of some grandiose computer with a multitude of departmental and clerk keys. The machine should be sophisticated to meet today's demands because, as we mentioned at the beginning of this book in our section on bookkeeping, your accounting procedures will be a reflection of the exposition of your cash register tapes. Your register will be the machine into which you feed daily sales and disbursements and out of which should come a resume tape that will be transcribed directly into your bookkeeping system. So it should be sophisticated, but not to the point where the investment you put into such a machine is far greater than you can ever hope to gain back in either service or information. Keep in mind that you pay for any and every extra key you ask for on your register; it makes good sense to keep the key count down to what you feel you will need.

You may want individual department totals. . . 3 or 4 keys that will tell you at the end of each day what you have done in the fish department, dog and cat department, bird department. But our feeling is that 4 should be adequate. One could be fish dry goods. A second could be dog and cat dry goods. Three could be a bird and small animal dry goods. A fourth could be all livestock. At the end of the day, when closing out the register, you would be able to get up-to-the-minute sales information on those 4 categories. Thus, at any point in the year's business, you would know which department or departments were ahead. You would then have the figures to make adjustments in both space and inventory to increase the department that was falling down or push ahead to greater heights that department that was doing well.

Figure 30 shows 2 registers typical of those adequate for the pet shop retail business. We are not suggesting one machine over the other; for that matter, we are not suggesting either machine. But these are typical and you should apprise yourself of all available register information before making the investment. A new register can run from $1,000 to $18,000 and this kind of an outlay should demand careful consideration.

There is, of course, another approach and that is the used register. Many fixture and supply houses handle used cash registers. Although your motto should be one of caution where a used machine is concerned, it is often possible to pick up a good used machine at a bargain price. Let The Buyer Beware is still a good slogan and like a used car, you can make a dandy deal and then again, you can buy a lemon.

PRICING INSTRUMENTS

Satisfactory marking machines are often put off until the day the initial order arrives. Then there is a rush to the office supply house to pick up something that will mark that first order. If the machine is too big or too complicated, it is used for part of that first order and then put aside for some other easier, quicker method. The thing to avoid is buying something in the beginning that is too big or too complicated. So before that first inventory comes rolling in, let's take a good hard look at what's available that can do the job in your store.

The simplest devices are the grease pencil and marking pen. But both of these items, while inexpensive and flexible, are too slow to mark any amount of merchandise. Also, they lack the look of professionalism which is a necessary factor even when we consider pricing merchandise. At the other end of the marking spectrum is the sophisticated machine that turns out stick labels or string tag labels as you turn a handle to feed the labels past the inking-pricing mechanism. These are time-honored machines that are used today by all types of retailing businesses. But our feeling is that they still lack the flexibility necessary for fast marking. They are used universally by department stores because more than one line of figures can be printed on each tag. One line can give a cost code, one line can give the code date when the item was purchased and a third line can give the selling price. And it could well be that you might want to put all this information on your selling tags. But our feeling is that you should not.

Well, then, what kind of marking system can you use? Figure 31 shows 3 kinds of marking systems that will work well in a pet shop. Label-Matick (SIA) is a handy machine that can be carried around the shop and will affix a pressure sensitive label on any object. It will work as well on boxes as it will on cans and as well on choke chains as it will on a bird cage. If you wish to keep a record on the selling tag as

Pet shops come in all shapes and sizes. Just about any location and/or shape has been successful as long as the basics of livestock knowledge, product merchandising and promotion are followed.

A rather inexpensive yet effective way to hold a pet shop together is by signing. But the signing must be neat, concise and the graphics consistent.

*Most grooming shops and grooming departments within pet shops
set aside a small product display adjacent to the grooming
area to capitalize on impulse sales.*

Your shop's aquarium department offers great potential for decorative beauty. Many choose to highlight their tanks with lighting; others decorate the entire department in a consistent style.

Pegboard is the pet shop's best friend. With the pegboard as a base, the ease in changing fixtures and displays is limited only by your imagination.

One of the most unique in-store fixtures we've seen is this Disney-like fish which serves as the entrance to a shop's fishroom. It is startling but also inefficient as the shop must always have two people, one covering the fishroom and the other the checkout counter.

Retail fixtures can be as modern as you want. Just check a fixture manufacturer's catalog. You'll be surprised and pleased!

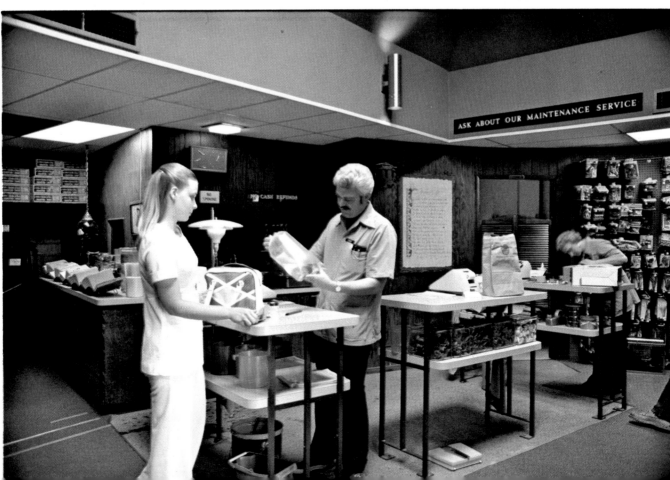

Too many pet shop owners think of promotion only as advertising. Publicity
is usually easy to obtain and most always free. Maybe your local TV or radio
station is looking for an expert on pets?

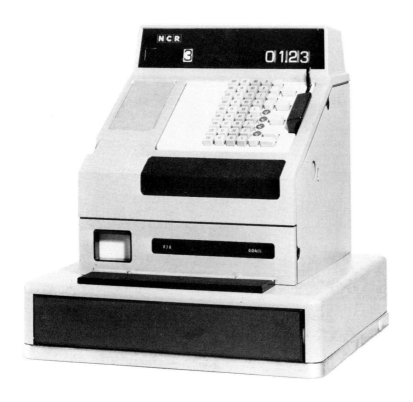

FIGURE 30 *Cash registers are expensive but form the core of your accounting system. Here are just 2 of the many models on the market.*

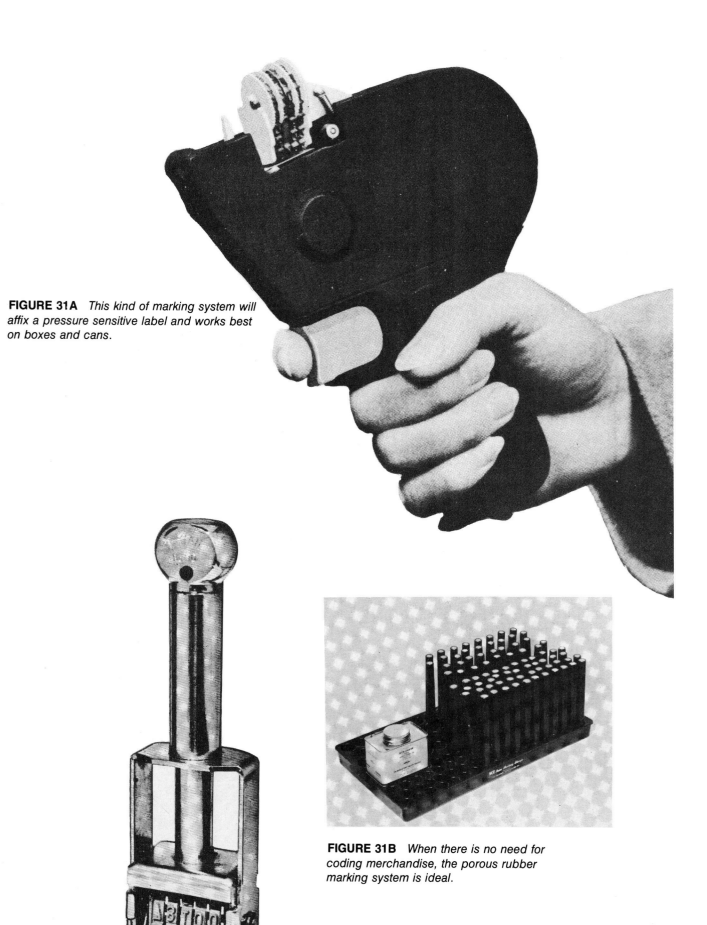

FIGURE 31A *This kind of marking system will affix a pressure sensitive label and works best on boxes and cans.*

FIGURE 31B *When there is no need for coding merchandise, the porous rubber marking system is ideal.*

FIGURE 31C *This marking tool is similar to that shown in Figure 31B but is not well-suited to marking small and/or flexible objects like dog toys.*

to when you purchased an item, use different colored labels. White could represent January, green could represent February, red, March, yellow, April and so on. If you run out of colors for the labels, then have different colored inks represent the various months.

Where there is no need for coding the merchandise as to date purchased or cost price, then the porous rubber price marking system such as the one by NCR, Figure 31B, will do a splendid job. Each stamp has one price on its end. The particular one we show will give you 500 to 800 quick-drying price marks without re-inking. These stamps come in a set and will cover just about any price you will ever have in your store. For marking case goods, where all the prices are the same for a 12 or 24 count, they are the easiest and quickest method devised. Because of the slimness of the stamp tube, they are also ideal for marking items such as small latex dog toys, air pump parts, cat collars. They also work well on round objects such as heater tubes, aquarium ornaments (ceramic type), balls, bird toys. However, since they are stamped directly on the object, they

would be a problem with a dark object such as a black leather collar or an object such as a choke chain.

Another type of marking machine which will do a similar job to the porous individual rubber stamps is the one shown in Figure 31C. Containing its own ink pad, the numbers can be changed on the machine by merely turning the dial. This type of a machine is quite versatile and again, like the porous rubber stamps. is ideal for case goods. But for small objects and especially flexible objects such as dog toys, this particular type of marking equipment is difficult to use. It is also useless on black leather goods and choke chains. Like the porous rubber stamp, the only answer for this type of merchandise is to stamp the price on a pressure sensitive label and then affix it to the item.

A pet shop should have a marking machine that can be carried around the store. The 3 examples given here fill this need. A marking machine should be able to mark all kinds of merchandise and all kinds of materials. With few exceptions, these machines will cover every situation.

chapter 6
You Must Become An Expert In Livestock!

The day you open your pet store you are an authority on all pets. Like the doctor hanging up his shingle, the cook putting on his chef's hat or the pilot sliding into the cockpit, you are, because you are running a pet shop, an expert on pets. You would never open a shop without knowing the vast quantities of information needed to dispense advice to all who come into your store. Or at least this is what the public believes. And of course, they are right. After all, why did you go into business unless you could talk with knowledge on the subject of pets?

Because of the nature of the store, the girl in the discount house is not expected to be expert on all phases of pet health and pet products. But you are. And it is important that you take a cold, objective look at yourself and determine if you really know pets. If you decide that you are weak in certain areas, you must determine where and how fast you can absorb the required knowledge. Those already in the business learn fast or else. If you are just in the planning stages of a shop, you must have basic facts about all pets before you put your first pencil mark on your store plans. Your knowledge can't just be confined to pets you plan to carry. When people see "pet shop" on the store front, it's an invitation for questions on all types of livestock.

The more knowledge you have before you spend your first dollar for shop stationery, the better off you, and your customers, will be. How you obtain this knowledge is not as important as the fact that you get it. The first suggestion is that you read. This is particularly important for the established retailer. He must continually refresh his knowledge of pets in addition to gleaning the new techniques and points of information constantly being developed. The scope of this

Suggested Reading List

AQUARIA

☐ Atlas of Fish Diseases, Elkan/Reichenback-Klinke, T.F.H. Publications, Inc., 211 W. Sylvania Ave., Neptune City, NJ 07753.

☐ Breeding Aquarium Fishes, Books II & III, T.F.H. Publications, Inc., 211 W. Sylvania Ave., Neptune City, NJ 07753.

☐ Exotic Aquarium Fishes, Innes, T.F.H. Publications, Inc., 211 W. Sylvania Ave., Neptune City, NJ 07753.

☐ Fish and Invertebrate Culture, Spotte, Wiley & Sons, Inc., John, 605 Third Ave., New York, NY 10016.

☐ Fish Behavior: Why Fishes Do What They Do, Adler, T.F.H. Publications, Inc., 211 W. Sylvania Ave., Neptune City, NJ 07753.

☐ Freshwater Fishes of the World, Sterba, T.F.H. Publications, Inc., 211 W. Sylvania Ave., Neptune City, NJ 07753.

☐ Manual of Aquarium Plants, Roe, Aquarium Stock Co., Inc., Book Div., 27 Murray St., New York, NY 10007.

☐ Marine Aquarium Keeping: The Science, Animals, and Art, Spotte, Wiley & Sons, Inc., John, 605 Third Ave., New York, NY 10016.

BIRDS

☐ Diseases of Cage and Aviary Birds, ed. by Petrak, Lea & Febiger, 600 Washington Sq., Philadelphia, PA 19106.

☐ Parrots & Related Birds, Bates & Busenbark, TFH Books, 211 W. Sylvania Ave., Neptune City, NJ 07753.

CATS

☐ Cats, An Intelligent Owner's Guide, Henderson, Mead, Transatlantic Arts, Inc., North Village Green, Levittown, NY 11756.

☐ Complete Book of Cat Care, Whitney, Doubleday & Co., Inc., 501 Franklin Ave., Garden City, NY 11530.

DOGS

☐ Behavior Problems in Dogs, Campbell, American Veterinary Publications, Inc., Drawer KK, Santa Barbara, CA 93102.

☐ City Dog, Wolters, E.P. Dutton & Co., Inc., 201 Park Ave. So., New York, NY 10003.

☐ Complete AKC Dog Book, 15th edition, Howell Book House Inc., 730 Fifth Ave., New York, NY 10019.

☐ Grooming All Toy Dogs, Kalstone, Howell Book House Inc., 730 Fifth Ave., New York, NY 10019.

☐ International Dog Encyclopedia, Dangerfield, Howell, Howell Book House, 845 Third Ave., New York, NY 10022.

☐ Poodle Clipping & Grooming Book, The Complete, Kalstone, Howell Book House, 845 Third Ave., New York, NY 10022.

☐ Successful Dog Showing, Forsyths, Howell Book House Inc., 730 Fifth Ave., New York, NY 10019.

☐ Understanding Your Dog, Fox, Coward, McCann & Geoghegan, Inc., 200 Madison Ave., New York, NY 10016.

☐ What to do Till the Veterinarian Comes, Pommery, Chilton Book Co., Radnor, PA 19089.

MISCELLANEOUS

☐ Living Mammals of the World, Sanderson, Doubleday & Co., Inc., 501 Franklin Ave., Garden City, NY 11530.

☐ Living Reptiles of the World, Schmidt, Inger, Doubleday & Co., Inc., 501 Franklin Ave., Garden City, NY 11530.

☐ Merck Veterinary Manual, Merck & Co., Inc., Rahway, NJ 07065.

☐ Names For Pets, Kolatch, Jonathan David Publishers, 68-22 Eliot Ave., Middle Village, NY 11379.

☐ Retail Pet Supply Manual, Miller, Book Dept., Pets/Supplies/Marketing Magazine, One East First St., Duluth, MN 55802.

☐ Sales Promotion Handbook, ed. by Aspley, Riso, The Dartnell Corporation, Chicago, IL 60640.

☐ Snakes: the Keeper and the Kept, Kauffeld, Doubleday & Co., Inc., 501 Franklin Ave., Garden City, NY 11530.

PERIODICALS

☐ American Cage Bird Magazine, 3449 N. Western Ave., Chicago, IL 60618.

☐ Aquarium Industry, Toadtown, Magalia, CA 95954.

☐ Audubon Magazine, 1130 Fifth Ave., New York, NY 10028.

☐ Cats Magazine, P.O. Box 4106, Pittsburgh, PA 15202.

☐ Dog World, 10060 West Roosevelt Rd., Westchester, IL 60153.

☐ Kennel Review, 828 N. LaBrea Ave., Hollywood, CA 90038.

☐ Marine Aquarist, The, P.O. Box 35, Marlbora, MA 01752.

☐ National Wildlife, Box 343, Wakefield, MA 01880.

☐ Pet Age, 2561 N. Clark St., Chicago, IL 60614.

☐ Pet Dealer, The, 225 W. 34th St., New York, NY 10001.

☐ Pets/Supplies/Marketing, 1 East First St., Duluth, MN 55802.

☐ Pure-Bred Dogs American Kennel Gazette, 51 Madison Ave., New York, NY 10010.

☐ Simian, The, Box 343, Wakefield, MA 01880.

☐ Tropical Fish Hobbyist, 211 W. Sylvania Ave., Neptune City, NJ 07753.

U.S. Retail Pet Organizations

(Retail pet associations, all regional in nature, are surfacing all across the country. Below is a listing of known groups as of January 1976. It is our strong feeling that every retailer should belong to a trade association. If there is not one in your area, start it.)

☐ American Groomers Guild, Ltd., 185-22 Union Turnpike, Flushing, NY 11366.

☐ Illinois Retail Pet Supply Association, 5408 S. Harlem Ave., Summit, IL 60501.

☐ Maryland Association of Pet Industries, Inc., 1250 Columbia Mall, Columbia, MD 21044.

☐ Michigan Pet Retailers Association, Inc., P.O. Box 1144, Southgate, MI 48195.

☐ National Dog Groomers Association of America, Box 101, Clark, PA 16113.

☐ National Retail Pet Supply & Groomers Association, 14126 E. Whittier Blvd., Whittier, CA 90605.

☐ Pet Dealers Association of New Jersey, 61 Park Ave., Rutherford, NJ 07070.

☐ Pet Retailers Organization of New York State, 18-14 Parsons Blvd., Whitestone, NY 11357.

☐ Professional Pet Association of America, 9680 Blackwell Rd., Central Point, OR 97501.

☐ Tri-State Pet Dealers Association, 3135 Dixie Highway, Erlander, KY 41018.

☐ United Pet Dealers Association Inc., 2601 E. 16th St., Brooklyn, NY 11235.

☐ Washington State Pet Dealers Association, P.O. Box 16031, Seattle, WA 98116.

☐ Western Pennsylvania Pet Dealers Association, Rte. 19, West View, PA 15229.

book prohibits a full discussion of the care and treatment of livestock. However, a comprehensive list of publicatons and associatons is presented on these pages in addition to a recommended reading list for beginner and veteran alike.

Along with a constant program of reading, the beginner would do well to work in a pet shop for a time. Most retailers will be glad to help out a beginner providing your new shop is not planned for the teacher's trading area. There is no better way to learn the business than by becoming involved on a day-to-day basis. Every problem, every sale, every complaint becomes a lesson first hand. Compensation in money is really not important; the compensation in information and experience could well be worth a thousand times over the immediate monetary compensation. Continuing conversations with pet supply distributors and livestock wholesalers is a good idea. If they are in the business of supplying pet shops they should know something about shop operations. Interchange of information with other retailers is also beneficial. Retail trade associations are another area for such interchange. As a beginner you should try to attend meetings and should have no problem in gaining permission. Read and listen. Remember, the one cardinal rule is to provide a service to your customer. . . a service not available elsewhere.

The knowledge you gain must become a part of your daily business life. It must be natural and spontaneous. It must be born of a certainty that you know exactly what you are talking about. And this knowledge must be imparted to your customer in such a way that he has confidence in you and your advice. Be assured that there is no advantage gained in picking up a package or box and reading from the directions. The customer can do the same . . . unless he can't read. Reading labels takes little

initiative or intelligence. And your customer should never have to read a label because you know what's on it and can relate to him much more . . . and in a much more personal manner. You know why the undergravel filter works the way it does; you know how much air that green vibrator will pump. You know how different types of dog muzzles work. You can hold up a can of flea spray and tell a customer what the killing ingredient is and how safe it is for his dog.

The answers are as endless as the questions. Furthermore, you not only need to know your products but you must also know why what you sell is better than what your competition handles. It isn't necessary to run down the other dealer to make a sale. Your concern must always be for the customer and his pet...and not necessarily in that order. Be fair. Sell your particular item because you know it will do the best job. Be sure, and know why you are sure. The classic example of this is the story about the retailer who examined a parrakeet for a customer to ascertain what was wrong. As the retailer was looking over the bird, it gave one last quiver and died in his hands. The bird was thin; it obviously had not been receiving the proper nourishment for some time. "What kind of seed have you been feeding," the confident retailer asked gently. The customer named a popular brand found in any grocery store. "Ah," sighed the dealer, "that's what killed your bird. You should have been feeding our special mixture. If you had, this would never have happened." The retailer turned away to reach for a package of the special seed. "Here's what you should have used. People just never learn." The customer looked at the package of seed, then to the dead bird, then back to the seed. "But," he said, "this is the seed I've been feeding him for 13 years." So much for the need to know!

chapter 7
How Do You Set Up An Aquarium Area?

Probably the most important piece of construction in any full-line pet shop is the fixture known as the set-up stand for aquariums. And here again, as in all things, you have a choice as to types available. There are only 2 basic formations that can be achieved functionally but there are possible variations to these. The first type is the so-called Step-Up design; the second type, where the tanks are mounted directly over each other, is the Vertical design. Figures 32, 33 and 34 show the Step-Up design and Figure 35 illustrates the Vertical conception.

The plans shown here and discussed further on are for set-ups designed to go against a wall and to be worked from the front. However, when we discussed store layout earlier, we had 2 illustrations of aquarium set-ups that would be worked from the rear. (Figures 15 and 16). The Vertical design, shown in Figure 35, is the only design that can be efficiently used for rear service. If you have a store layout in mind similar to those in Figures 15 and 16, go right to the section here that deals with the Vertical design. Step-up racks are just not designed to be used as partitions or to be worked from the rear.

The one inescapable problem that faces you regardless of which plan you adopt is: The lower you bring the top tank, the less you can see of the bottom one. And conversely, the higher you take the bottom tank, the more difficult it becomes to get to the top row. The only ideal, but impractical, solution is to have just one row of aquariums at eye level. This you cannot have, so let's look over the 2 available plans, plus a modification of one, and discuss the good and bad points of each. We'll start with the

Step-Up design shown in Figures 32, 33 and 34.

In Figure 32 the total depth is 2'8'' and the overall height is 6'3'' with the first tank sitting 25'' from the floor. This puts the first tank a little on the low side. You can move it higher, but if you do, you'll put that top row of tanks out of sight. You see, this really becomes a matter of give and take—a problem of finding that happy ...or practical...medium. The bottom row of tanks sits on a shelf that is wider than the other 2 shelves above it in order to accommodate a catching jar, a net, you name it. That extra shelf width comes in handy so be sure to work it into whatever design you use. Also, note that all 3 shelves are wide enough to allow a 2¼'' space between the back of the tank and the vertical riser. This space is necessary to allow for a heater, filter tubes, manifold pipe or for some sort of aquarium background decoration. One thing you should note before I go any further at this point. Don't box yourself in by not allowing enough space. One inch, one little old inch, can make a lot of difference!

STEP-UP DESIGNS

Looking at Figure 32, you will note that the tanks extend out over the tanks below and it is up under this cantilever that the lines of fluorescent fixtures are installed to provide illumination for the aquariums. By arranging the fixtures up out of the way in this fashion, no reflectors are needed. (By reflectors, we mean one of the fabricated stainless steel hoods made by various manufacturers for home aquaria.) The system that you see here minimizes wet wires and inhibits condensation on the electrical parts. Even more important, perhaps, is the great savings affected with this plan because it is far more economical to install these simple fluorescent fixtures up under that cantilever than it is to install ready-made stainless steel reflectors.

Now check Figure 33. The same rack Step-Up design is used here but now the cantilever has been eliminated. Why should we bother with such a design when the one in Figure 32 would do? Again, it is a question of weighing good points against bad and laying down your money. The rack in Figure 32 is only 2'8'' wide but it is 6'3'' high. So it might not come out from the wall far enough to be a bother, but it could be much too high for a short clerk to reach the top row without a ladder. Now look at Figure 33. This rack is only 5'1'' from the floor. Most any clerk could reach up to dip fish. But this rack does come out and steal a little more of your floor space.

In Figure 34 we offer a more improved design of Figure 32. Such a plan requires more running

space because, as you will note, only 2 racks of aquariums can be accommodated. If space is available, Figure 34 could well be ideal for you. First of all, as shown here, it is only 4'10'' high, low enough for your shortest clerk. And it comes out but 2'4'' from the wall, ideal if your store is long and narrow. The first shelf for the first row of tanks is 2'2'' from the floor and is shown as being 1'4'' wide, wide enough for a 10 gallon tank with background behind it and still some room for a work shelf in the front. Like in Figure 32, the fluorescent tubes are situated up under the facia of the overhanging shelf, safe and out of the way. At the same time the fixture top offers another work shelf for the rack of aquariums above.

Looking at this design quickly you might suspect that it is nothing more than what you saw in Figure 32 except that we have cut down one row of tanks. Not so!! In Figure 34 we find a very workable rack that will not only be easy to build but easy to service. First of all, the shelves containing the fluorescent fixtures do not carry any other weight but their own. The second row of tanks will not bear on that shelf. So construction of the shelves for the lights need not be as sturdy (or as costly) as in Figure 32. Also, you will note that between the first row and the second there is a 5 inch opening running the full length of the rack. This opening is closed off by sliding doors, 3 of which have been opened (in the illustration) to show the manifold pipe and pipe valves for air hoses. Just above the manifold pipe and out of sight is the wire molding into which heaters or individual lights can be plugged. True, this 5 inch opening raises the second row of tanks by that much, but the great convenience that these ports offer far outweighs the extra height necessary. With such a panel you can regulate every air outlet in every tank without bending over.

Rack 34, as illustrated, has the first row of tanks 2'2'' from the floor. You can have it higher if you prefer. The height in this design is not a criterion. You might wish to make that first row of tanks 2'8'' from the floor (which is about table height). That's fine! It will just mean that your second row will be higher by that much. But even that would not be too high for the normal man or woman to reach the top tank. What we are attempting to do here is illustrate the convenience of these sliding manifold doors and the savings in money and future aggravation by having the fluorescent tubes safely hidden and out of the way.

Figure 32 offers built-in inexpensive illumination. Figure 33 demands separate fabricated hoods or reflectors with their accompanying wires. The question well asked at this point—why even consider the design in Figure 33 if the alternative seems to have all the advantages? The answer is that the design in

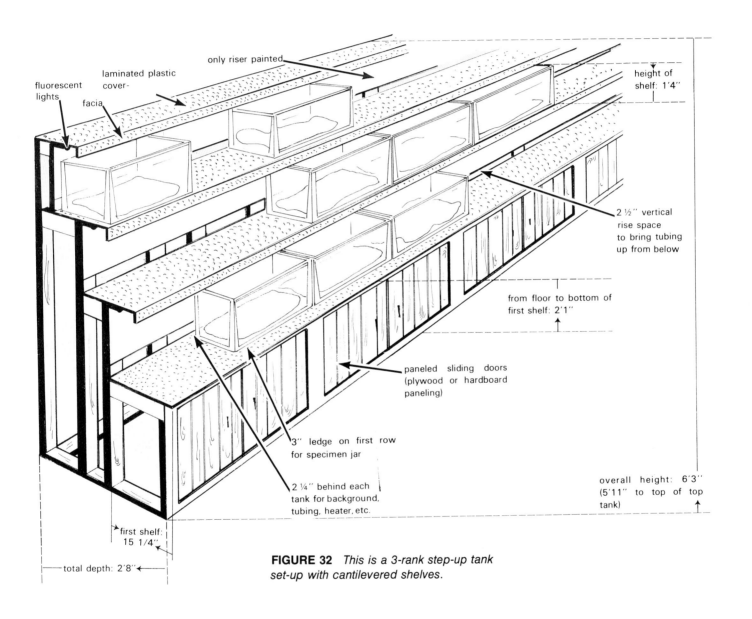

fluorescent lights

laminated plastic cover-

facia

only riser painted

height of shelf: 1'4"

2 ½" vertical rise space to bring tubing up from below

from floor to bottom of first shelf: 2'1"

paneled sliding doors (plywood or hardboard paneling)

3" ledge on first row for specimen jar

2 ¼" behind each tank for background, tubing, heater, etc.

overall height: 6'3" (5'11" to top of top tank)

first shelf: 15 1/4"

total depth: 2'8"

FIGURE 32 *This is a 3-rank step-up tank set-up with cantilevered shelves.*

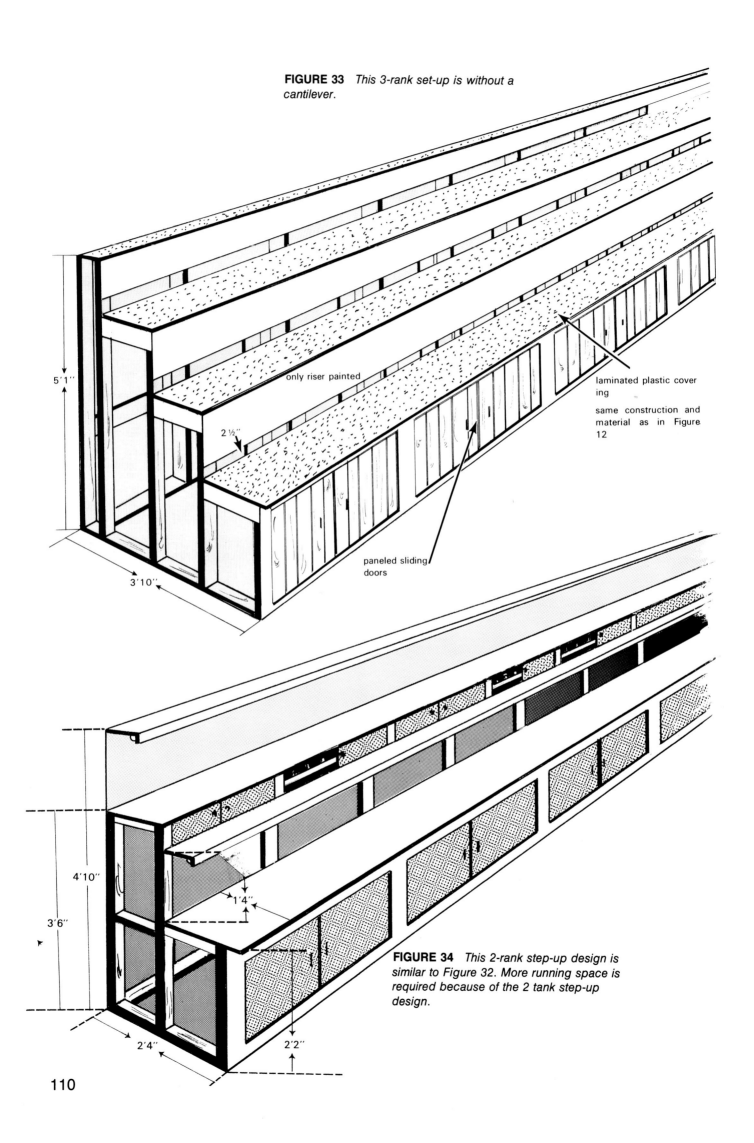

FIGURE 33 *This 3-rank set-up is without a cantilever.*

5'1"

only riser painted

2½"

laminated plastic covering

same construction and material as in Figure 12

paneled sliding doors

3'10"

4'10"

3'6"

1'4"

FIGURE 34 *This 2-rank step-up design is similar to Figure 32. More running space is required because of the 2 tank step-up design.*

2'4"

2'2"

Figure 33 can be erected quite easily. Many pet shop owners, new to the business, long on hopes and ideas but short on cash, have constructed this design out of 2'' by 2'' or 2'' by 4' lumber, covered the shelves with rolled plastic laminate, put ready-made sliding doors below, and were in business. Even if you go to a contractor. . .which you should. . .to have a professional job done, Figure 33 is the easier to build. Figure 32 demands the cantilever and such a cantilever requires bracing. This particular design is often constructed of welded iron in order to give strength to the cantilever. But this is really not necessary. The only part of the entire rack that would need any metal (should you elect to build it yourself of lumber) is the cantilever. There you would definitely need metal supports to give the shelf enough rigidity to carry the weight of the overhanging tanks above.

In all designs you will notice that the space below the first shelf is used as a storage area with laminated plastic wood grain ¼'' material used over sliding plywood doors. Laminated plastic covering such as Formica should be used under the tanks on all shelves. Easy to clean, it offers no water-absorbing surface in case of a leak. And there will be leaks. Also, notice that the vertical risers shown in Figures 32 and 33 have a 2½'' opening the entire length of the rack and that they are not protected with any type of plastic covering, as are the shelves, other than 2 good coats of a water resistant paint. The reason for this 2½' opening is so that all air lines and heater cords can be led from the tanks down to the outlets or to the manifold pipe supplying air. Once gravel and background are put in the aquariums, this opening will be covered from sight. So do not permit your carpenter to drop that riser all the way down. Allow the recommended room.

We have been discussing custom-built, in-place wooden or wood and metal step-up racks. Another alternative is a ready-made set up of metal available through several aquarium manufacturers. Shown in Figure 36 is a rack that comes knocked down but that can be assembled with bolts and nuts in a half hour. Depending on your location, the initial cost might not be any greater than having your own rack built to specifications but these metal racks, by their very simplicity of design, do present a rather cold appearance. Hinged or sliding doors can be mounted below the tanks inside the angle iron frame but this sort of thing will run the cost up. Another advantage with this type set-up is that the lights are usually built in, doing away with a reflector over each tank. How then does speed of delivering and assembly stack up against the custom-built appearance of a built-in-place formica and wood rack? You lay your money down and take your choice.

VERTICAL DESIGNS

Figure 35 illustrates the Vertical design which has gained in popularity in the last few years. In essence, this arrangement is much like putting 10 gallon tanks, or larger, on rows of shelves built simply of wood or metal. The front edges of these shelves are finished off and a door installed to allow access to the top of the tank. The finished look is one of 3 rows of tanks, each in a picture frame. Nothing disturbs the eye; all attention is focused on the tanks and the fish. As you can see, a space must be left between the top of one tank and the bottom of the tank above to allow for dipping fish, feeding and cleaning. Eight inches of space is minimal and is what is shown here. However, it is because of this space that the Vertical design becomes the tallest of the 4 discussed. The overall height in Figure 35 is 6'8'' counting the height of that top row of tanks and providing you start the bottom row a mere 18'' from the floor. Nevertheless, despite its height, this system can be called ideal from many points. It takes up little floor space, jutting out into the room never over 15 inches. It is simple and inexpensive to construct. And finally, it utilizes inexpensive lighting fixtures.

But as we have said before, its one condemning feature is that most set-ups of this type have the bottom row of tanks too low and the top row too high for easy accessibility. Construction of this design, as with others we have discussed, can be of 2'' by 2'' or 2'' by 4'' lumber or of angle iron. Regardless of the material used, it should be painted with at least one coat of an epoxy paint. Spilling water is inevitable in all set-ups, but particularly here where the tanks are back in their separate cubbyholes. The problem of rotting wood or rusting iron can be avoided quite easily by the use of the epoxy coating.

Once the framework is put up, a strip fluorescent reflector fixture is installed along the back uprights high enough to illuminate the tanks below. Facing material of either a good quality pre-finished wood paneling or a wood tone plastic covering such as Marlite or Formica is then used to cover the supports and the door over each tank. The 8 inch high door is made to swing either out and up or back and up. Whichever you prefer, a magnetic catch or an automatic locking brace should be used on each door. When you are catching fish for a customer or when you are working on a tank, a door that keeps falling on your arm can be annoying as well as painful. As with the other designs, sliding or swinging doors can be installed below the tanks for storage. And a note should be made here: It is not mandatory that doors be installed below the tanks. It is perfectly acceptable to leave that space open, finished off and used as

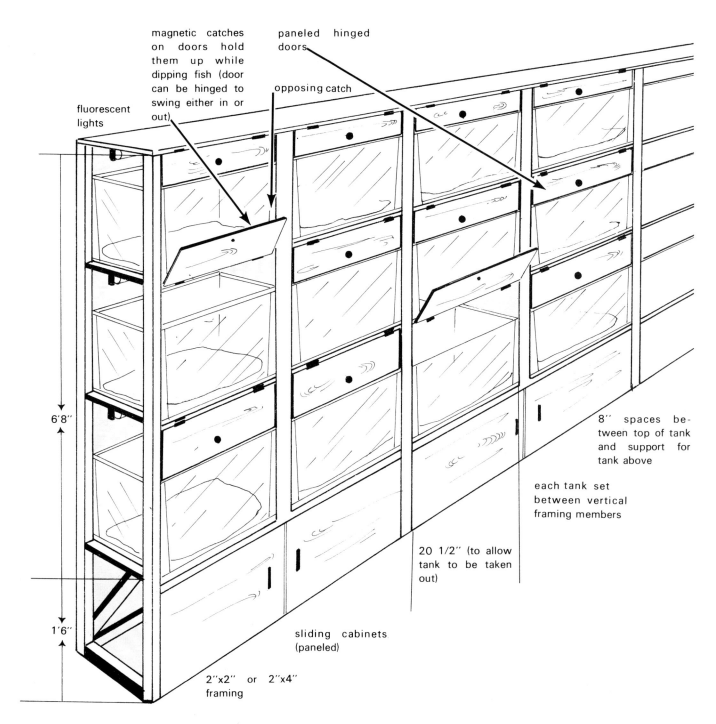

magnetic catches on doors hold them up while dipping fish (door can be hinged to swing either in or out)

paneled hinged doors

opposing catch

fluorescent lights

6'8"

1'6"

8" spaces between top of tank and support for tank above

each tank set between vertical framing members

20 1/2" (to allow tank to be taken out)

sliding cabinets (paneled)

2"x2" or 2"x4" framing

FIGURE 35 *This is a 3-rank vertical tank set-up.*

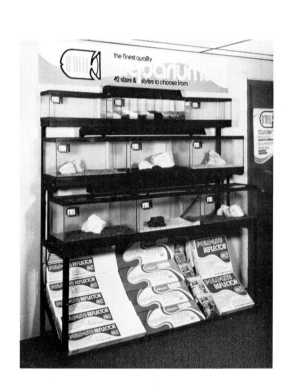

FIGURE 36 *Tank set-ups need not be customized. This metal fixture comes knocked-down and can be assembled in less than an hour. (Courtesy of O'Dell Mfg. Co.)*

FIGURE 37 *Commercial vertical tank set-ups are also available. (Courtesy of General Cage Corp.)*

storage for plants or aquariums or any other stock that you wish viewed by your customers. It is simply a matter of preference and sometimes a matter of space as well. But leaving the bottom completely open invites youngsters to play in the water (if you put tanks of plants down there) or runs the risk of an accidental kick smashing out the side of one of the tanks stored down there. One thing more before we leave the matter of tank set-up designs. The 4 Step-Up designs shown in Figures 32, 33, 34 and 36 are for wall use, and although they could be placed back-to-back, we have never known of a case where this was done. Because of their width, they demand wall space. Figure 35, however, can be placed against a wall or placed back-to-back to form a double display. Back-to-back, such a set-up would be no wider than a floor gondola for merchandise. In fact, 2 vertical set-ups back-to-back would be narrower than most merchandise gondolas.

The Vertical design set-up need not be home-made. Figure 37 shows a commercial set of fixtures that can be obtained for ten gallon, 15 gallon or 55 gallon tanks. In function it is identical to the rack in Figure 35; because it is predesigned and engineered, it can be assembled quickly where time is of the essence. Bear in mind that two qualities are necessary for satisfaction in a rack of this type. Over and above the initial price, the metal must be sturdy enough to carry the water weight without extra wall or ceiling support and the paint job must be of such a quality to inhibit rust formation, especially if saltwater tanks are to be used. Corrosion is always a problem with metal racks, even more so when saltwater is used.

PUMPS, MANIFOLDS

Any tank set-up must be discussed in terms of the type of pump and manifold you consider. More than that, it must be discussed in regard to where this pump and manifold will be situated for easy service to both pump and air valves. Years ago, a store pump was usually an intermittent type mounted on a storage tank similar to what you see at most automobile service stations. When this pump was in operation it was capable of pumping air to a pressure of up to 100 psi. Normally, it would cut off at 45 to 50 psi. The air would drain from this storage tank into the aquariums as needed through a pressure regulator valve that brought the pressure down to a mere 3 or 4 psi, sufficient for pet shop aquarium use. This type of compressor was noisy, especially as it got older; it was expensive and took up a more-than-necessary number of valuable square feet.

In recent years, the trend has been to use a smaller, continuous operating pump designed to furnish sufficient air at the normal required pressure (3 to 4 psi) for whatever number of tanks desired. The concept is one of fitting the pump to the number of tanks rather than having a larger compressor than necessary and bleeding off excess air. Belt driven and direct drive rotary pumps, such as those shown in Figures 38A, 38B and 38C take up little space, can be mounted just about anywhere and are perfectly adequate for any set-up providing the proper capacity compressor is used. Here we are dealing with a central compressor hooked into one or several manifolds feeding air into the tanks. At the end of the section titled Manifold Location you will find an alternative to this central compressor concept that could be of some value to the potential tropical fish department.

It has been estimated that a square bottom filter with charcoal and glass wool takes about 40 cubic inches of air per minute in a 10 gallon tank. Thus, a dealer with 50 tanks is looking for a pump that can deliver a minimum of 2,000 cubic inches of air per minute. If he should choose undergravel filters, he will need more air than with the square bottom filters. This increase in air requirement is a variable factor, however, and is directly proportional to the amount of gravel used in the bottom of each tank. Two inches of gravel on the tank bottom, for instance, requires 30 percent more air than the square bottom filter. But using only one inch of gravel requires only a little over 10 percent more air than the square bottom filter.

The best policy when considering any compressor is to compute your needs and then add 25 percent for future expansion. This really is not too difficult a task. Most manufacturers can be trusted to recommend the correct pump to do the job you desire. One point before you give final approval on any particular compressor—any compressor, no matter how small, makes a noise. And any compressor, no matter how small, needs proper ventilation if it is to perform at its optimum. Plan ahead as to where you will situate this machine. Not under the set-up. The noise will be enough to annoy and it's constant. Just over the stock room partition at the end of the set-up? You're not kidding anybody. The sound of the pump in that location will be as bad as it would have been under the tanks. You might consider a sturdy shelf in the lavatory. There's enough air in there for the pump and with the door closed, very little sound will escape. Granted, you won't take as long to wash your hands, but that can have merit too. Or you might consider putting it outside, either up on the side of the building where it can be protected from the elements and out of reach or in a special groundlevel

FIGURE 38A *This 1/12th hp rotary air pump develops a constant 14 psi at 1,725 rpm and will handle 30 to 40 10 gal. tanks. (Courtesy of Bell & Gossett.)*

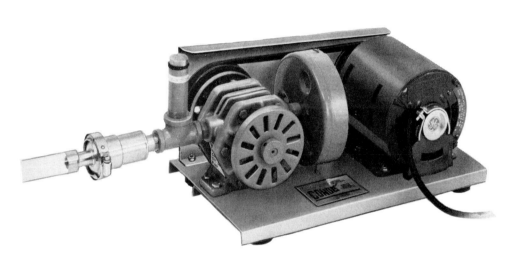

FIGURE 38B *This pump will handle 100 10 gal. tanks and will develop 1,360 rpm. It can aerate 1,000 gals. of freshwater or 600 gals. of saltwater. (Courtesy of Conde Pump Div.)*

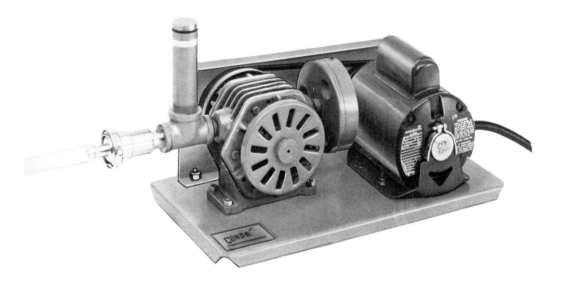

FIGURE 38C *Slightly larger than the pump in Figure 38B, this unit will aerate 5,000 gals. of freshwater or 3,000 gals. of saltwater at 1,360 rpm. (Courtesy of Conde Pump Div.)*

cage, but again protected from rain, snow and dust as well as the curious.

If all of these suggestions are impractical in your particular store, you might construct an insulated box large enough to cover the entire compressor. The core of this box would be of inexpensive plywood covered inside with heavy insulation. Holes would have to be drilled to give it ample ventilation, but even with these holes, the noise factor would be reduced dramatically. All this might sound like so much trivia now, but what a shock it can be to mount the compressor under the tank set-up and then stand back in amazement the day you plug it in. Just because the advertisement said "this is a quiet pump" doesn't mean your customers can't hear it.

There is an alternative to the large compressor-manifold system that works well and comes in at about the same cost as the set-up discussed on the last few pages. Figure 39 shows such a system. A heavy-duty vibrator pump is used for every three or four tanks. Normally the pump is placed above the tanks but this is not a "must." Advantages? Well, twenty of these heavy-duty vibrators combined would not put out the noise of one back room compressor. No manifold is necessary—3/16 inch airline tubing can be used directly from the pump to the tanks by using tees. If one vibrator breaks down only 3 or 4 tanks are effected. A broken back room compressor can tie your air system in knots for hours...unless you are far sighted and fortunate enough to make provisions for a spare machine.

Disadvantages? Your electrical outlets would have to be increased by one outlet for each 6 to 8 tanks. Also, should you wish to include a 55 gallon or larger tank in the system, it might require one heavy-duty vibrator by itself. A heavy-duty compressor would and should have extra power and air to spare. This extra margin would not exist with the heavy-duty vibrators.

The cost of installation of either a backroom compressor or a group of heavy-duty vibrators is just about equal. Here are some cost comparisons. For a 24 tank set-up a single large compressor will run between $80 and $90. Manifold pipe and brass pipe valves for 24 tanks would run an additional $35 or a total cost of between $115 and $125. Using one vibrator for every 3 tanks, the cost would be $95 to $110. For a 48 tank set-up, the total cost for a single back-room compressor with brass pipe valves and manifold pipe would run $160 to $180. Using heavy-duty vibrators, the cost would be $190 to $210. For a 100 tank set-up, the total cost for a single back-room compressor with brass pipe valves and manifold pipe would be $470 to $510. Using heavy-duty vibrators, the cost would be $390 to $430.

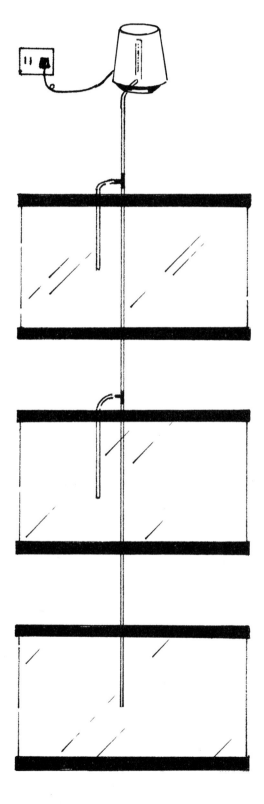

FIGURE 39 *The use of heavy-duty vibrator pumps for every 3 or 4 tanks is an alternative to the compressor-manifold system.*

THE AIR SYSTEM

The compressor is hooked up. The tanks are filled with water. Now we need a functional method of conveying air from pump to tanks. The easiest, most efficient way to do this is by means of a large tube or pipe mounted close to the tanks that will act as a manifold. Into this pipe, at designated places along its length, are fitted brass or plastic valves. Onto these valves go lengths of 3/16 inch plastic tubing which connect to each filter and/or to each underwater aerator.

The diameter of the tube is not critical. A 1/2, 3/4 or even 1 inch pipe can be used. The larger the diameter the easier it is to tap and insert the valves because of the thickness of the pipe walls. Metal pipe, once the standard for aquarium air systems, has been replaced by plastic rigid pipe or flexible tubing. Plastic is easy and quick to work, does not require elaborate equipment to install and will give years of trouble-free service. You have the option of buying the long sections of rigid plastic (PVC) pipe (10 or 16 foot lengths) or a coil of the more flexible plastic tubing. The flexible tubing might be a little cheaper than the rigid; the rigid pipe, however, looks a bit nicer when installed with pipe brackets. Tubing, because it comes in a coil, has a tendency to wave along the wall when mounted. As long as that doesn't bother your aesthetic taste, there is no problem. Schedule 40 PVC pipe is standard for water systems in homes. It is made to withstand normal urban water pressures. That strong a pipe is not necessary for your air system which would never require more than 7 pounds pressure. You might look for something less than Schedule 40 with the knowledge that a small saving in cost could be affected.

Drill 3/8 inch holes along the length of your pipe or tubing. Put them as far apart as you feel necessary for your system. Three to 4 inches seems to be the norm but it really depends on how many outlets you desire for now and for future expansion. Once the holes are drilled, screw in the three-way valves. No tapping is necessary. The valves will seat themselves as they go into the softer plastic. You can put a bead of silicone sealant around the base of each valve, but generally this is not necessary. If the valve goes in straight there will be no air loss under normal operating pressure.

Elbows, tees, unions and end caps can be installed on your line with ease. One container of PVC Cement puts you in business. It's just as easy as brushing glue on the fitting and the pipe and putting them together.

The control valve, shown in Figure 40, is usually of brass, threaded for insertion in any of the manifold materials we have discussed. There are plastic pipe valves on the market which work quite well and can be cemented to the plastic manifold pipe easily and quickly. They are not machined with the close tolerance found in the brass valves and, therefore, will not regulate your air as well as the brass type. Also, the plastic valves can only be used with plastic pipe. However, they are inexpensive and where installation costs and time become big factors, these plastic valves have value. For the more permanent installation, go with the higher cost and use brass.

As a point of discussion here, let us assume that you mounted your compressor on a corner shelf in the lavatory, high enough to be out of the way on a shelf sturdy enough to bear the weight and take the constant vibration. Since most compressors come mounted on rubber feet and the whole unit locks down on a base, in this case your shelf, if your materials are strong enough there should be no problem with anything tearing loose. Your object is to carry the air through the lavatory wall and out to the manifold pipe in your tank set-up. Depending on the outlet fittings on your compressor, this conveying can be done with either flexible copper tubing or flexible plastic tubing anywhere from 3/8 to 1/2 inches in diameter. Since plastic tubing is the cheapest, most dealers go this route. A hole is made in the lavatory wall large enough to accommodate the flexible tubing coming through. The tube is then run from compressor outlet, through the lavatory wall, out across the stock room (securely fastened to wall or ceiling) and then through the partition into the retail area. Whether you run this tube high or low doesn't matter. You're only trying to keep it from sight wherever possible and to get it to the fish tanks as unobtrusively as can be managed. Meanwhile, you have installed your manifold pipe with its many valves under the aquarium set-up. Keep in mind that you will need to get to these valves daily so they should be completely accessible. Many, many dealers obtain their regular exercise in contortionism every morning because they have installed their manifold too quickly and without thinking. Therefore, place the manifold so that you can watch the tanks as you adjust the valves. Put it out of sight and you'll need another person to help regulate the air coming through the filters. The dialogue between 2 people trying to guide each other adjusting air to filters when the manifold is hidden under the tanks is something to hear: "Yeah, just a little more. No, that's too much on that one. Cut it back. No, not that one, the one next to it. Fine. No, just a little more. Good. Leave it alone. Now go to the next one."

Let us pin down the manifold position. In Figure 32 the manifold would go just inside the sliding doors, high up under the first tank shelf, so that it would be out of the way to permit storage of merchandise without hitting the

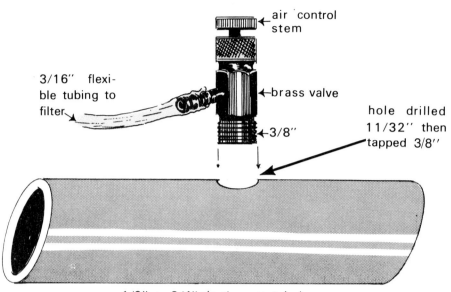

air control
stem

3/16" flexi-
ble tubing to
filter

brass valve

hole drilled
11/32" then
tapped 3/8"

3/8"

1/2" or 3/4" plastic or metal pipe

FIGURE 40 *Detail of air control valve and
manifold.*

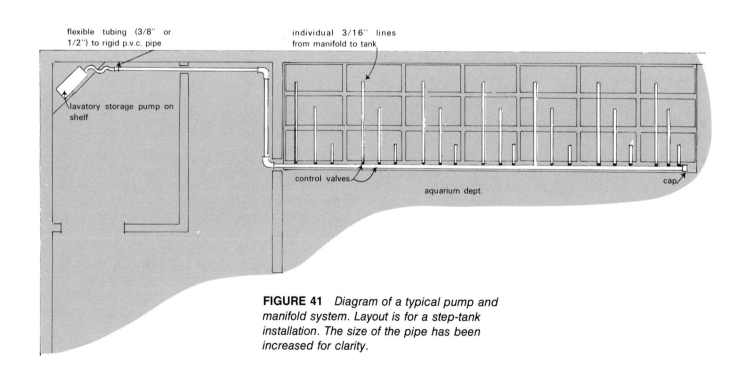

flexible tubing (3/8" or
1/2") to rigid p.v.c. pipe

individual 3/16" lines
from manifold to tank

lavatory storage pump on
shelf

control valves

cap

aquarium dept.

FIGURE 41 *Diagram of a typical pump and
manifold system. Layout is for a step-tank
installation. The size of the pipe has been
increased for clarity.*

manifold. In such a position the operator could regulate valves while watching the filters. In Figure 33 there are 2 possible positions. One would be inside the sliding storage doors as noted for Figure 32 and the other would be along the top of either the first or second riser. The middle riser would be the most convenient. Putting the manifold on a riser, however, brings it into view which might detract from the aesthetic beauty of the arrangement of tanks, lights and fish. However, this situation is mentioned because it is one that is seen frequently because it is easy to install and because the filters can be watched as the valves are regulated. Figure 41 gives an accurate diagram of a typical pump to tank layout for use with the Step-Up design.

For the Vertical design, as in Figure 35, the manifold would be run at the very back of the set-up, probably in back of the second row of tanks. Easy to install yet hidden from sight, this position is just about ideal from every aspect.

There is a variation to the one manifold design for the Step-Up tank set-up. This is where separate manifolds are installed for each row of tanks (3 lines) so that each valve is positioned right above the tank it regulates. More costly, by far, than the single manifold, it does offer the elimination of long lengths of 3/16 inch feeder tubing from manifold to tanks. To the best of my knowledge, it might be much neater in appearance but it offers no advantage for air control in the filters.

The 3/4 or 1/2 inch plastic tubing routed from the compressor is now hooked into the manifold (or series of manifolds), and as shown in Figure 40, valves are then inserted or screwed into the manifold every 3 or 4 inches along the entire length of the pipe. From each valve exhaust attach a piece of 3/16 inch flexible tubing to the filter or aerator in each tank. If a straight manifold is used, a cap is glued onto the far end to prevent air loss. If more than one manifold is used, the 2 ends can be hooked together to form a continuous manifold.

Once the tanks are filled with water to the point you intend to keep them . .. which should be about 1½'' from the top . . . and filters have been installed and hooked into the system with the 3/16 inch tubing from the manifold, go down the line and turn off every valve. Once you are sure they are all off, start up your compressor. Now moving to the tank furthermost from the pump, open the valve just enough to notice air bubbles coming from the filter. Then move to the next tank and open the valve until a steady flow of air bubbles is rising. Move from tank to tank, row upon row, until you have moved down the entire line, always moving toward your source of air, the compressor. Once they are all in operation, go back and check the first tanks you worked on to see if they are still bubbling. If not, then you have opened all the other valves too far. By checking individual filters and making regulations here and there, all tanks should be operating satisfactorily after you have made the second round of adjustments.

But they won't stay that way; they will need some attention at least once a day. As dirt accumulates in the filter, air pressure is effected which in turn effects the performance of the filter. At this point you will understand only too well why we suggested that you put your manifold in a convenient position so that it would be hidden yet available enough to regulate the air flow by sight.

Traditionally, the 10 gallon glass tank has been used for store set-up. But in recent years there has been a swing to larger tanks. Fifteen and 20 gallon sizes are being used more and more. This gradual change and its effect needs an explanation. The 10 gallon tank is the fastest seller in terms of units sold at the retail level. Because of this, all reflectors, filters and other aquarium accessories are geared first to the 10 gallon size. Thus, a set-up that uses this tank is the easiest to outfit. But above and beyond availability, the 10 is really the most suitable to a large fish department. Twenty-five swords or 50 zebras can go into a 10 gallon tank very nicely. Use a 15 and you must either stock more fish of one specie to fill the tank or you must add a second specie which complicates catching. You can use a tank divider but that defeats the reason for the larger tank in the first place. In summation, there is no rule that says you should not or cannot use a tank size larger than a 10; just remember that through the years the 10 has remained the most popular because it is also the most practical.

THE LIGHTING SYSTEM

When we talk about illumination for the tank set-up, we think of 2 objectives which are not necessarily compatable. One is the problem of simply lighting the tank. The other is the problem of covering the tank. And lighting a tank and covering a tank simultaneously may or may not be accomplished with one object. In Figures 32 and 35 the problem of lighting is solved quite easily. The fluorescent fixtures, the least expensive available, are installed up out of the way of water and customers. There are no wires hanging loose. Illumination is complete and positive and there is very little that can corrode from the prevalent high humidity. In a tropical fish set-up as in Figure 33, we have a different matter. Here the reflectors must be placed either directly on each tank or suspended from chains from the ceiling to hang directly over each tank; or lights must be installed between each tank.

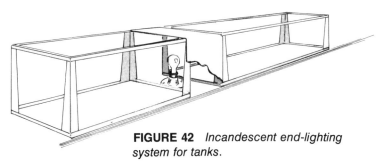

FIGURE 42 *Incandescent end-lighting system for tanks.*

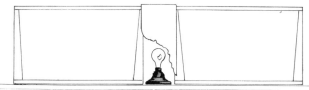

FIGURE 43A *Heavy-duty plastic strip reflector available for all tank sizes and for incandescent or fluorescent lights. (Courtesy of O'Dell Mfg. Co.)*

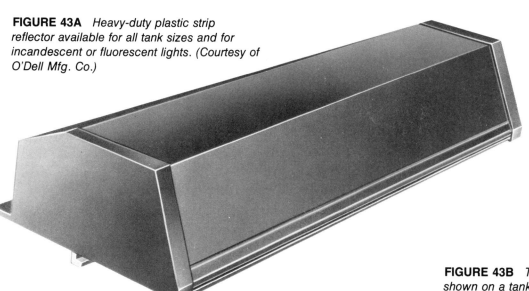

FIGURE 43B *This is a plastic strip reflector shown on a tank and in conjunction with a sliding glass top used to prevent fish and water loss. (Courtesy of O'Dell Mfg. Co.)*

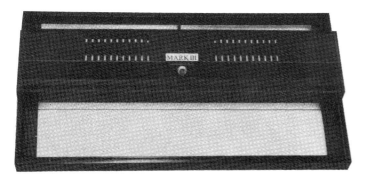

FIGURE 43C *This full hood with sliding glass front is available for fluorescent lighting. (Courtesy of Metaframe Corp.)*

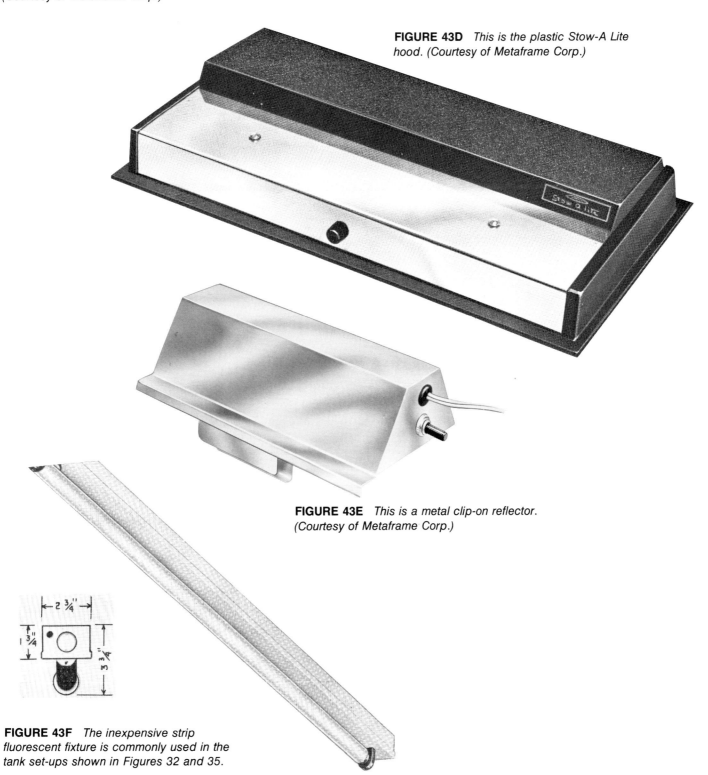

FIGURE 43D *This is the plastic Stow-A Lite hood. (Courtesy of Metaframe Corp.)*

FIGURE 43E *This is a metal clip-on reflector. (Courtesy of Metaframe Corp.)*

FIGURE 43F *The inexpensive strip fluorescent fixture is commonly used in the tank set-ups shown in Figures 32 and 35.*

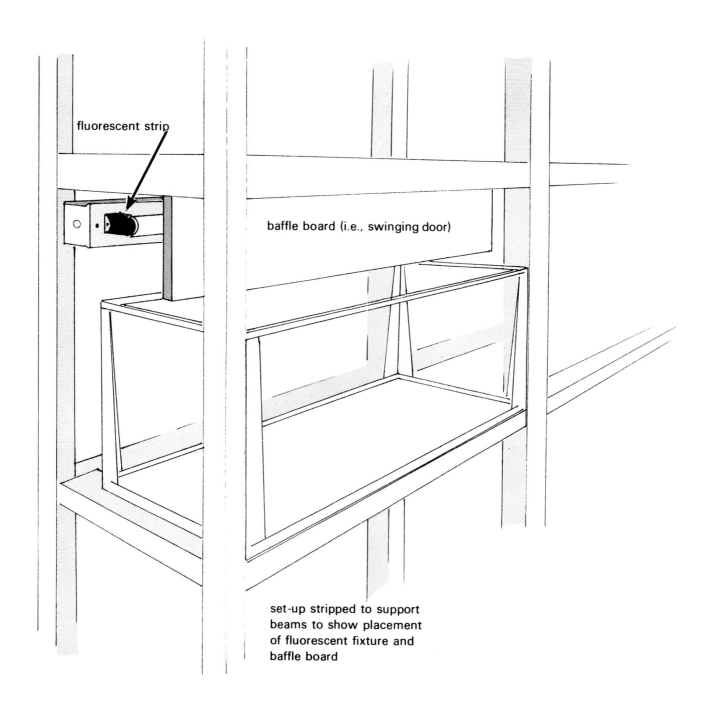

fluorescent strip

baffle board (i.e., swinging door)

set-up stripped to support
beams to show placement
of fluorescent fixture and
baffle board

FIGURE 44 *A different method of lighting tanks in a vertical tank set-up is to eliminate the over-the-tank swinging door at the front and move it back to hang free in front of the light.*

122

Right away you can see that Figure 33 will present a problem and so we will concentrate for the moment on this situation.

A method of lighting tanks popular some time ago, but which has fallen into disuse of late, is that of putting lights between the tanks as shown in Figure 42. Here, a 5 inch space is left between each tank and in this space a 4½ inch weatherproof recepticle is installed. A 25 watt regular or a 40 watt appliance bulb is screwed into this recepticle and an inverted 'L' shaped piece of stainless steel or even Formica over aluminum is cut to fit over this space and hide the light bulb and fixture.

Inexpensive and quick to install? Yes, but there are drawbacks. You must allow at least 5 inches between each tank. That means on a 3 row set-up of 45 ten gallon tanks, you would give up 70 inches to these fixtures, almost 6 valuable feet. The other bad feature is that the heat created by the incandescent bulbs can be very significant during hot weather and the side algae produced in conjunction with the heat can become a real problem. We mention this type of illumination here simply because it has been so very popular. And where space is of no concern, it can be a very economical method of providing light along with plenty of heat. It does have 2 other advantages. One, the light is completely out of the way when you are trying to catch fish or work on the tanks. Also, there are no wires to get in the way, become frayed or corroded.

In Figure 43 you see an array of reflectors available for store use. Every one shown can be used for both store and home, the thought being that what is good for the store is also good for the customer. The incandescent or fluorescent strip reflector (Figure 43A and 43B) must be used in conjunction with some type of tank cover to inhibit the fish from jumping and to prohibit use of the tank as an ashtray by customers. (You would be surprised at the things customers will drop into your tanks.) A strip reflector is inexpensive but if kept to the front of the tank, it must be moved backward whenever fish are to be caught. The full hood in Figure 43C is a stable variety of the strip reflector and is available in all popular sizes. The Stow-A-Lite Hood in Figure 43D has long been a favorite with hobbyists but it has a serious drawback in its use in the store. The Stow-A-Lite has its reflector with the fluorescent tube in the front which is the portion that hinges up to allow access to the tank. When open, the light shines in your eyes instead of into the tank. Where a more ornate appearance is sought or as an example of what is available and workable, the Stow-A-Lite might be considered for a group of tanks.

As manufacturers become more aware of the need for functional beauty in an aquarium, new and more delightful designs will become available to you. Stainless steel gave way to the glass tank with a wooden base. That succumbed to the glass tank with the black plastic top and bottom. Now that has been replaced by a woodgrain effect in various hues to fit any decor. Whatever you start out with as a store set-up will, in time, be revised as you keep up with the changes and refinements that must come as the industry grows.

There is one other lighting adaptation which is not in wide use but has merit. This system is shown in Figure 44 and is suitable only for a Vertical design. In this plan, the door, shown at the very front over the tanks in Figure 35, is moved to the back at least 6 inches from the front edge of the tank. It is hinged at the top so that it can swing freely. It hangs down to within an inch or so of the top of the tank. As shown in Figure 44, a fluorescent strip fixture (shown in Figure 43F) is mounted on the rack supports behind this door, or more correctly, behind this baffle. The baffle is painted with white or aluminum paint on its back side to increase reflection. There are now no doors to worry about. The fixture is still hidden, but its light, reflected from the baffle, does a perfect job. However, now that the door is gone, a glass or a plastic cover must be put over the tank to prevent jumping and, more especially, garbage disposing.

The small 8 inch clip-on reflector is mentioned here and shown in Figure 43E as a possibility for special lighting effects. This reflector can be used on just about any tank, whether in your regular set-up or on a special display tank. It is not seen too often but is highly recommended where special effects are desired.

In recent years there has been a tremendous growth in the use of fluorescent fixtures for aquarium use, both in the regular familiar white light as well as the plant stimulating type that so enhances fish coloration. For longevity, for brilliant color and for operation with a minimum of heat, our suggestion is most certainly the fluorescent tube, and more specifically, the plant stimulating tube. Your initial fixture costs will be higher, but in the long run you will save on operating costs. More important, the kind of light you use in your display will determine the kind of light your customers will desire.

Before closing this section on lighting, let's summarize briefly points to keep in mind when planning your aquarium lighting set-up.

1. It should provide adequate lighting and do so conveniently.

2. It should provide adequate light safely...and by this we mean with a minimum number of wires getting in your way and with adequate protection from corrosion for all electrical components.

3. It should provide adequate lighting as economically as possible.

THE FILTRATION SYSTEM

It would be so simple to say there is just one way to put your pet shop together. It would make less reading and take many a decision from your shoulders. Unfortunately...or fortunately, depending on how you look at it...there are several alternatives for each phase of planning and building and stocking a pet shop. Your filtration system for the tank set-up is no exception. At present, there are 3 fundamental filtering concepts that you can follow and all filters now in use fall into one or another of these groups. The 3 are undergravel filters, bottom filters and outside filters (which includes both motorized and air driven). There are as many proponents of one method as there are of the others. I do not intend to get in the middle. Each system has its pros as well as its bad points. Why don't we consider them one at a time.

The easiest to install and the easiest to service in terms of hours in operation is the undergravel type of filter shown in Figure 45A. The flat plastic grid is placed on the empty bottom of the tank with the 2 air stem returns coming up in the far corners of each side of the tank. These stems have a large tube inside of which is a smaller tube. Once the filter is in position, gravel is placed on the grid along with plants and rocks and whatever else in the way of decoration is desired in the tank. A 3/16 inch diameter air hose from the pipe valve on the manifold is connected to the smaller tubes from the filter, one at each end of the tank. When the pump is turned on, air is forced down the small tube under the grid. Once under, it seeks to escape, and does, back up the larger tube. As it comes to the surface it carries a small amount of water with it. Since water is displaced and its density is lessened because of the air, more water moves into its place under the grid. This moving of water down through the gravel through the tiny holes in the grid causes tiny particles of waste matter, food, etc., to be pulled down into and through the gravel. Eventually these tiny particles are captured either deep under the gravel or down under the grid itself where bacteria can work on this material and change much of it into harmless gases which pass off up the large tube into the atmosphere.

Herein is the secret of this filter. The entire bed of gravel acts as a large filter. Over a period of time, beneficial bacteria multiply and build up in this gravel bed and as the water is pulled down through the bed, these bacteria literally chew up the toxic wastes and transform them into harmless gases. This type of filter is completely out of the way with the exception of the corner riser tubes. It requires no service other than daily checking to make certain that air bubbles are coming up from sides of each tank. Bubbles should rise evenly, steadily, not causing the water surface to "boil." Keep in mind that as those bubbles break they throw tiny water particles into the air. If the filter...and this applies to any filter...throws bubbles too fast and too high, every piece of equipment around the breaking pattern will become saturated with water droplets and in time will start to corrode.

The only bad feature about this filter is that not all the dirt particles are pulled into the gravel and destroyed. Many larger pieces of debris must be syphoned out of the gravel. They will simply not go down into the gravel until they break down to the point where they can move downward to the grid. Then again, much of the waste material accumulated in the gravel will rise as a great cloud when the gravel is disturbed. That this waste material is beneficial to plant life in the aquarium is of little value since most store set-up tanks are devoid of live plants. One method of assisting this type of filter is to stir up the gravel in the front of the tank periodically. Once the debris have settled down on the gravel, go back and pick it up with a syphon hose.

The second type of filter common in store tanks is the bottom filter. They come in various shapes: triangular, round, rectangular or square as in Figure 45B. But operation is about the same for all types. Here water is drawn in through the bottom slots, passes up and through the filtering media placed in the central portion of the filter, is caught by the bubbles from the air stone and is moved out and up through the large lift tube. Both types shown are very efficient filters, are simple to operate and the amount of air required per filter is less than that required for the undergravel type. Further, they can be watched from the outside of the tank for signs of dirt saturation. The Bubble-Up Filter is an inexpensive filter similar in design to other box filters on the market. To clean it you must take it completely out of the tank. Whether or not you take off the airline depends on how much slack line you happen to have. But out of the water it must come. Most bottom filters are cleaned in this way. The Maxi-Flo Filter, although a bottom box filter, is designed so that the portion containing the filtering media can be taken out without disturbing the rest of the filter, changed and replaced. Although its cost is considerably more than other bottom box filters, the advantages of its design should be considered.

Well then, what's wrong with these types of filters? Well, for one thing, they just never appeal to the aesthetic sense sitting quite phlegmatically on the tank bottom. Also, in a stock tank, where fish are netted daily, bottom filters can be quite a problem once fish learn to hide behind them. Often it is necessary to dislodge a filter to catch an elusive specimen.

FIGURE 45A *Two examples of the undergravel filtration system. Courtesy Kordon Corp. and Metaframe Corp.)*

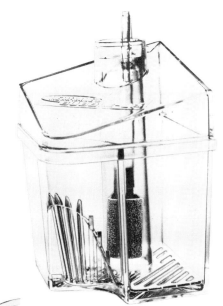

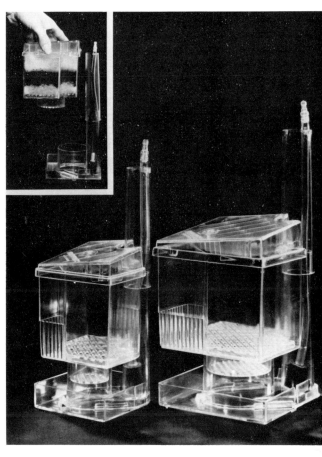

FIGURE 45B *Two examples of inside bottom filters. (Courtesy Marineland Aquarium Products and Metaframe Corp.)*

FIGURE 45C *An outside air filter. (Courtesy of Metaframe Corp.)*

FIGURE 45D *An outside motorized filter. (Courtesy of Hagen U.S.A.)*

Nevertheless, they are popular filters. Another point to keep in mind when making a comparison with the undergravel filter is that these bottom filters do require glass wool (or polyester wool) and charcoal and that they require that these two agents be changed periodically. It's one more chore not known to the undergravel filter enthusiast.

Outside filters should be considered only if you are contemplating a Vertical design set-up and then only when the Vertical design set-up is used in the shop layout shown in Figure 15. Outside filters, as their name implies, hang onto and operate outside of the tanks (Figure 45C), and generally on the backs of the tanks. Outside filters all work one of 2 ways. One is where the water flows into the filter from the tank by syphoning action after which it flows down through a layer of glass wool and charcoal to the bottom of the filter where it is pumped back into the tank by air or by a motor-driven impeller. In the second system, water is pumped into the filter by air action where it flows to the bottom and up through glass wool and charcoal and then back into the tank by gravity action. The most commonly used system is where the water is introduced into the filter by syphon and is returned by power.

Outside filters, by and large, perform a more thorough filtering job and circulate more water per hour than either the undergravel or bottom filters but they do have the great disadvantage of not adapting themselves to the majority of store set-ups. And there is one other significant disadvantage even when and where they can be used. Outside filters that depend on syphon tubes to carry water from the tank into the filter demand a water level in the tank at all times equal to or higher than the bottom of the discharge tube that goes into the filter. As long as the water in the tank is high enough to keep the bottom of that discharge tube covered, and there is no air in the syphon, the water will continue to flow from tank to filter. This cycle will continue as the water seeks the lower level of the filter and is returned to the tank. Should the air stop, this syphoning will continue until the level of water in both tank and filter box coincide. If you dip water from the tank as you catch fish and succeed in pulling enough water from that tank to expose the bottom of the syphon tube hanging in the filter, your syphon will stop and no further filtering will be possible until you fill the tank to its original level and start the syphon once again.

The water is returned to the tank in an outside filter by air or by a motor-driven impeller. Air carries the water in the same way it functioned in the bottom filter, i.e., it is forced to the bottom of the filter and allowed to escape, whereupon it immediately heads for the surface carrying tiny particles of water up and over into the tank via the plastic return stem. Other water particles replace those carried to the surface and this rising and replacing of water sets up a current and a continuation of the syphoning action. Motor-driven types have an impeller that throws the water up and over through a return tube into the tank. The function is the same with an impeller as with the air powered types; however, the action is much faster, giving a faster water turnover and thus increasing filtration.

THE HEATING SYSTEM, COVERS

In recent years, the trend has been away from individual tank heaters to central heating for the store that maintains proper water temperature. The modern, insulated pet shop with a reliable heating system and with tanks situated away from the entrance to avoid cold air from traffic flow is now able to keep a close 78 degrees in the tanks year round. It really gets down to this: If you can maintain the optimum temperature of 78 without using individual heaters in each section, good. This section can offer you nothing; if not, read on.

There are 2 types of heaters available. One is submergible and is placed on the bottom of the tank, often under the gravel, and depends on a thermostat placed at some other point in the tank or some other tank; to regulate its action. The second is the heater that is affixed to the back of the tank by a clip or thumb screw and which has both heating element and thermostat contained in one tube and which cannot be completely submerged. This is the most popular and most practical heater and examples are shown in Figure 46. Held tight to the back of the tank, it is out of the way more so than a bottom heater.

However, a word on heaters in general. Regardless of the type you choose, a heater is one more item in the tank and adds more wire to contend with in your set-up. And should you allow the water level to drop below the bottom of the heater, either when cleaning the tank or by sheer negligence as you dip for fish, and should you allow the heater to stay on, the tube will overheat and crack. Any water that gets into a heater will short it out. This means no heat for that tank and always the possibility of electrocuting the fish, you, or both. Heaters are necessary for your customers, but if you will plan now to maintain a 78 degree air temperature in your fish section, you can eliminate the heaters. Should you need them later on, you can install them quickly enough as long as you provide the electrical outlets now.

If you decide to use the Vertical design set-up or the Step-Up design shown in Figure 32 or should you elect to use a

126

FIGURE 46 *Here are 2 types of clamp-on heaters suitable for all tanks. (Courtesy of O'Dell Mfg. Co. and Metaframe Corp.)*

FIGURE 47 *Two kinds of tank covers—The stainless steel screen and the sliding glass cover. (Courtesy of Metaframe Corp. and O'Dell Mfg. Co.)*

FIGURE 48A *Here are just a few of the many 3-D backgrounds now available. (Courtesy of Penn-Plax Plastics.)*

FIGURE 48B *Crystallizing and 3-D effects such as this can be obtained through the use of paint, metallic foil and optical plastic. (Courtesy of Penn-Plax Plastics.)*

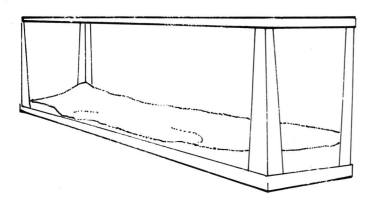

FIGURE 49 *The first step in aquascaping is the placement of the gravel. Most experts suggest the gravel slope away from the front and middle of the tank. The second step is to place rocks and/or ornaments and, finally, position the plants. Plastic plants are best for the busy shop.*

reflector that does not cover the entire top of the tank, then you should have some type of cover for the open water surface. There are sound reasons for this. Newly introduced tropical fish, especially livebearers, will almost always jump until they have become acclimated to their new surroundings. And not only will they jump, but they will, and can, jump through the smallest openings imaginable. We've seen swordtails go through an opening in the top of a tank no bigger than a 5 cent piece. This sort of thing can be expensive to you and darn frustrating to the fish who jumps out and lands on the floor instead of in another pond of water. So for this reason, a top cover is very wise. Second, should you leave the tops of your tanks open to the public, they might use your tanks as disposal recepticles for assorted junk. Cigarette ash, as an example, can cause more than cancer in a tank of neons. Third, you should always attempt to keep down the loss of water through evaporation. Warm, aerated water evaporates quite readily if the tank surface is left exposed. And as the water evaporates, it leaves minerals in the water behind. Adding new water gradually increases the build-up of these minerals. Constantly adding more water to a tank that has rapid evaporation thus increases the hardness of the water.

To give you an idea of what is available in the way of covers, look at Figure 47. There is a stainless steel screen that fits over the entire tank, covering all top edges and fitting on the tank much like the lid of a box. Excellent for prevention of jumping, it cannot be used to stop evaporation and will not inhibit customers from using the tank as a trash can. Some reflectors will fit over the screen cover, some will not. If you desire to use this type of cover in conjunction with a strip (partial) reflector, check your reflector first to be sure they will fit together. Any reflector that fits on any inside edge of the top of the tank will not work with the screen cover.

There are several manufacturers offering glass or plastic tank tops. This one slides in grooved plastic tracks positioned at the end of the tank; others are hinged and lift up rather than slide. Whatever the material and whatever the means of entry, keep in mind that you need to get into your stock tanks often and quickly, conveniently and without spilling water. Illumination and containment are very important to the overall fish operation but not to the point that looks makes function secondary. Whatever you choose, whether made to your specifications or available through your local wholesaler, keep uppermost in your mind the need for practicality.

TANK DECORATION

One of the most difficult tasks to accomplish successfully is to make each tank in your set-up look like a picture or like a piece of furniture that the customer would want in his own home. In the store the aquarium's major purpose is to act as a holding tank. But at the same time you must attract customers by the sight of your tanks. Unfortunately, too many dealers set up one or more 55 gallon tanks, elaborately decorated with rocks, plants and large fish, to act as show pieces while they allow their 10 or 15 gallon stock tanks to become dirty and dull. That new customer, the novice, is not thinking about a 55 gallon tank with large show fish. He's thinking how nice it would be to own a small tank and he is looking at your set-up for help. Well then, the problem is to create some beauty in these tanks and yet leave enough room in each to catch fish.

First, you can decorate the outside back of the tank. There are several things that can be used and you should try to use everything that you will be selling in the store. One effective item is crystallizing paint. (See Figure 48A.) Available in red, green, blue or gold, it will form a jack frost pattern on the back of the tank and does a remarkable job of blending well with plants yet setting them off to advantage. Crystallizing paint must be applied to a horizontal surface to be effective and, thus, must be painted before the tanks are set into place and filled. Regular household flat or gloss paint is often used on the backs of tanks but this is never really satisfactory. The very opaqueness of regular paint is too stark; it

lacks the depth found in crystallizing paint. You can also apply several different types of paper or plastic to the backs of the tanks. Many are metallic and have the same crystalline designs formed by paint. These backgrounds come in a variety of colors.

Next are the molded plastic backgrounds that are actually 3 dimensional and give a feeling of depth to the picture when viewed through the tank. These backgrounds are available in many different designs. (See Figure 48B) All fit on the outside of the tank and are self-adhering. These backgrounds take up from ¾ to 1½ inches in depth. This space requirement must be taken into consideration when you plan your tank set-up. Finally, there are several different types of backgrounds made with natural rock and a few synthetic designs which fit inside the tank. These are hard to beat for underwater realism. Now, which should you use . . . paint, foil paper, plastic or real backgrounds? Use all of them with the exception of the household paint. You'll be selling the crystallizing paint and the foil and the plastic and rock backgrounds so why not display them as they should be. Remember, if you display it, you'll sell it. What you have in your tank set-up is what your customers will want to purchase. Which is as it should be, because you're going to be the expert and what you use must also be good and right for your customers.

Now add colored gravel. Use between 1½ to 2 lbs. per gallon and be sure to vary your color combinations. For instance, use 8 lbs. of lavender and 8 lbs. of black and 8 lbs. of fluorescent red against a red or gold background. In another, use all black or all yellow with just a handful of chartreuse. You should make up your own color combinations but be sure to stagger the colors from tank to tank. Also keep in mind how each tank looks next to its neighbor.

Slope your gravel away from the front and middle of each tank; high points should be at the back and on the ends. You might add 1 or 2 plastic plants per tank. Plants add some color and at the same time provide a haven for shy fish. And if in netting fish you should upset them, no harm done. They can be replanted quickly enough. Rocks should be avoided, especially if you use a square bottom or corner bottom filter. Rocks would be just one more problem to circumvent when catching fish.

That's about all there is to decorating your set-up tanks. But allow your imagination to run riot when you set up your larger show tanks. These are the tanks that you will set out on the floor as demonstrators. With these you should bring to bear all your decorative and artistic skills. Use plenty of rock, specimen plants and large exhibition fish. Make up here what you had to forego in the 10 or 15 gallon tanks. Figure 49 summarizes the 3 basic steps for the interior decorating of any tank.

before: If you build your own kennels, individual taste and space allotment will have a lot to do with the particular size you choose.

Figure 50A shows a simple 5-sided box using 3/4 inch plywood held together by both nails and glue. If you would prefer, a one inch flakeboard could be used just as well. (If you use flakeboard, however, gluing is absolutely necessary.) Figure 50B shows the same size kennel, but plastic hardboard such as Formica has been added to the inside for easy cleaning and to resist moisture. At the same time, the builder has used this plastic hardboard to round out the bottom corners effectively. Last, an aluminum grill door has been added.

In Figure 50C the wire grill door has been replaced by a wooden frame in which 2 sliding glass doors give access to the kennel. A small slot has been cut in the frame above the doors and covered with screening. In the back of the kennel, close to the ceiling, a similar wire-covered slot has been cut. This second slot is connected to a forced ventilating system which pulls fresh air into the kennel over the door, across the top of the kennel and out the back. If the store is air conditioned, this venting system need not be too powerful. If no air conditioning is available, then the ventilating system would have to be powerful enough to pull a steady flow of air through the screens.

Figure 50D shows a solid wire front but with Dutch doors in the back to give access to the kennel interior. This type of cage, as well as 50E, where solid glass is used in the front, can be used for a store set-up such as we discussed in Figures 15 and 16 back in the chapter on layout. In both of these set-up designs, the cages were facing the public but they could not touch an animal unless they opened the door. All feeding and cleaning would be done from the rear.

Wooden cages can be built quite inexpensively compared to steel or fiberglass, but you must remember that wood, no matter how well protected with paint, is subject to deterioration, especially on the floor of a cage because of bacteria and fecal matter. Where there is the smallest crevice in which urine can collect, bacteria will go to work on it, creating odors which are difficult, if not impossible, to eradicate. Seams at the bottom of any wooden cage should be water tight. In fact, the best solution is to line the entire inside of any animal cage with a good plastic surfacing such as Formica or a similar product which will not absorb water and body wastes yet will be easy to clean and easy to maintain. Certainly there is no great objection to wooden kennels providing you follow the simple rules of construction and sanitation mentioned.

It goes without saying that cages should be built to look professional. If you are a craftsman,

chapter 8
What About The Other Departments?

Depending on the number of puppies, kittens and other larger animals you wish to keep, the facilities needed to confine these pets can be as expensive and extensive as your tropical fish set-up. Since the dog and cat business is variable, the equipment needed for this department is necessarily relative to the expected volume.

At the very outset let us assume that any cage we buy or build for a dog will be suitable for a cat or other animal of comparable size. A cubic module determination is important for consistency of decor as well as keeping your sanity; so, whatever we talk about in terms of a dog pen or a cat pen will be the same size. If more room is needed, you have the latitude of putting 2 cages together, taking out the middle partition and coming up with one big cage. But at least, in the beginning, you will start with a single predetermined module to be used throughout. Like everything else we have discussed thus far, there are various approaches to the building or the buying of animal cages. Again, we have a few choices, to wit: Wood, fiberglass, galvanized steel or stainless steel.

Wood is the most versatile material if you have do-it-yourself tendencies. It is flexible, inexpensive, but unless properly coated, it can give you a sanitary fit. One thing to be said about wooden cages, whether you make them or have them built, is that you can provide doors at the back of the cage as well as the front if you so desire. Most of the metal and fiberglass cages that come ready-made can only be entered through the front. In Figure 50 we show some examples of wooden kennels. These kennels all run about 35″ wide by 32″ high by 28″ deep. But bear in mind what we said

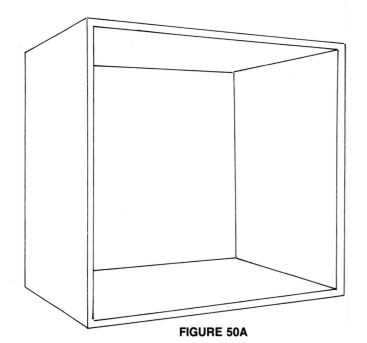

FIGURE 50A

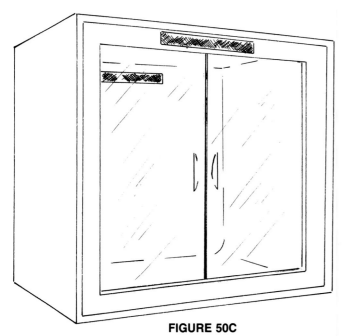

FIGURE 50C

FIGURE 50E

FIGURE 52 *Here are 2 galvanized kennel units that may be stacked. (Courtesy of General Cage Corp.)*

FIGURE 51 *This is an example of formica covered wooden kennels with anodized aluminum doors. (Courtesy of Snyder Mfg. Co.)*

FIGURE 53 *This bank of stainless steel kennels comes in various sizes. (Courtesy of General Cage Corp.)*

FIGURE 54 *These 5 fiberglass units can be fitted together to form any arrangement. Here we see 4 single and one double unit, all with false wire bottoms. (Courtesy of Safari Kennel Prods.)*

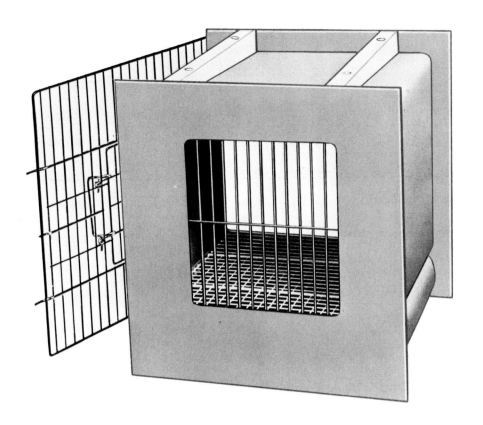

FIGURE 55 *Where rear servicing can be done, this wall unit can be used. Since animals cannot be cared for from the front with this cage unit, you will need more than one clerk if you decided to clean the unit during store hours. (Courtesy of General Cage Corp.)*

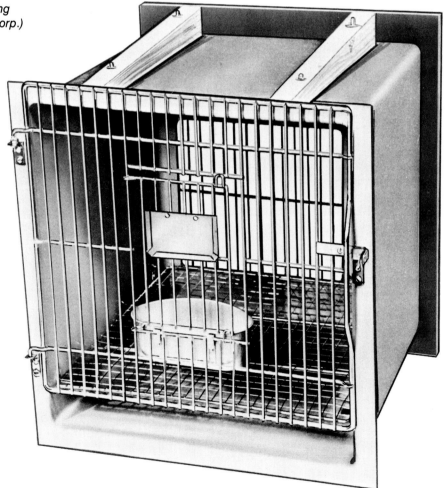

cleaning easier, hides fecal matter and by adding an enzyme to a small amount of water in the tray can help maintain an almost odor-free kennel.

You might notice that the stainless steel kennels in Figure 53 are on rollers. All kennels can be fitted with rollers. Depending on how much moving you intend to do with your cages for cleaning and/or display purposes, you might give the roller base idea serious thought. It will certainly make a bank of kennels more flexible, especially if they are to be used in a grooming operation. Some cages come with or without the roller bases and they can be added later if not purchased initially. Other manufacturers stipulate that they must be ordered with rollers at the outset and conversion later is costly. Be sure to decide which way you will go before you purchase.

FEEDING DISHES

A good time to discuss the various types of feeding dishes for dogs, cats and other larger animals and birds is right here in the cage section. For the pet owner at home a cute plastic diner or a set of light aluminum pans can be quite attractive and quite functional. For your animal cages, however, where space is so limited and durability so important, feeding dishes must be heavy, kept out of the way and durable under sanitizing procedures. And they must be easy to clean. Figures 56A-H show a galaxy of feeding dishes that are adaptable to most any kennel design. Figures 56A, 56B and 56C show types of hanging feeder-waterers. Hanging dishes seem to be more satisfactory in the majority of cases because animals would be hard put to get into or upset dishes of this type; for this reason alone they are more sanitary than anything placed on the floor. Figures 56D and 56E show dishes that are sold to the consumer trade but which are quite satisfactory. The crockery feeding dishes (56F) are inexpensive and are available in three sizes: 5, 7 and 9 inches. A crockery dish cannot be picked up by the average puppy. For that matter, a pup would have difficulty moving it at all. Plastic dishes will also work so long as they are weighted (56G). Pups have a tendency to chew and plastic is usually chewable. That one drawback not withstanding, the plastic dish is easy to clean and the weighted feature makes it very difficult for a pup to move or turn over. For water, any of the above dishes can be used but in Figure 56H is shown the "lick-type" watering apparatus that hangs on the outside of the cage and allows the pup access to water whenever desired without giving him the opportunity to step in or upset a dish. Medications are easily

given in the water with this method; it is by far the most practical and sanitary method of watering yet devised.

Any of the cages we have discussed can be used for larger, more exotic animals. In fact, with some alterations, they can be used for the larger birds as well. However, these cages are intended to perform as sanitary housing for dogs and cats. They perform this function perfectly. But they cannot be made to look glamorous or help create an exotic atmosphere unless you go to some lengths to remodel them.

As holding pens for a large assortment of exotic creatures, any cage we have discussed will work well enough. But where you are seeking the unusual cage, it will be necessary, in all probability, to have it custom-created. If you need a large display cage for a pair of scarlet macaws, your best bet would be to design what you want and then visit your local ornamental iron worker. He can put together what you require. Since this custom work is consuming and a one-shot affair, you can expect to pay more per cubic foot than you would for one of the ready-built cages we have been discussing. But for effect and for spaciousness, something of your own construction in this case will be the best answer.

BIRD ENCLOSURES

With birds we are allowed a good deal more flexibility than with animals because wood can be used to a greater degree than with dogs, cats and exotics. Fecal waste from animals is death to any metal unless it is stainless or galvanized. Wood saturated with urine becomes intolerable. With birds the situation is different because of the very physical nature of their fecal matter. All seedeaters have a low moisture content in their waste material. Because of this, the droppings dry readily and are no problem. The exception is with what we call soft-billed birds such as the toucans and mynas. There are many soft-billed birds but only toucans and mynas are found regularly in pet shops. Since these birds require foods with a high moisture content (fruits, meat, soft vegetables), their excrement is more liquid and can play havoc with any metal surface. But even with the soft-billed bird species, absorbent materials can be used on the cage floors to soak up moisture and prevent corrosion (sand, cat litter, cedar shavings). Since wood can be protected with little trouble and because of the very nature of the droppings of most birds found in pet shops, large wooden cages are often built that reflect one's own individualism.

To give you a better idea of what can be done with different store designs, let's go back to

FIGURE 56A *Aluminum coop cup. (Courtesy of General Cage Corp.)*

FIGURE 56B *Kidney bean aluminum coop cup. (Courtesy of General Cage Corp.)*

FIGURE 56C *Stainless steel coop cup. (Courtesy of General Cage Corp.)*

FIGURE 56D *Spun aluminum feeding dish.*

FIGURE 56E *Stainless steel feeding dish.*

FIGURE 56F *A typical set of crockery feeding dishes.*

FIGURE 56G *Weighted plastic feeding dish. (Courtesy of Suburban Plastics.)*

FIGURE 56H *"Lick-type" animal watering set-up. (Courtesy of Oasis Pet Prods.)*

Figure 14. In this layout there was a separate bird room which was, as we said, to help shield the livestock from the customers as well as the customers from the livestock. Starting from scratch, this was just a room with pegboard on the back wall and both side walls. The front was of glass to allow the customers to view the birds. On the pegboard walls vertical metal shelf standards were fastened and then the shelf brackets and the shelves were installed. At this point the room was complete to the point of being lined on 3 sides with shelves. On these shelves cages were placed...small individual cages that would hold 2 parrakeets or 2 finches, possibly a pair of lovebirds or a male singing canary. This type of cage is known as a shelf cage and Figure 57A shows what one looks like. Slid up on the shelves side by side, they are easy to take down for cleaning.

For a larger group of birds, such as 2 dozen parrakeets or a similar number of finches, a large community cage is provided. This type of cage is known as a flight cage. It offers the birds more flying room but it also makes them more difficult to catch. This flight cage can also go in the bird room as shown in Figure 14.

Finally, there is the large, commercial cage used to house mynas, parrots, toucans and other large birds. Like the flight cage, this one can be put in the bird room too, but usually it is hung from the pegboard with hooks rather than mounted on a shelf because of its size (Figure 57C). A parrot cage is 14 inches wide or wider and attempting to put such a large cage on a shelf would be difficult.

Well, you say, but I'm not going to have a separate bird room. My birds will be right out where customers can come up to them. Can I still use the shelf cages, the flight and parrot cages? Absolutely. That separate room was only to confine the birds more closely. It was also intended to keep drafts from hitting the cages. Drafts on all birds can be deadly and in a room such as the one in Figure 14 you would be free of this problem. Again, birds, especially parrakeets, are constantly shedding tiny feathers which go floating about the store with the slightest puff of air. On top of that, seed-eaters (canaries, parrakeets, finches, parrots, lovebirds) always hull their seeds quite daintily, which, if you'll pardon the pun, makes a hull of a mess should some get kicked or scratched or blown out onto the floor. That is why a separate bird room makes such good sense. (Another logical reason is that it is much easier to catch an escapee in a small room than in a large pet shop.)

For the store layout in Figure 15, you would most probably build wooden cages of varying dimensions to house different sized birds. These cages would have wire fronts and would be mounted on roller bases. They would be cleaned from the rear. For observation by the public, they would be pushed up to the glass partition windows. To clean the floor of feathers and seed hulls, they could be pushed back away from the window.

In reviewing a bird set-up, let's say that small birds can be housed in individual shelf cages or in groups in a large flight cage. These cages can be hung from pegboard or they can be placed on shelves along a wall area. Some type of an enclosure is desireable, i.e., either glass doors in front of them or completely isolated in a room of their own. Bigger birds in bigger cages can be put in a separate room or in special custom cages. Or they can be kept in ready-made commercial cages at various positions around the pet shop where people can see them, but not tease them, and where they are out of the way of drafts.

Figure 58 is an illustration of a custombuilt flight cage divided into 2 sections and with tropical greenery painted on the back and side surfaces. (The illustration is shown without the front wires.) Done in sharp, brilliant oil colors, this type of interior cage decoration can be very effective and is quite inexpensive. Made of ½ inch plywood, the wire spacing on the front will depend on the size of birds you wish to contain. For a group of large birds, such as medium parrots or toucans, a nice size for each section would be 4' long by 3' high by 2½' deep. Welded wire mesh 1'' by 2'' would be suitable for the front. Where smaller birds would be kept, 1'' by 1'' welded wire could be used or even ½'' by 2'' for finches and canaries. (Welded wire in these sizes can be obtained through any of the large mail order houses that sell lawn, farm or garden supplies.) On a cage of this size, one mistake is often made: that of making the entrance door too small. You need plenty of elbow room in this kind of cage. Make the door large enough to get a 6 inch catching net into the cage.

SMALL ANIMAL DISPLAYS

Favorites of the children are mice, hamsters, gerbils, turtles, caimans (South American alligator), snakes, horned toads, chameleons and other small pets that can be kept in a small space. Cage requirements for these animals and members of reptilian groups are not too much different from other animals except that, being smaller and often quick to discover the smallest hole, they must be confined with great care. Snakes are the worst offenders and probably head the list as escape artists. They seem to be able to slip through the slightest aperture.

In Figure 59 a 10 gallon tank, with a built-on

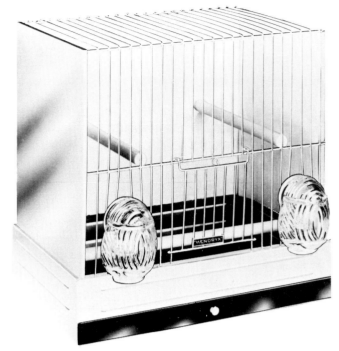

FIGURE 57A *This shelf cage can hold 2 parrakeets, 2 finches, a pair of lovebirds or a male canary. (Courtesy of Prevue Metal Prods.)*

FIGURE 57C *This large parrot cage can also be used for toucans, mynas, etc. (Courtesy of Prevue Metal Prods.)*

FIGURE 57B *This flight cage can hold 24 parrakeets, finches or a lesser number of larger birds. (Courtesy of Prevue Metal Prods.)*

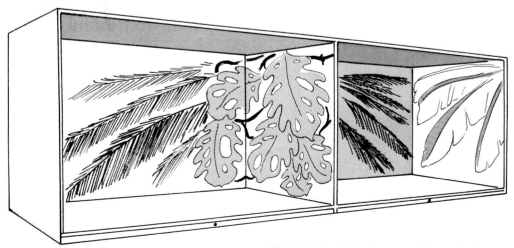

FIGURE 58 *This large partitioned flight cage (front wires are omitted on illustration) shows what can be done with a little decoration.*

FIGURE 60 *Commercial small mammal units are available from various manufacturers. (Courtesy of General Cage Corp.)*

FIGURE 59A *A slide cover tank with sand, rock and cactus can make an excellent display for reptiles.*

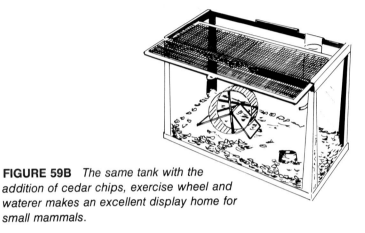

FIGURE 59B *The same tank with the addition of cedar chips, exercise wheel and waterer makes an excellent display home for small mammals.*

FIGURE 59C *Gravel piled high at one end with a few inches of water at the other makes a ready display for amphibians.*

screen sliding cover that is available commercially, has been decorated 3 ways to show a variety of uses. In Figure 59A fine sand, one or 2 rocks, live cactus and a small water cup are all that's needed for many of the reptiles that like dry conditions. This is a perfect display for horned toads, chameleons, snakes and some of the fancy lizards. Figure 59B shows a typical hamster or gerbil set-up. All that's required is an exercise wheel, waterbottle with holder and a small container for food. Mice, rats, gerbils, hamsters, flying squirrels fit very nicely into a setting such as this. Figure 59C would be used for turtles, alligators (caimans), salamanders, and frogs. Nothing to building this display. It's merely a question of piling gravel high on one end of the tank and using a rock or 2 to hold it in position.

The size tank shown in Figure 59 is 10 gallon. These tanks, however, are available up to 20 gallon. Most tanks fitted with the sliding screen covers shown in the illustrations can be locked. If you keep small animals in tanks of this type in a separate animal room as in Figure 14, or behind glass out of the reach of customers as in Figures 15 and 16, locks will not be necessary. But should you elect to keep these display tanks out in the main selling area, it's best to have locks. Figure 60 is a commercial small animal unit that is just great for the small store or where a small animal department is desired as an addition. Self-contained, it can be moved to any location with little effort. This type of unit would not supplant a total animal room; it would be right where a small investment in store fixturing is necessary or where space is limited.

chapter 9
Display Is Your Key To Turnover!

Back on the opening pages of this book, when we talked about the full-line pet shop, we said that 40 percent of the business, on the average, was in fish; that 40 represented the dog and cat business and the remaining 20 percent went to birds, small animals and grooming. Making the assumption here that you are contemplating a full-line pet shop, it becomes a simple matter to allot percentages of your total inventory capital approaching the 40, 40, 20 ratio and to make up an order accordingly. Now there are natural progressions in putting together just about any pet shop that will occur time and time again and here is the progression for the opening inventory that works best year in and year out.

Your first step is to contact your products distributor. We assume that you have done that long before you approached the shelf-stocking stage. You have met with him, obtained his catalog or price list, and are now completely apprised of what he stocks. Perhaps it has been necessary to contact more than one distributor. He is fully aware of what you are planning and throughout your entire preliminary discussion with landlord and contractor, this distributor has been in touch with you, giving you advice and keeping abreast of your progress in getting the store into position for inventory.

The first order to write is that of the store set-up tanks and everything relating to that set-up. You want that order in first and set up before any other merchandise comes in. If you intend to have backgrounds on the tanks, filters in them, heaters and reflectors for each tank. . . whatever you have decided as being right for you . . . that order should be made up and delivered. Then, once the tanks are cleaned, filled, the air circulating, you can give some serious thought to the initial dry goods inventory. Again, contact the distributor's salesman and sit down with him. At this point there are 2 methods to approach the first inventory. One, you can write out the entire order by yourself and merely present it to him. This saves him a tremendous amount of work. He has no decisions to make. He copies your order onto his invoice and the job is done. On your shoulders rest the responsibility of your decisions. There's nothing wrong with this system; it's done all the time. But if you make a mistake and order either too heavy or too light anywhere along the way, it's your fault. Or, you might let your distributor have the complete responsibility for that first inventory. What you lose in self-satisfaction putting together the first order can be easily outweighed by the gain in time. For as you near the completion of your shop, there are so many, many details to sap your attention that the load of ordering could well be entrusted to the folks who know the business.

A word here about wholesalers. A pet supply distributor who has been in business for many years knows your business. When you visit his offices and inspect his warehouse, you should find, along with neat, orderly rows of merchandise, an air of optimism and understanding for your undertaking. If this company is to be entrusted with keeping your store stocked, you must have the confidence to lay out all your plans, discuss your finances and project your future aims and intentions. A good distributor will take this information and use it all as a guide to present you with a workable, sufficient and saleable inventory. At the same time, he should point out any holes in your plans, any doubts he may have on any phase of your intended operation. A good distributor should not be only your supplier but your advisor on every aspect of your business life. He needs you as much as you need him. Out of this mutual dependency can be formed a very profitable relationship. Thus, in the beginning, when time is short and many small details are still left unfinished, it might be well to consider giving over to your distributor the task of working up your first inventory.

THE FIRST INVENTORY

And then comes that day when the cock crows, the truck rolls up, and endless streams of cartons and boxes come pouring forth to rest in the middle of your store. Good grief. Where will it all go and where do you begin? At this point, the ideal situation is for the tropical fish tank set-up to be operating, but with no fish, and the holding cages for birds and animals all installed, but with no livestock on hand. For now is your opportunity to concentrate on marking and putting up the dry goods. For this task you have assembled all available help, both free (like relatives except your mother-in-law) and paid-for help plus marking instruments. You should also have on hand enough liquid refreshment (soft drinks) to keep the entire crew going far into the night. (It must be soft drinks . . . anything stronger makes for a more jolly time but for less work.)

The first and cardinal rule that goes into effect now, and holds from this time forward, is that every item taken from a box is to be checked off the distributor's invoice. Every case, every box, everything you mark, must be reconciled with a corresponding entry on one of the invoices. Most distributors mark the invoice number(s) on the cartons. This is essential when you have hundreds of boxes of merchandise. (And you will have hundreds of boxes on that first order.) It's important that you be able to match each carton with a specific invoice and to do this it is necessary that the distributor so mark each box delivered. The majority of distributors will also put the suggested retail next to each item on the invoice to guide you in marking. Should he fail to do this, it will be necessary to have at least one complete catalog of pet supplies that shows the retails for the items you are stocking.

One person is now going to be pricer and locater. If you can spare a second person to check off the merchandise on the invoices, fine. Otherwise, the pricer-locater will also check off the items. A carton is opened and a box is taken out. The invoice is found that covers that carton and the box from inside is checked off the invoice as being recieved. The pricer then marks the retail price on the top of the box with a heavy felt-tipped pen and pulls one item from the box and places that one item on the shelf. He has now located that item on its designated shelf spot. The marker that comes along behind him will take out the remaining items from the box, mark them and put them on the shelf with the one pilot set up there by the pricer-locater.

Now the question always arises at this point as to whether the merchandise should be put up by manufacturer's name or by usage. We feel that every item should be shelved according to its usage. Thus, if you were putting up dog remedies, you would not put up one section of Sergeants, one section of Pulvex, one section of Holiday, one section of Lambert-Kay, and so on; rather you would put all the shampoos of all the companies together, all the flea-killers of all the companies together, all the vitamins and diet supplements of all the companies together. It is far easier for you to inventory your stock at some later date if the shelves are filled by manufacturer's name. But let's face it, the customer wants to buy an item from a selection.

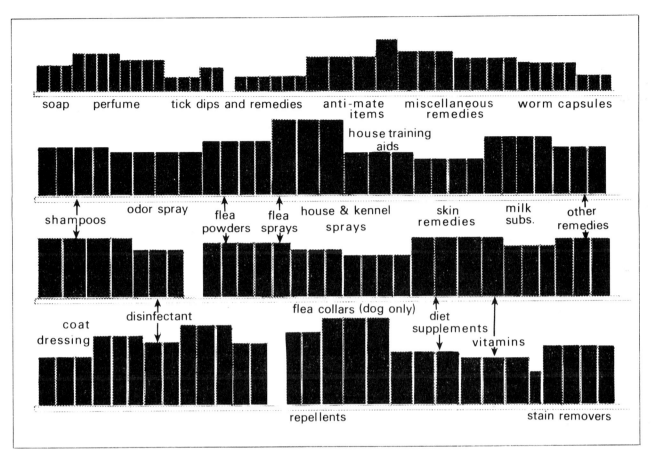

soap   perfume   tick dips and remedies   anti-mate items   miscellaneous remedies   worm capsules

house training aids

shampoos   odor spray   flea powders   flea sprays   house & kennel sprays   skin remedies   milk subs.   other remedies

coat dressing   disinfectant   flea collars (dog only)   diet supplements   vitamins

repellents   stain removers

FIGURE 61 *Here is an illustration of a possible grouping of products on a gondola following the vertical display theory.*

He wants to choose one can of flea powder, let's say, from many different brands, not look over several manufacturer's lines to pick out his preferential can of powder. In similar manner, put all the dog items in one section and all the cat items in another. And if you happen to have a few items that are applicable to both dog and cat, split up your count and put half in the dog section and half in the cat section. It's the customer you must think about, not how easy taking inventory will be.

VERTICAL DISPLAY

The next thing to consider when laying out your shelves is whether you wish horizontal or vertical display. In Figure 61 you see vertical display. Horizontal treatment would be where all the shampoos were spread along one shelf, all the repellents on another and so on. There is

always controversy over which system is best but the leading department stores in the country today insist that vertical display will sell more merchandise. The eye, they contend, travels up and down easier than it does from side to side. As the person moves along a shelf, the eye, moving from top to bottom, catches sight of all the items available. Now, obviously there are some items, such as soap or perfume that do not permit vertical stocking. But keep in mind that wherever possible, this system will produce the best sales results.

In Figure 62 you can see the reason for our suggesting pegboard space near all of the shelf areas. We can think of no group of items in the pet business today that is packaged strictly for shelving. Dog remedies, grooming items, bird foods, toys, accessories, whatever group you can think of that was originally packaged for shelves, now has several items available for peg hanging. You can see this in Figure 62. Notice how there are clippers and boxed brushes,

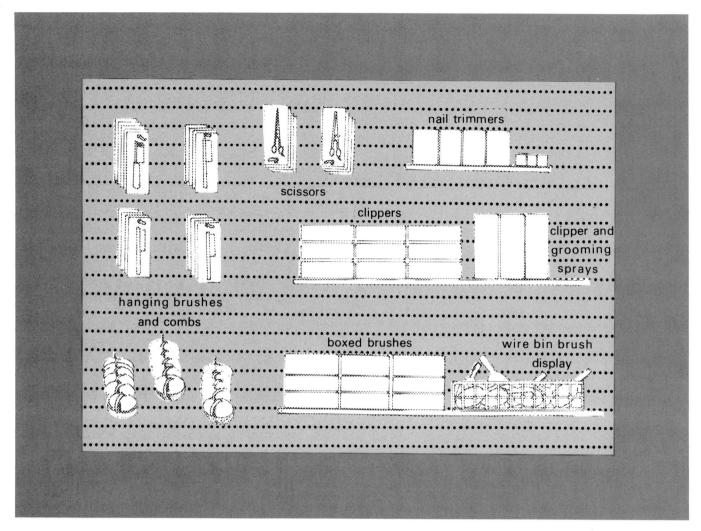

FIGURE 62 *The flexibility of pegboard and its component hooks and shelves is amazing. Here is just one display example.*

clipper sprays and nail trimmers . . . items that go neatly on a shelf. But what do you do with combs on a card or brushes that do not come boxed? The combs that are carded (and the grooming scissors as well) should be hung from pegboard. We have also installed a wire bin to hold brushes which cannot be hung and will not stack on a shelf. But the picture we are trying to get across is that these grooming items are all in one area of a gondola or wall display. To put shelfable items on a gondola shelf and those that can only be hung over on some distant pegboard wall is pure death. Or to throw the carded combs and scissors in a wire bin, or throw them out on a shelf haphazardly, is just as criminal. If they'll peg, peg'em. Just make certain you keep them with their relatives.

And so, shelf by shelf, gondola by gondola, you will unpack, check off, mark and display the entire initial inventory order. There will be arranging and rearranging. You'll put up merchandise, stand back and look and then change it with items from another shelf. You'll think you have enough room on one section of a gondola to finish out a line and find that you haven't allotted enough space. You'll end up moving the line to another spot. But all this is par for the course so don't become discouraged. In weeks and months to come you'll constantly change things around until they are just right for your operation. You'll never do it all the right way the first time.

MERCHANDISING SPECIFICS

Wicker beds and metal beds can be displayed on an end gondola, or end flat, or right out on the floor in pyramid display, largest bed on the bottom, naturally. Mattresses can be handled the same way but they should be in a wire rack to keep them from sliding helter-skelter onto the floor. Large, bulky items, such as cat litter and cedar bedding, should be placed on the bottom shelf of a gondola. Conversely, light, small items, will go at the top shelf of the gondola. A good rule is that the larger the item, the further down it should be displayed. Another good rule is that the fast moving items should always be put at a lower level; slow moving, high profit items are best shown at eye level. Basically, we all take the path of least resistance, even when looking for pet items. Fish at eye level will sell faster than fish at knee or top of head level. And it is just as true with dry goods. Wild bird houses and wild bird feeders should be displayed from an old dead tree with a base or just a pole with a base and cross arms. Never get into the position of displaying them on a shelf. Wild bird seed, sunflower seed and suet cakes should always be displayed close to the feeders.

Coats, sweaters, blankets and raincoats, as we discussed under store fixtures, can be hung from skirt hangers on a pole, whether out from a wall or from a freestanding floor unit. They can also be piled on a table or on a gondola end, but this method means more work for you in attempting to keep them segregated by size. People will just not keep them straight for you when you display this way.

During the months just before Christmas, cat and dog toys sell exceptionally well. You might decorate a nail keg which is filled with toys and put out on the floor for impulse sales. Dump displays (as they are known) will amaze you with the products they can sell. A dump need not be fancy. That nail keg works fine. A cardboard box, decorated with fancy paper, will work just as well. Display as many tanks, completely set up on the floor, as space will allow. Keep at least one of each size tank on display at all times; the remainder go in the back room. Display aquarium ornaments where the customers can get to them. Put them out of reach of the little children but keep them readily available to the curious adult. Holding and touching an item is the first step in creating the desire to buy.

Any item that can be hung from a peg should be displayed in this manner. There is no finer way to show off merchandise than by hanging. . . providing, of course, that the manufacturer has packaged his product in such a way that it can be hung. But again, as we mentioned in talking about the arrival of the first inventory, keep related items together. It might be necessary to lose in display effect here or there by doing so but it is essential to keep like subjects together. Finally, take a page from your department store or supermarket neighbors who build "mass end displays" of one item to promote maximum movement.

Whatever you are featuring for any particular weekend, week or month should demand prime floor space in your store. Usually that means the end of a gondola that can be seen by every customer coming through your door. Make sure that the items you use for this "Head-On" display are timely items, pertinent to the season. Use items that normally turn well, that are favorites. Wild bird seed, sunflower seed, suet cakes, cat litter, flea and tick collars, flea powder and spray, shampoos, indoor (or outdoor) repellents, tie-out stakes and chains, sweaters and blankets, wild bird feeders and wild bird houses, dog training items—these are popular items that a mass display will push out.

It is important that for an end display you use an item that is a fast seller. You might, as an example, have an affinity toward thermometers that is beyond belief. And you might build the most beautiful, the most grandiose display of thermometers one could imagine. The customers almost trip over the mass of thermometers you assemble. It would never be worth the time, effort and space. Thermometers, no matter what you do with them or to them, will never have the appeal, the dollar volume, the movement, to warrant anything more than shelf or pegging space. To be worth the space and display time involved, the item must be either popular or have a high dollar value. It cannot, as in the case of the thermometers, be a small ticket item with medium turning power. Space is money. Use it wisely.

WINDOW DISPLAYS

Sad to say, most pet shops are prone to neglect their windows and their display signs. The window becomes a chore, which, after the first time, is put off for longer intervals until finally, one dusty and uninteresting conglomeration of faded boxes and crepe paper remains to remind the passerby that a rather lethargic and unimaginative pet shop operator lives there. A good looking window, like the inside of the store, requires thought, effort and time. If you decide to change your window every week, do it. If you decide that a window should remain for at least 2 weeks, fine. Keep it intact for 2 weeks. Then tear it down and put something else in. Your adherence to a methodical schedule is of the utmost importance. It is a ritual that you cultivate actively and conscientiously. No matter what happens, change that window when it's time.

The most attention-getting window is one where live animals, birds or reptiles are displayed. Guaranteed! There is no better way to draw people than with a gaily colored bird flitting back and forth. But don't keep the live animal display constant. Change to merchandise every so often. Or combine them.

FIGURE 63 *Every retailer should work toward building a monthly sales graph which shows sales by month and percent.*

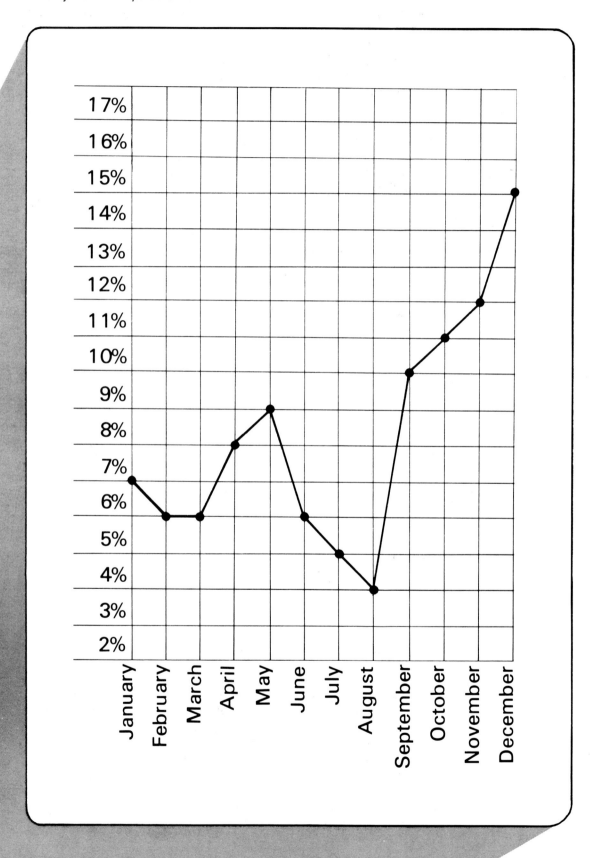

One of the most effective displays I have ever seen was in a northern New Jersey shop one fall. In front of the window were 2 corn shocks, ears of corn still on them. At their bases were pumpkins. Bags of sunflower seed and wild bird seed mix were piled on each other in one glorious display of fall cornucopiousness. And in the back part of that window, and going its entire length, was an enclosed cage in which a pair of golden and a pair of ringnecked pheasants strutted. You had to look twice to see the cage, so effectively had the owner hidden the wires. From the outside it looked as though the birds were free among the shocks and wild bird seed. It was a beautiful window display that brought traffic to a standstill.

In-store signs can often fall into the same sad shape as the front window. You see them day in and day out and they become part of the landscape. You look past them rather than at them. Your customers, on the other hand, especially new customers, view them as part of your store's decor. They notice the condition of the signs, whether or not they match the merchandise over which they preside, whether or not they mention current prices. Never laugh away signing.

All department stores and chains depend on signs to carry the short, sweet message of price and quality. It is true that large department stores have their own signmaking machines, something prohibited to the general pet shop, but there is never an excuse for dirty, outdated signs. If you feel that a sign service is too expensive for your budget, buy inexpensive white cardboard and make your own price and sale signs with a large black felt-tipped pen. Most stationery houses of any size stock cardboard signs preprinted with headings of "Sale Now" or "Special Price" or "This Week's Special," etc., that can be used as the basic stock for your own handiwork. But whether you go commercial or do-it-yourself, make signs work for you. They are designed to help inform your customers; see to it that they perform this function properly by keeping them clean, correct and current.

SALES BY MONTH

That first inventory, even with the help of an experienced distributor, will be 20 percent guesswork. There will be many items that you'll go heavy on only to find they just do not move quickly enough in your area. There are also many items that you will keep light only to find you're out of stock in a few days. This, then, is the problem with the first inventory. From there on, as you become accustomed to your merchandise and to your customers, you will gain knowledge and experience as to the optimum level of inventory for each item in your store.

However, keep in mind that this knowledge of individual products does not always tell you the full story, does not tell you the rate of increase of decrease necessary in your total inventory from month to month. How much more merchandise should you have in total in December, let's say, than in August? Or how much should you have in April in relation to September? If you could know the highs and lows of the public's buying habits it would give you part of the picture; you could regulate your buying accordingly.

We went to one of the country's foremost retail chains to get some idea as to what can be considered average percentage-wise for each month of the year. Figure 63 shows graphically the hills and valleys of business in this national chain of department stores. Note that June, July and August are the slowest months of the year. This is also true for the pet business as a general rule across the country. Notice that beginning in September, business climbs to a high, peaking in December. Here again, the same is true in the pet industry. Note that 48 percent of the year's business for this chain is done in the last 4 months of the year. That's almost half of their yearly business in only a third of the year. Notice, too, that in January, sales slump back down to 7 percent, drop again in February, level off and then climb during the spring months.

The drop in the pet business is not quite so severe after Christmas as we show in Figure 63. We find that business can be up around the 10 percent mark in our industry in January. Now, this peaking and slumping does not mean that you must carry a greater inventory or a lower inventory of just certain items. It means that you must try to keep a balance of total inventory to sales with this chart in mind. Maintaining such a chart might not be possible at the start, but by the beginning of the second year you should have enough information that you can set up a chart of your own that will show the relationship of each month's sales to the total yearly volume.

chapter 10

What Do You Need To Know About People?

You may have the best designed, best stocked store for miles around, but, if your customers are not serviced properly and courteously, you won't see them again. It has been proven over and over that good personnel make a fair store good and a good store great. If you ever feel that you are not getting the potential sales and profits out of your store, one of the first areas to look at should be your employees. In the next few columns I will attempt to give you some guidelines to help you hire, train, supervise, motivate and, unfortunately if needed, terminate store employees. This is in no way meant to be a cure all; it's for you to use, to build on with your experience and, possibly, make your store a little more efficient.

In our industry, personnel is probably the single largest problem. How many times have we said or heard someone else say "if I only had the help." There are certain things you should do on a routine basis to help yourself. Every position in the store, from the manager on down, should have a description of what his job entails, what his specific responsibilities are. When you are interviewing for a position, using this description leaves nothing to be misconstrued by either party.

Also, all employees should know there are certain guides as to how much they can earn. They should know how they will be rated to determine if they are eligible for a raise. In general, like jobs, pay exceptions will happen but the more you minimize salary discrepancies the better off you'll be.

In a specialized industry such as ours, probably every store worker comes in contact with some customers during the course of the day. I think it's necessary to establish some basic requirements you should look for in each new worker.

a. Overall Appearance. Well-groomed, neat, someone you would be happy to talk to about your pet.

b. Personality. A person who is going to come in contact with people should not be too timid. He should be able to carry on a routine conversation with you. Be aware that interviews tend to make all of us nervous, but you should be able to distinguish between nervous and timid.

c. Comprehension. The person should be able to understand the job responsibilities and be seemingly able to carry them out.

One of the best sources for new help is sometimes overlooked. Ask your current employees if they know any qualified people who might be interested in working in your store. Next, have a set of signs (one for the window, one at the check-out) notifying customers of a job opening. Your customers like pets, usually understand the maintenance part of the job, and with careful selection, probably would make good employees.

If you still haven't come up with your new worker, I would recommend the local paper. The rates are inexpensive, and unless you are hiring for a manager, probably just as effective. You can usually dominate the help wanted section of these local papers with a larger ad than normal at a very reasonable cost. Be sure you have the people at the paper help you write the ad and make sure you have all phone applicants talk to you personally. This will save you some unneeded interviewing.

As do most retail stores, you should also keep a current file of job applicants (back 6 months.) It helps to go back and review this file. Maybe 2 months ago a young man or woman you talked to impressed you but you didn't have an opening at the time. Make a call; the person might still be available.

Other alternative sources for workers include school programs. Many high schools and technical schools have programs where students interested in retailing get special permission to work on the job several days per week. Also check church groups and, of course, your local employment office.

Be sure any applicant fills out an application form. If you see any questionable areas, ask the applicant about them while he's there. Don't you be timid. And be sure to follow up on references. Too many people today don't check these out. It will save you a lot of grief later on.

Now that you have hired a potentially good worker, he has been given a complete job description, it's into on the job training. Setting the details of the training schedule, the timing of the schedule and the responsibilities for the

schedule, is your first order of attention. If you have confidence in your store personnel, it's a good idea to have them help in the training but you must always be aware of the new worker's progress. While the new person is learning his or her specific responsibilities, he should also be learning some of the basic store policies concerning other personnel, customers, outsiders other than customers. This will probably come naturally, but a review with the new person after a definite period of time is a must. And make sure you spot check during the training period with both the trainee and trainers to see how things are going.

You might have a training salary and then an automatic increase to the normal salary structure after 30 to 90 days. It's an incentive for the new person and a form of protection for you. Make a big deal out of someone finishing training (after you personally have seen to the person's satisfactory completion). Give them their own store jacket, name tag, throw a little coffee and cake party. It's not how much you necessarily spend, it's the recognition that counts. Let the new worker know that the learning process continues on by exposure to customers, store associates, yourself. They should also be constantly learning from materials in the store, books, product labels, trade magazines, manufacturer's catalog sheets. Their learning process should (just as yours) never really stop.

ONGOING SUPERVISION

There have been so many books and articles written on supervision and its varying philosophy that it would be impossible to go into depth on any one aspect. So what I will do is highlight, based on conversations with all size retailers. I will try and impart some of their suggestions to you. Good supervisors have some common traits in dealing with personnel.

a. Knowledge of the jobs of their workers.

b. Treatment of all workers equally.

c. Fairness in their praise or criticism and evaluations.

d. Honesty and forthrightness with their employees.

e. Treatment of all workers the way they would like to be treated themselves.

These 5 traits should be present in you or your supervisor. We all may feel we have them but it never hurts to try and improve on all or any one of them. Every person in a store contributes to that store's success, *they are all part of a team*. A good supervisor will set goals for his team to meet and then assist them in meeting them. Because the supervisor has all the traits listed, he establishes total communication. He gets feedback from his workers on various aspects of their jobs or on the general store operation. He's a good listener. If he finds a suggestion from an associate worthwhile, he will implement it and give at least verbal credit to the associate (credit where credit is due).

If you are honest with your people, you will have to chew them out once in a while. All people expect to make mistakes and want to be corrected and then helped so as not to make the same mistake again. So it's not the correcting action that usually causes problems, it's the how, where and when you do it. I can remember being in a store when the manager started to dress down an associate on the sales floor—everything stopped, the customers all turned to look, the other store workers stopped what ever they were doing and the poor salesman wanted to crawl away and die. I hope that manager learned that his mistake was probably greater and more damaging to the store than whatever the clerk did. Always talk to your people in private when you are criticizing or reprimanding them. If need be, take them off the sales floor at the time the problem arises; if it's not that big of a deal, make a note and talk to them before they leave that day. They'll appreciate it more and you won't have the other employees wondering when they'll be embarrassed.

In summary, a good supervisor accomplishes his goals by forming a team that has mutual respect for each other; he then works with them to accomplish the job. He remembers that the team works well so long as all the individuals are contributing.

Setting the store atmosphere through good supervision is the first step in motivating store personnel. But somewhere along the way, you want to be sure you retain their enthusiasm. When you set up your salary guide, it's a good idea to make provisions for periodic salary increases. I would recommend every 6 months a review be made with each worker and, based on his job performance, he be considered for an increase. The increase does not have to be large but as a matter of general consensus, a periodic small increase is the most effective method.

Somehow each worker should be compensated if the store makes its sales goal. This compensation should be in real dollars, no matter what the amount. At certain times during the year, you may have specific merchandise you want sold. If the profit margin allows, give your people 25 cents per unit sold. I guarantee it will help move those goods for you.

Every once in a while run an "On The Spot" Contest. Whoever has the highest sales tally today gets $25. Whoever has the biggest individual sale gets $10. Whoever sells the most

puppies today gets $5 per dog. Or make up your own list of potential contests and run them as you see fit. Before we leave this section, two words of caution. Check your competition. Try to pay the going rate. Don't skrimp when it comes to your people. Promotions should be made from within whenever possible. If this cannot be done, at least talk with the people in your store who might feel they are eligible for the promotion and tell them your views before you start to look for an outside worker.

Equally important to most people (although they won't admit it) is psychic income. This might be derived from any number of sources. Probably the single most effective form of psychic income is recognition. Recognition by one's boss and one's peers on the job makes some otherwise bad days bright and cheery. When you get a pleasing letter from a customer about one of your employees, frame it and display it prominently. When your worker goes out of his way to help a customer and you see it, praise him (this time, in front of the group is OK). When someone puts in some extra time for you, tell him how much you appreciate it. You might consider one of the following.

1. Employee of the month award.
2. Customer service award.
3. Store news letter (for customers as well).

Every so often hold an early morning meeting (you supply the coffee and donuts). Have a general agenda but be sure to let the individuals contribute to the meeting with their ideas and suggestions.

Let your employees design and make-up in-store signage and displays (if they are qualified and with your guidance). Let them do your window displays, let them work on seasonal and promotional events.

Whatever combination of motivating factors you use, you will reap the benefits in greater sales and profits. A smooth running store, with minimum personnel problems and great esprit de corps, will allow you to feel at ease when you are away from the store.

Every well-run store must have a set of rules to protect both the owner and the workers. When any of the rules are broken, there must be some disciplinary action taken. It might range from a strong reprimand to immediate dismissal. Anytime you have to reprimand an employee, do it in writing (and have the worker sign, if possible) and place it into their personal file. If for some reason you must dismiss the employee at a later date, you will have the backup you may need. Failure to take disciplinary action when it is called for will not rest easy with your other people. "Firm but fair" is the rule of thumb. If you have to let someone go, try to get from them the reasons behind their poor actions. Maybe you will learn something and be able to prevent it from occurring again.

chapter 11

What Should You Do About Promotion?

One of the ongoing factors in the success of your store will be your desire and ability to promote. There are many types of promotion and the first you should be concerned with is the "grand opening." There are 2 schools of thought on a grand opening. One is that it should be held as close to the actual store opening as possible; the other is to delay the formal opening for 3 or 4 weeks. I favor the latter.

Those first few days when you open will be hectic enough without adding any other burdens to your feverish mind. You might have been the one who put every piece of merchandise up on the shelves, but let a customer come in and ask for a specific item and you go round in circles trying to remember where you put it. Just learning the daily swing of talking and selling to customers, suggesting and cautioning, answering questions and finally making the sale can take several days, several weeks. Piling onto that a grand opening schedule of advertising and prizes, gimmicks and ballyhoo, can be too upsetting for comfort. For that reason I suggest you get your feet on the gound and then, once you know your store, have an opening that you'll be proud to look back on.

A grand opening should encompass prizes, specials and gimmicks. Your object is to get the greatest number of people into your store in the shortest space of time, and as they say about playing an organ, you pull out all the stops. A grand opening should not be too long. A good schedule would be Friday and Saturday, or Friday, Saturday and Sunday. Local radio spots will help. Local newspaper ads are a must. You want everyone to come so the more you tell your story, the greater will be your results. You can also add flyers to your radio and newspaper advertising. Inexpensive, they should have color and zip, and can be circulated by children (trustworthy boys and girls) to houses in the community or placed under the windshield wipers of cars in every area parking lot.

Be sure you have samples on hand, all kinds of samples. If your distributor hasn't sent them with your initial inventory let him know when your grand opening will be and ask that he contact various manufacturers for samples. Any vendor with a sampling program is more than delighted to provide whatever you might need. The more samples he sends the more exposure his products obtain. Should your distributor be unable to provide whatever samples you require, ask him to write his suppliers and have the samples sent direct from the factory.

THE GRAND OPENING

You should work out a prize or give-away program for the grand opening. This can be done in the form of merchandise; it can also be in the form of money; or it can be in the form of prizes totally unrelated to the pet shop. My feeling is that prizes given in the form of pet merchandise are the most meaningful, the easiest to obtain, and will do the most to insure a return of the recipients. At least 8 weeks before the grand opening spend one evening sending letters to every manufacturer whose products you handle. These names can be obtained from your distributor or from one of the trade magazines. Your letter should explain that you are stocking their merchandise and that on such and such a day upcoming you will be having a grand opening and that you desire they participate by supplying one of the prizes to be given away at the opening. Most manufacturers, realizing the publicity and advertising value of your opening, especially when you are featuring their items, will usually donate some gift. More often than not this will be their own merchandise. They can send this to you directly or through your distributor. However it is accomplished, there will be an accumulation of merchandise, both dry goods and livestock, for your opening.

You now have the option of giving that merchandise away at the opening or translating the value of the items donated into retail dollars and giving gift certificates away instead of the actual merchandise. An example of what we mean would be: If a supplier donates 12 dozen packages of fish food for your grand opening, it would be rather awkward trying to give fish food away. However, translating that 12 dozen into what the total retail dollars would be, and then allowing the winner the value of the food in any

merchandise he might choose, would be a more efficient way of utilizing the food gift. Customers coming into the store during the opening festivities will sign a slip which they will place in a fish bowl or brandy snifter or a hamster cage, etc. Every hour or every 2 hours, depending on the amount of merchandise accumulated, you will hold a drawing, notifying the winner whether he is in the store at the time or not. Now you will not only have built up good will with those who win but you will also have the foundation of a future mailing list. Always try to have more small-size drawings rather than a few large ones. Everyone likes to win and the more winners you have the more customers you can expect in return. And that's the name of the game.

One great idea at a grand opening . . . and it's an old stunt by this time but still works like a charm . . . is the giving away of free goldfish or free tropical fish. It works everytime. Thousands of goldfish in a wading pool placed right on the floor of the store has an appeal that little else can match. You can even let the customers dip their own if they wish. Guppies work equally well. And once in a poly bag, what do the winners do if they have no food, gravel, or bowl or net, at home? Why, they buy it from you right then and there.

In many cases we have seen grand openings advertised with coupons in the ad that had to be brought into the store for the free fish. Sure, you would give them the free-bees just the same, coupon or no coupon, but it gives you some measure of the paper's ability to draw people; it also gives more value to the fish. "Two Free Goldfish Will Be Given To Each Child On Presentation Of This Coupon When Accompanied By A Parent." And if you leave room on the coupon for a name and address, you have another way of building up a mailing list.

Another useful gimmick is a "One Cent Fish Sale." Buy one at the regular price and get the second one for a penny. A guppy goes for 19¢ or 2 for 20¢. A medium black mollie goes for 69¢, the second one for a penny. But don't go too high in price with your fish on this promotion. Stay around the 89¢ level unless you have a source that will back you up all the way. What do we mean? Well, should you fail to put a ceiling on the cost of the fish to which this penny sale applies, someone will come in and buy a Betta for $2.25 and get the second one for a penny. That would be a beautiful deal for the customer but too much of that sort of thing will break your grand opening wide open. Keep the fish for this sort of special below one dollar retail and you'll be all right.

Balloons, buttons, whistles . . . all are eye stoppers and traffic getters. Nothing wrong with them. Figure that anything you spend is advertising for that one big day and the stronger you can hit, the more benefits you can reap later. But like all things, the economics of such festivities must be taken into consideration. It would be wonderful to have a catered affair with food and drink for everyone, but if that type of splurging would shorten your inventory next week, forget it. Rely on signs, newspaper advertising, samples from your suppliers and inexpensive gimmicks.

REGULAR ADVERTISING

For the multiple store operation, heavy and consistent advertising is very practical; for the single store, this degree of advertising can become a debilitating financial drain. Advertising, therefore, must be economical, well thought out and well executed. And of course, it must be effective. A man with 9 outlets has no problem running one ad, the cost of which can be economically apportioned among the stores. His choice of items for the ad is not too critical because he has 9 chances to obtain movement. And if his 9 outlets are within easy driving time of each other, his inventory problem in covering the ad is not one of great concern. As one store depletes advertised merchandise, stock can be moved in from another outlet that is not doing as well.

The best advertising advice is to "be cautious." Even before your store is open, there will be newspaper advertising salesmen knocking at your door for that half page guaranteed to bring in customers from 70 miles away. The radio ad man will be in next and the T.V. guy won't be far behind. Each is going to promise to double your business if you follow his advertising expertise. He might be right; he could be wrong.

The yellow pages of the telephone book is a time-honored, proven method of advertising. The agency salesman would love for you to subscribe for an entire page but, in fact, a 4″ by 5″ ad is more than enough for the single shop operation. In fact, for starters, a 4″ by 2½″ ad is sufficient. The difficulty with yellow pages is if you are in a large metropolitan area that publishes sectional yellow page books. You will have to decide in which books you want coverage. Or, when the agency man comes by and not only offers you more than one yellow book, adds: "You have a full-line shop, Mr. Jones. Now, do you want an ad under Pet Shops, under Dog Kennels or under Aquariums & Supplies?" Caution is necessary! With a little sales effort you could end up with 3 ads in more than one yellow page book. And that costs a bundle.

Like the yellow pages, newspaper advertising becomes a matter of how large an area you are trying to cover. If you do business in a large urban area such as Los Angeles, New York or Chicago, there is a question as to the effectiveness in advertising with a paper that covers the entire city. The exposure you need probably covers no more than a 30 mile radius from your location. Any newspaper coverage beyond decreases in effectiveness. But the advertising rate you pay is geared for the entire city and not just for the area you want. Should you be in a city the size of Cleveland, Boston or San Francisco, advertising in the classified section could generate business. This type of column exposure would blanket the city, be reasonable in cost and would be as effective a means of calling attention to your store as any.

The next advertising vehicle to consider would be that of the local newspaper. The term "local" does not necessarily imply small town; it could indicate that type of coverage given by smaller papers located in the shadow of the larger cities. These papers came into being when a new suburban development was established beyond the clamor of the large metropolis. These are community papers, county papers that fill themselves with happenings in and around a small area. Their advertising rates are usually quite low and their coverage is normally quite effective. Pet shop advertising in this sort of media can be very rewarding because not only does your advertising dollar buy more space but you are hitting only those people who shop in your area.

Radio on a regular basis is an "iffy" subject. As mentioned earlier, the multiple shop operation should be able to handle radio "spots." But single shops in a large metropolis find it hard to justify this kind of advertising outlay. Prime time is always the most expensive. And who wants to advertise at 2 a.m. if that's all their budget will allow? Again, as with the newspapers, local radio stations can offer more effective advertising simply because they are beaming your message to a higher percentage of potential customers.

Television should not be tried except in one specific situation. Many stations, large and small, run daytime features on pets. With some gentle pushing on your side, participation in the show can be obtained. It means going to the station now and again with animals that will be shown to the audience but it also means free advertising. This is the only television exposure a single store can afford.

We have discussed the obvious advertising forms. But there are many other effective and economical avenues for you to explore that are only limited by your imagination. Earlier we talked about grand opening promotions of goldfish and "one cent" tropical fish sales. These are just 2 of many such promotional

FIGURE 64 *All promotion need not be advertising. Just a few examples of promotion techniques are shown here.*

techniques that do not confine themselves to grand openings. Inexpensive handouts can be prepared for whatever special you offer. These can be distributed house to house, car to car or mailed. If you happen to be located in a mall or shopping plaza that initiates its own promotion, it becomes a matter of tailoring your specials to fit the center's theme of the moment. Sidewalk Sale, Mardi-Gras Days, pre-Christmas Sale, Circus Days . . . whatever it might be, you should be able to fit it in. If you are not situated in a shopping center and must generate your own traffic, here are some ideas that have worked over the years.

Tropical Fish Sale. . .5 for $1.00 Mix 'N Match!

This Friday, Saturday & Sunday Only. . .10 FREE Tropical Fish when you purchase this 10 Gallon Set-up at our Low Price of. . .!

Hamster FREE when you buy this attractive cage and diet kit!

Mr. M. Rice, famous German Shepherd judge and breeder, will be here from noon until 5 p.m. this Saturday to answer your questions on dog nutrition, care and training.

Come in and register now for our Valentine's Day Parrakeet & Cage Give-A-Way!

All you need is the idea, merchandise to back it up and the advertising technique to make people aware of what you are doing. Since you sell live animals that require food, remedies, litter and vitamins, there is that customer "return factor" on which you can build an advertising program. Suppose you give a small card out to each customer buying a 10 gallon tank or larger. This card could be the size and weight of a credit card. Figure 64 shows such a card. On the front side would be your advertisement with the months of the year around the edge. On the back would be room for the customer's name and address. The card would entitle the buyer of the 10 gallon tank (or whatever you would wish to use as a base) to 6 or more free tropical fish, available one per month when the customer would bring in the card. A simple paper punch could cancel the month out on the edge of the card. Such a promotion would tend to insure the customer's return once a month for as long as the free fish offer was in force and the total cost to you would never exceed $1.50 for the 6 fish. This is advertising at its cheapest. And the information on the flip side of the card would give you a built-in customer mailing list.

A similar idea would be to insert a give-away coupon in the local paper as part of your shop ad. When returned to the store, the coupon would be good for a free chew bone for the dog, a pair of fancy guppies or a partridge in a pear tree. You name it! Whatever you can use economically that will initiate the desire on the part of some reader to clip that coupon and bring it in for his freebie will cause your promotional idea to be a success. The goal is to lure as much traffic into your store as possible. How you do it depends only on your imagination!

chapter 12

Adding A
Second Store
Can Be Difficult!

Your first store is operating successfully and you are starting to think of a second store. Your commitment to this second store changes your role from owner/manager to supervisor. You will have to develop the ability to work through people; you simply won't have the time to do it all yourself. This is a function overlooked all too often. You will have to accept the fact that some decisions will be made without your knowledge and your work day and its frustrations will increase significantly. Systems and procedures (policies) will have to be developed to give your employees guidelines to work by in your absence. If you have looked at these considerations and still have a positive commitment, the next step is to decide when you and your business is ready to expand.

Timing is all encompassing. It really means that you are personally ready emotionally, financially and you have the necessary personnel with appropriate systems and procedures to go on to a second store. Let's take a look at some of these considerations and see what they are all about.

Obviously you must already have a successful business from a profit and loss standpoint. You should have been able to draw a livable salary and still show a good profit on your first store. You should be meeting all your financial commitments on a current basis. There should be enough reserve funds in the bank to carry you through a period of slack business. Take a look at your current profit and loss statement. If you don't have one, ask your accountant to make one up for you. You will need it for presentation to the bank or small business administration when applying for a loan and for getting a good look at your fixed expenses—bank notes, rent, insurance, utilities, etc.—so you can use it in planning for your expansion.

You will probably want to borrow some money for your second store (rather than use your own cash). Your business performance from your first store (P & L statement) plus security in the form of fixtures and inventories from both stores should be enough to generate a loan. You should have an estimated profit and loss statement for your new store when you apply for the loan. The key here is fixed expenses; you can always cut back on personnel, advertising and promotion. But even in the worst periods you should be able to meet your bank, rent and insurance obligations. The bank may make the loan itself or ask the Small Business Administration to guarantee it.

Equally as important as your monetary investment is your own assurance that you have qualified people to run both your original store and your second store. Hopefully, the personnel you need are already working in your current operation along with their potential replacements. If all goes well, you can have promotions all around. Everyone is happy and morale is high. But beware! Make sure you have discussed your plans with your key people. Sally may be the best salesperson, the most trustworthy, seemingly the most intelligent and obviously made to manage the second store. But does Sally want to be a manager? Does she want to drive across town, does she and her family want her to work longer hours? Only careful discussions can find out the answers and you must know these answers before you make your decision.

When you have multiple stores, your employees will be a step removed from you. As they will be talking amongst themselves, be sure you establish policies for salaries, benefits, holidays and work conditions. Make yourself available (open door) to all your people; don't shut yourself off. Make sure you personally communicate all important information so you know it can not be misinterpreted. A personnel manual is a great help. When a manager has a specific policy to adhere to there is little chance for his misinterpretation. It makes the manager feel more comfortable in his administration and it makes the employees feel they are being treated equally. And it should give you enormous peace of mind!

Adherance to Federal and state regulations regarding employees should remain your responsibility. You must, however, make your managers aware of their legal responsibilities to the store personnel and advise them on procedure should a problem arise. Having qualified, happy, well-motivated people is an ongoing job that you will find reaps untold benefits for your company and for your .

STORE SYSTEMS

Having more than one store means that you cannot be present during all routine jobs. It, therefore, becomes necessary to layout some systems and procedures for store personnel to follow. Everyone, from the manager on down, will feel more comfortable if they know what their responsibilities are. Let's just highlight some basics.

1. Store Maintenance. The cleanliness of your store and its overall appearance should be as important as hearing the cash register ring. If the customer has a pleasant shopping experience in your store, he will undoubtably return. You should set up a cleaning schedule that includes duties prior to store opening, during store hours and after closing, laying out what's to be done, how it's to be done and approximately how long it should take. This would include covering jobs such as maintenance of animals, housing/kennels, cages, displays, aquariums, feeding of animals, possible medication, restocking of livestock and dry goods and general dusting, wiping and mopping. You should also list such things as routine maintenance on your store equipment, HVAC system, compressors, hot water tanks, drains, all of which, if adhered to, will save you that big surprise expense down the road. As you develop the systems, try to spell out even the name of the products you want your people to use. You might develop a daily check-list with your managers. This would help them check themselves and give you yet another evaluation tool.

2. Merchandise Flow. In order to achieve your sales goals, you must have merchandise to sell. Whether dry goods or livestock, if it's not on the floor, it's not going to sell. You must have a method to be certain your stores will be in stock. Because the average pet shop carries so many dry goods items, it's a seemingly impossible task. As in other businesses, we have products that have very good turnover and some that have poor turnover. A starting point might be to form a "Never Out Book." This book would consist of your top 50 selling items. You would have to know sales of the item per week, the delivery time from the date you place your order and what you want to have on hand at all times. It then becomes a simple calculation to determine when and how much to order. This may be expanded to cover your entire inventory if you see fit. If you have confidence in your manager, he may fill in the book and place the order for you.

Because livestock is such a fluctuating market both in price and availability, I would recommend that all purchasing be done by yourself. The quality of your livestock cannot be compromised and you should retain tight control on this aspect of your business. Ordering weekly will obviously maximize your cash flow and minimize your out of stocks.

3. Cash Protection. All sales taken in by your store are CASH. Whether its actual cash, a charge or finance contract that you'll be reimbursed for later, its CASH. You must set up certain safeguards to insure proper handling. You should have daily register statements set up so that you can see where your sales are coming from (which department?) and have all transactions accounted for. Obviously, you want to know exactly what came in and what went out of the register. You also want the draw to be balanced daily. A daily bank deposit is mandatory (no exception), whether you do it yourself or the manager does it. Cash lying around is too great a temptation. The deposit slips can be attached to the register statements so that you can double check the cash transactions and balance to register statement and deposit slip.

Most businesses will get stuck with a bad check from time to time. Make sure you have a firm policy on checks. Use whatever you feel you need in your area to keep these losses to a minimum. Whenever possible, limit the number of people handling cash. If there is more than one person, try and give them separate draws or keys. Don't make it too tempting or you will be the one who pays.

Sales goals sometimes lead a good salesman to fudge a little on a contract to get the credit approved. Inevitably, the finance company turns down the application. Never let any financed merchandise out of the store unless you have the approval of the finance company manager. You may do a goodly portion of your business via credit cards. Are you sure your employees are processing the cards? This is cash! Check daily to see they are processing the credit charges. You might have each store manager fill out a summary of charge transactions daily and, if possible, have a separate key on the register for charges so that you can balance them out.

Everyone hates inventories but they must be done. Do them twice a year. An inventory will quickly tell you of any theft problem when you balance against your book inventory. Sure, there are probably some poor entries and a few wrong extentions, but if you are a great deal short in inventory, it's from theft.

LOCATION

A good portion of your success in your first store was probably due to location, so equally important in the search for your second store must be the location you choose. Here are some considerations when looking for a site.

a. Trading Areas-Radial Draw—How far will customers come from to shop my store? 1. In-town store (5 miles). 2. Strip Center (10 miles). 3. Regional Mall (25 miles).

b. Demographics—1. Population (In households in your area). 2. Average income per household.

c. Accessibility Roads—1. Main Roads, Rts., Highways, in area. 2. Ease of locating your shop in area.

d. Competition—1. From yourself—Your first store. 2. From others—According to the area you expect to draw from.

e. Physical Store—Based on your initial experience, does this store possess the size, lighting, frontage you need to run a smooth operation? Is it in good repair?

f. Zoning and Licensing—Be sure you check out the zoning, licensing conditions not only for a pet store but for such things as the size of the store sign you may erect, the health regulations regarding your livestock, requirements for in-store grooming.

g. Lease—The world is negotiable; so is your lease. Retain a good attorney and try to get as many concessions out of the landlord as you can, but know when to stop pushing. Each site will have some good and some bad features. You should evaluate all of them and then make your decision.

Go back and review your first store. Make a list of your successes and failures during your first opening. What should you repeat? What would you never do again? This experience will probably be your biggest asset. Based on this knowledge from your first store, things you've seen in other pet stores and ideas you've seen in other types of stores, draw a rough shop layout. Things to consider are the division of the sales floor and reserve area, placement of livestock and dry goods—wall units, gondolas, placement of check-out. All through this exercise your main consideration should be customer traffic. How do you get them to walk through your store? It is usually the combination of livestock placement and store design. The landlord will supply you with a rough print of the store for you to work with. Make several copies; you will probably change it quite a few times.

No matter where your store is located or how it is designed, you want to get identification from the walk-by, drive-by trade. The store sign is that vehicle. There are usually local township regulations on the size a sign may be (or lease restrictions) but you may sometimes get special dispensation. The bigger the better, especially in a strip center, small town or any other free standing location.

Shop around for fixtures. Many times a fixture company will help you layout your store. And remember, most studies show that women buy the larger portion of pet supplies so be sure your stock is geared to the average women shopper. If you look at some drug store fixtures for comparison, they may help you to judge size and height.

You should have down on paper just what merchandise you need to meet your customer's needs and to make an interesting and unusual presentation. If you have any over stock in your first store, you should use this merchandise first (provided it is in good condition). Your plan now becomes a buying tool. Let us say that, at cost, you have a $3,000.00 to $8,000.00 order. Go to your local distributor but be a buyer. What is he going to do for you on your initial order? Be sure to get all the store opening specials that are offered (sometimes silently) by manufacturers. Have your distributor assemble your order a week or so ahead of your schedule so as to be sure of his in-stock position. Also, if you can get your livestock suppliers to help, do so.

Open your store and run it for a week or two before you go into normal operation. You'll be able to work out the bugs. All the steps should have some timing schedule placed against them. Usually you have, upon the signing of the lease, 30 days for construction and merchandising so the more you have done ahead of time the better. Keep yourself on schedule and see that any workmen you have are on schedule as well.

The most important thing to remember is that you have people who will help you. Pet supply manufacturers, distributors and, most important, your successful experience with your first store!

ALASKA

Alascan Pet Distributors, Inc.
2803 Arctic Blvd., Anchorage, AK 99503
907—277-5824

Alaska Pet Wholesale
4233 Mt. View Dr., Anchorage, AK 99504
907—274-0941

ARIZONA

Harris Aquarium & Pet Supply Co.
2006 S. 16th St., Phoenix, AZ 85034
602-257-0753

Southwest Distributing Co.
3301 N. Park Ave., Tucson, AZ 85719
602—888-1205

CALIFORNIA

Aquarium Supplies Unlimited
11080 Talbert Ave., Fountain Valley, CA
92708
714—557-8761

Boston's Pet Supply, Inc.
P.O. Box 1818, 75 Industrial Way, Buellton,
CA 93427
805—688-3816/3844

Dog Show Specialties (Inc.)
2180 Darby St., San Bernardino, CA 92405
714—887-1825/1800

Feathers Co., Inc., Ben R.
800 E. 8th St., Oakland, CA 94606
415—452-2917

Ginn Pet Supplies, Inc., Chris
12510 S. Bellflower Blvd., Downey, CA 90242
213—869-1183

Inter American Sales
15018 Marquardt Ave., Santa Fe Springs, CA
90670
213—921-8576

Merchants Pet Supply Co.
14105 S. Avalon Blvd., Los Angeles, CA 90061
213—321-6083

Mission City Aquatics
3008 Kifer Rd., Santa Clara, CA 95051
408—246-5773

NOR-CAL Pets
115 Jordan St., San Rafael, CA 94901
415—453-3852

Norso Distributors, Inc.
8383 Capwell Dr., Oakland, CA 94621
415—632-3250

Pet Dealers Supply Co.
22361 S. Wilmington Ave., P.O. Box 4668,
Carson, CA 90745
213—549-2700

Pet Dealers Supply Co.—San Francisco Div.
175 Sylvester Rd., P.O. Box 2026, So. San
Francisco, CA 94080
415—589-3454

Pratt's Tropical Fish
155 W. 35th, Suite C, National City, CA 92050
714—426-1344

San Diego Pet & Laboratory Supply
4580 Federal Blvd., San Diego, CA 92102
714—264-6061

Trico Aquarium & Pet Products
6911 Valjean St., Van Nuys, CA 91406
213—997-7394

Westcoast Aquarium SUpply
32 Clement St., San Francisco, CA 94118
415—752-7245

Western Kennel, Inc.
9546 E. Rush St., So. El Monte, CA 91733
213—579-5833

Wright's Marine
6000-C Reseda Blvd., Tarzana, CA 91356
213—881-5600

COLORADO

All West Pet Supply Co.
1300 Lamar St., Lakewood, CO 80215
303—233-3497/4635

Mountain States Wholesale Co.
1125 S. Inca St., Denver, CO 80223
303—777-2661

Western States Wholesale Co.
3891 Forest, Denver, CO 80207
303—338-3215/6061

CONNECTICUT

Connecticut Tropical Fish Dist., Inc.
146-156 High St., Milford, CT 06460
203—877-1331

Smith-Worthington Saddlery Co.
287 Homestead Ave., Hartford, CT 06112
203—527-9117

WIllis Distributors, Inc.
1901 State St., Bridgeport, CT 06430
203—334-9485

FLORIDA

Allison Pet Supply
531 Osceola (P.O. Box 2530), Jacksonville,
FL 32203
904—388-1494

Bill Aquarium Supplies, Inc., C.
112 Robin Rd., Altamonte Springs, FL 32701
305—831-5515

Carlson's Fish Supplies
U.S. Hwy. 41 S., Gibsonton, FL 33534
813—677-9287

Crown Aquarium Supply, Inc.
680 Woodruff Ave., Jacksonville, FL 32205
904—388-6588

Exotics Unlimited
513 S. 21st Ave., Hollywood, FL 33020
305—921-4019

Florida Pet Supply, Inc.
1043 N.W. 1st Ct., Hallandale, FL 33009
305—983-7821/947-8845

Holiday Pet Supply, Ltd.
3503 Alt. 19 N., Holiday, FL 33589
813—937-8852

Kanine Products
2123 Fowler St., Fort Myers, FL 33901
813—332-2615

Nu-Age Farm Supply Co.
2826 S.W. Broadway, P.O. Box 1257, Ocala,
FL 32670
904—622-6801

Paramount Pet Supplies Inc.
Jet Port Commerce Park, 5456 Jet View
Circle, Tampa, FL 33614
813—886-7177

Peterson Pet Supply Co.
7391 NW 78th St., Miami, FL 33166
305—885-3538

Seminole Pet Supply
1013 W. 2nd St., Sanford, FL 32771
305—322-8215

Traex Distributing Co., Inc.
529 W. 28th St., Hialeah, FL 33010
305—885-1708/887-1791

GEORGIA

Bamboo Aquatic & Pet Salon
1346 S. Indian Creek Dr., P.O. Box 1227,
Decatur, GA 30031
404—294-7855

Bennett's Exotic Fish Farm, Inc.
1057 Lee St., S.W., Atlanta, GA 30310
404—755-1616

Appendix I: U.S. Pet Supply Distributors

Cappet Corp.—Atlanta Div.
5194 Minola Dr., Lithonia, GA 30058
404—981-2660

Hastings Co., H.G.
6095 Boat Rock Blvd. S.W., Atlanta, GA 30336
404—349-6600

Tucker Leather Goods Co., Inc.
3401 Lawrenceville Hwy., Tucker, GA 30084
404—938-4322

HAWAII

Hawaii Pets & Supplies, Inc.
1130 N. Nimitz Hwy., Honolulu, HI 96817
808—523-1304

Honolulu Aquarium & Pet Supplies
3209 Ualena St., Honolulu, HI 96819
808—841-8987/847-2377

Tom's Pet Supply
98-125 Lipoa Place, Aiea, HI 96701
808—488-5030

IDAHO

Pendleton Enterprises
Rt. 6 Box 24, Idaho Falls, ID 83401
208—523-3092

ILLINOIS

American Pet Supply Co.
3701 W. Touhy Ave., Chicago, IL 60645
312—674-1020

Area Pet Supply
9818 W. Farragut, Rosemont, IL 60018
312—671-3355

Auburndale Goldfish Co., Inc.
14 N. Sangamon, Chicago, IL 60607
312—421-0152/3/8

Consolidated Pet Supply, Inc.
840 Madison, Chicago, IL 60607
312—733-5896

Eddie's Pet Supplies
Rt. 1, LaSalle, IL 61301
815—223-0043

Intra-Pet Distributors
929 S. Main, Lombard, IL 60148
312—620-1556

Krause & Sons, Inc., M.P.
3450 S. Archer Ave., Chicago, IL 60608
312—247-7676

McElheney, Inc., R.H.
16975 Westview Ave., P.O. Box 497, South Holland, IL 60473
312—596-3010

Middle West Distributors
7554 Central Ave., River Forest, IL 60305
312—261-8026/369-8885

Midwest Aquarium, Inc.
639 N. Thomas Dr., Bensenville, IL 60106
312—766-4155

NAPCO Distributing Co.
2434 E. Oakton St., Elk Grove, IL 60007
312—437-5880

Pets Plus, Inc.,
19015A W. Franklin Ave., Franklin Park, IL 60131
312—451-1570

Pioneer Pet Supply Co.
3845 Carnation Ave., Franklin Park, IL 60131
312—678-3640/625-0660

Tempel's Tropical Fish & Pet Supplies
2005 E. Olive St., Decatur, IL 62526
217—423-1414/1445

INDIANA

Atlas Pet Supply, Inc.
2042 Stout Field, W. Drive, Indianapolis, IN 46241
317—247-4457

King Pet Supply, Inc.
251 2nd St., S.W., Carmel, IN 46032
317—844-1125

Sea Life Distrib. Inc.
207 Joliet St., Dyer, IN 46311
219—322-2250

IOWA

Hawkeye Seed Co., Inc.
905 Third St. SE, Cedar Rapids, IA 52401
319—364-7118

KANSAS

All Star Pet Supply
108 N. Chester, Olathe, KS 66061
913—764-4232

Dressler's Dog Supplies
1708 Steele Rd., Kansas City, KS 66106
913—722-2430

International Marine Process
7800 Kessler, Overland Park, KS 66204
913—266-8611

Kelley Aquarium & Pet Supplies Co., Inc.
601 E. 5th, P.O. Box 57, Topeka, KS 66601
913—235-5444

KENTUCKY

Storm Aquarium Supply
625 Birkhead Ave., Owensboro, KY 42301
502—926-4168

LOUISIANA

American Pet Supply
5359 Leake Ave., P.O. Box 15405, New Orleans, LA 70115
504—891-7456

Animal Industries, Inc.
3612 N. Foster Dr., Baton Rouge, LA 70805
504—356-5206

Howard's For Pets & Supplies
P.O. Box 4144, New Orleans, LA 70178

Martiny & Son, F.A.
2824 Magazine St., New Orleans, LA 70115
504—895-5701

Ozone Pet Supply, Inc.
P.O. Box 786, Berry Todd Rd., Lacombe, LA 70445
504—882-5328

MAINE

Bangor Pet, Inc.
1599 Union St., R.F.D. 3 Box 22, Bangor, ME 04401
207—942-1347

Carter, Marjorie
Tropical Fish Rd., Canaan, ME 04924
207—474-9118

New England Pet Supply, Inc.
75 York St., Portland, ME 04111
207—773-5822

Northeast Pet Supply
498 Congress St., Portland, ME 04111
207-773-6696

MASSACHUSETTS

Albon Pet Supply
343 Medford St., Somerville, MA 02145
617—776-5204

Brady Co., Inc., Joseph M.
1361 South St., Needham, MA 02192
617—444-0781

Draper Pet Supply Co., Inc.
149 Wason Ave., Springfield, MA 01107
413—781-7746/7/8

New England Serum Co., Inc.
U.S. Route 1, Topsfield, MA 01983
617—887-2368

Paradise Gardens
14 May St., Whitman, MA 02382
617—447-4711

Patnaude's Aquarium
1193 Ashley Blvd., New Bedford, MA 02745
617—995-0214

Stormont Co., John S.
335 Albion St., Wakefield, MA 01880
617—245-1550

Vet-Med Supply, Inc.
29 Dean Ave., Franklin, MA 02038
617—528-1444

MICHIGAN

Aqua Engineer Wholesale
250 Cedar St., Ortonville, MI 48462
313—627-3430

Burdick's Seed House
800 S. Washington Ave., Saginaw, MI 48607
517—753-3406

H & H Distributing Co.
410 Jackson Plaza, Ann Arbor, MI 48103
313—662-1931

Herman Bros. Sales Corp.
3005 Central Ave., Detroit, MI 48209
313—843-5444

Interfish, Inc.
3000 Middlebelt Rd., Inkster, MI 48141
313—326-5555

Wolverton, Inc.
16020 Lowell Rd., P.O. Box 28, Lansing, MI 48901
517—489-9035

MINNESOTA

AAA Pet Products
1510 Nicollet Ave., Minneapolis, MN 55403
612—336-1249

Christenson Pet Supply, Inc.
1740 Terrace Dr., St. Paul, MN 55113
612—636-4636

Mattson's Pet Supplies Inc.
3702 W. St. Germain, St. Cloud, MN 56301
612—252-5746

Northwest Wholesale Pet Supply Co.
1055 Nathan Lane No., Minneapolis, MN 55441
612—545-5611

Robbinsdale Farm & Garden Supply Inc.
4125 Railroad Ave. No., Minneapolis, MN 55422
612—533-2244

Vet-Aid Industries, Inc.
8716 Harriet Ave. S., Minneapolis, MN 55420
612-884-7494

MISSOURI

Beldt's Aquarium, Inc.
7029 Howdershell Rd., P.O. Box 146, Hazelwood, MO 63042
314—895-3356

Country Pet Supply, Inc.
3029 Olive St., St. Louis, MO 63103
314—533-5878

General Petco
Cherry St. Indus. Park, 3121 E. Elm, Springfield, MO 65802
417—865-8776

Kansas City Pet Supply
1225 Union Ave., Kansas City, MO 64101
816—221-7488

K. C. Pharmacal, Inc.
1234 Clay St., No. Kansas City, MO 64116
816—221-0779

Mo-Pet Supply, Inc.
6727 S. Broadway, St. Louis, MO 63111
314—351-6969

Prunty Seed & Grain Co.
620 N. 2nd St., St. Louis, MO 63102
314—621-0582

Vick's Aquarium & Pet Supply Co.
7248-50 Gravois Ave., St. Louis, MO 63116
314—352-3399

MONTANA

Graham & Ross Merc. Co.
815 7th St. No., Great Falls, MT 59401
406—727-2400

NEBRASKA

Nebraska Aquarium & Pet Supply
5106 S. 24th St., Omaha, NE 68107
402—731-7677

NEW YORK

All-Pet Distributors, Inc.
482 Mid Island Plaza, Hicksville, NY 11801
516—433-0026

Astro Pet Industries, Inc.
160 Orinoco Dr., Brightwaters, NY 11718
516—666-3400

Auburn Leathercrafters, Inc.
42 Washington St., Rear, Auburn, NY 13021
315—252-4107

Daleco Master Breeder Products
416 Glenalby Rd., Tonawanda, NY 14150
716—836-2582

Favor's Aquarium & Pet Supplies
251-61 Jamaica Ave., Bellerose, NY 11426
212—343-0700/516-352-0133

General Pet Supply Corp.
9 West 181st St., Bronx, NY 10453
212—584-7490

Great Eastern Pet Supply Inc.
1612 Madison St., Ridgewood, Queens, NY 11227
212—967-7300

Green Tree Pet Prod.
5020 Ave. D, Brooklyn, NY 11203
212—629-1678

Henry's Tropical Fish Hatchery
109-08 101st Ave., Richmond Hill, NY 11419
212—738-5140

Jez Dog Food Distributors, Inc.
269 Robbins Lane, Syosset, NY 11791
516—822-3310

Mohawk Pet Supply, Inc.
416 Mohawk Mall, Schenectady, NY 12304
518—374-3520

Quality Kennel Supply Ltd.
1330-B Motor Pkwy., Hauppauge, NY 11787
516—234-3732

Richter Co., Inc., Ben
85 Fifth Ave., New York, NY 10003
212—255-5373

Royal Pet Supplies
141 Central Ave., Farmingdale, NY 11735
516—293-0680

Schmidt, Alvin C.
2663 Seneca St., West Seneca, NY 14224
716—822-2969

Spring Valley Pet Supply, Inc.
24 Lake St., Spring Valley, NY 10977
914—356-1216

Syracuse Aquarium & Pet Supply, Inc.
4642 Crossroads Park Dr., Liverpool, NY 13088
315—451-0611

Stevens & Son, Inc., Walter B.
155 W. Broadway, New York, NY 10013
212—962-1157

Appendix I: U.S. Pet Supply Distributors

Suburban Pet Supply, Inc.
191 Marbledale Rd., Tuckahoe, NY 10707
914—779-3311

U.S. Specialties Co.
22-12 40th Ave., Long Island City, NY 11101
212—784-4848

Von Damm, Inc., Ace
900 Grand St., Brooklyn, NY 11211
212—782-2722

Viray Supply Co., Inc.
901 William, Buffalo, NY 14206
716—853-2799

Westchester Aquarium Supply Co., Inc.
184 Mamaroneck Ave., White Plains, NY 10601
914—948-0011

World-Wide Aquarium Supply Co., Inc.
2899 Nostrand Ave., Brooklyn, NY 11229
212-338-2420

NEW JERSEY

Animal Health Products Co.
1505 Heathwood Ave., Lakewood, NJ 08701
201—363-8460

Benro Supply Co.
269 Ellison St., Patterson, NJ 07501
201—797-6129

Central Pet Supply
221 Central Ave., Hillside, NJ 07205
201—372-5728/354-8492

Cherrybrook Distributors
Millbrook Rd., Box 15, Broadway, NJ 08808
201—689-7979

Fox Pet Foods, Inc.
East R.R. Blvd., Newfield, NJ 08344
609—697-3500

Garden State Pet Supplies, Inc.
31 Joralemon St., Belleville, NJ 07109
201—751-1416/17

Hall Co., Inc., Howard I.
291 Franklin Ave., Wyckoff, NJ 07481
201—891-5515

Kenlin Pet Supply, Inc.
118 Rte. 17, Upper Saddle River, NJ 07458
201—327-1168/9

Kennel Products Co., Inc.
474 Bloomfield Ave., Caldwell, NJ 07006
201—226-0755

Little Ferry Seed & Grain Co.
401 Liberty St., Little Ferry, NJ 07643
201—440-1344

M & G Pet Supplies Inc.
704 New York Ave., Union City, NJ 07087
201—866-0813

Reptile Aquatic Supply Co., Inc.
75 Route 208, Wyckoff, NJ 07481
201—445-3333

Ricci, Inc., Steve
291 Franklin Ave., Wyckoff, NJ 07481
201—891-2919

Steele Co., R. C.
51 Sullivan St., Westwood, NJ 07675
201—664-3343

Stirling Center Corp.
100 W. Main St., Bound Brook, NJ 08805
201—469-6988

Vanees Corporation, Inc.
84 Kent Ave., Marlton, NJ 08053
609—983-1104

NORTH CAROLINA

Ace Animal Supplies Co.
4410 Rozzells Ferry Rd., Charlotte, NC 28214
704—376-4978

Aqua Pets Supply, Inc.
2311 Eatonton St., Charlotte, NC 28208
704—399-3545

Berry Water Gardens, Inc.
P.O. Box 607, Berry Garden Rd., Kernersville, NC 27284
919—996-2611/800—334-2131

Brown's Tropical & Pet Supplies
107 Berry Garden Rd., Kernersville, NC 27284
919—993-2347

Hege's Aquarium, Inc.
P.O. Box 12, Piedmont Dr., Lexington, NC 27292
704—246-2757

Parker Seed Co.
306 S. Sampson Ave., Dunn, NC 28334
919—892-3009

NORTH DAKOTA

Lyons Den, The
1445 5th Ave. N., Fargo, ND 58102
701—235-0947

OHIO

D L Pet Supplies
R #2, Hwy. 250 South, Norwalk, OH 44857
419—668-2166

Loveland Pet Products, Inc.
3895 W. St. Rt. 3 & U.S. 22, Loveland, OH 45140
513—683-1930

Modish Craftsman Co., Inc.
1318 Kenton St., Springfield, OH 45504
513—322-5209

Oaks Feed & Pet Supply Co., Inc.
6142 Central Ave., Toledo, OH 43615
419—841-4111

Rainbow Aquarium & Pet Supply
2886 W. Market, Warren, OH 44485
216—898-5216

Tasty Foods
5219 Crookshank Rd., Cincinnati, OH 45238
513—922-0800

Verco Industries Inc.
1945 Jackson Rd., Columbus, OH 43223
614—276-6563

VIJAC, Inc.
One Angelfish Alley, Huntsburg, OH 44046
216—636-3877

OKLAHOMA

Oklahoma Pet Supply
1800 Linwood Blvd., Oklahoma City, OK 73106
405—235-8043

Roberts Dist. Co., Inc., Ray
1009 N.W. 68, Oklahoma City, OK 73116
405—848-2451

Wise Dist. Co.
3520 N.W. 23rd, Oklahoma City, OK 73107
405—946-3577/942-9007

OREGON

Arrow Pet Supply Co.
203 S. E. Alder St., Portland, OR 97214
503—233-5688

Pacoast Supply Co.
931 S.E. Sixth Ave., Portland, OR 97214
503—235-1332

Tucker Leather Goods
9003 S. E. Stark St., Portland, OR 97216
503—252-5595

PENNSYLVANIA

Bloom, Louis H.
2654 N. Reese St., Philadelphia, PA 19133
215—425-8350

Castle Pet Supply
Route 208 East, Box 253, Knox, PA 16232
814—782-3231

Decker, Inc., J.C.
Thomas Ave. (Box 127), Montgomery, PA 17752
717—547-2233

Haller & Co., Edward A.
Mars-Evans City Rd., Evans City, PA 16033
412—538-8116

Kassel Aquarium
108 Merle St., Clarion, PA 16214
814—226-9632

Leathercraft Co., The
374 Shurs La., Philadelphia, PA 19128
215—483-2277

Markey's Pet Supply
1518 Cumberland St., Lebanon, PA 17042
717—272-2111

Mechanic Co., Julius
1249 Kerper St., Philadelphia, PA 19111
215—342-0175

Nolts Ponds Inc.
3708-12 Quarry Rd., Silver Spring, PA 17575
717—285-5925

Northeastern Pet Supply Co.
103 Carbon St., Old Forge, PA 18518
717—457-9696

Pet-Master Products Co.
3439 N. Hutchinson St., Philadelphia, PA 19140
215—225-5700

Rice Pet Supply Co., Ken
R.D. 2 Box 24, Dallas, PA 18612
717—675-3505

T A Pet Supply Co.
3308 E. Thompson St., Philadelphia, PA 19134
215—426-7123

Westernesse Pet Needs
R. 50 Church St., Kingston, PA 18704
717—287-7182

Wilde's Tropical Supply
665 W. Corydon St., Bradford, PA 16701
814—362-1725

RHODE ISLAND

Petland
1465 Atwood Ave., Johnston, RI 02919
401—621-9796

Rumford Aquarium, Inc.
22 First St., East Providence, RI 02914
401—438-5476.

SOUTH CAROLINA

Carolina Pet Supplies, Inc.
R.D. #2, Box 613, Orangeburg, SC 29115
803—534-7611

C-K Products, Inc.
1411 N. Limestone St., P.O. Box 8, Gaffney, SC 29340
803—489-0549

TENNESSEE

E & S Supply Company
3083 Fleetbrook Dr., Memphis, TN 38116
901—332-2746

Mid-American Wholesale Supply Co.
2634 Faxon Ave., Memphis, TN 38112
901—323-5328

RAMFAB Aquarium Products Co.
151 Midway Lane, Oak Ridge, TN 37830
615—483-6367

TEXAS

Alamo Aquarium Supply, Inc.
400 W. Rhapsody Dr., San Antonio, TX 78216
512—341-8521

Anderson Pet Supply Co., L.E.
110 Fargo St., Houston, TX 77006
713—528-5371

Dallas Pet Products Inc.
5207 Bonita Ave., Dallas, TX 75206
214—821-0323

Fams, Inc.
9805 Monroe Rd., Houston, TX 77034
713—991-2570

Fritz Pet Products
2900 Executive Circle, Mesquite, TX 75149
214—288-6451

Hawaiian Marine Imports, Inc.
465 Town & Country Village, Houston, TX 77024
713—467-2408

House of Tropical Fish and Pet Supplies, Inc.
3316 S. Jones, Fort Worth, TX 76110
817—923-8888

K & K Sales Corp.
12936 Player St., Houston, TX 77045
713—729-1547

King-O-Pets, Inc.
1804 Texas Ave., El Paso, TX 79901
915—532-2634

Lone Star Pet Supply
2830 S. W. W. White Rd., San Antonio, TX 78220
512—337-4881

Marlin Distributors
3738 Roma Dr., Houston, TX 77055
713—462-6060

Sno-Co Supply
4622 30th St., Lubbock, TX 79410
806—795-6280

Southern Distributors
4943 Space Center, San Antonio, TX 78218
512—661-7201

Southwest Pet Supply
5737 E. Rosedale, Ft. Worth, TX 76112
817—457-0331/429-0932 (Metro)

Tamsco, Inc.
3328 N. Beckley, Lancaster, TX 75146
214—224-5511

Texas Aquarium, Inc.
3512 East T. C. Jester, Houston, TX 77018
713—688-0279

Tex-Pet Co.
806B McPhaul Rd., Austin, TX 78758
512—837-5182

UTAH

Bailey & Sons Co.
380 W. 5th So., Salt Lake City, UT 84110
801—532-3243

Edwards Pet Supplies Co.
733 W. Genesee Ave. (840 S.), Salt Lake City, UT 84104
801—328-3642

Tropical Pets & Supplies
1681 East 4500 South, Salt Lake City, UT 84109
801—277-4292

VIRGINIA

Cappet Corporation
4630 Eisenhower Ave., Alexandria, VA 22304
703—370-2300

Erickson Co., Inc., Roy
44 Waterman Dr., Harrisonburg, VA 22801
703—433-2761

Appendix I: U.S. Pet Supply Distributors

Appendix I:
U.S.
Pet Supply
Distributors

Schley's Hatchery & Distg. Co.
5212 Willow Lake Rd., Chesapeake, VA 23321
804—488-6554

Silverman & Co., Inc.
30 S. Quaker Lane, Alexandria, VA 22314
703—751-6046

Virginia Fisheries, Inc.
701—703 N. Daniel St., Arlington, VA 22201
703—527-6565/66

WASHINGTON

Avi-Cult Distributing Co.
118 105th Ave. NE, Bellevue, WA 98004
206—455-0696

Cascade Seed Co.
E. 121 Desmet, Spokane, WA 99220
509—327-6638

Marks and Thomas Wholesale, Inc.
858 Lind Ave. S.W., Renton, WA 98055
206—624-4833

Perrin Brothers, Inc.
27215 124th S.E., Kent, WA 98031
206—631-3210/3010

Puget Sound Pet Supply Co., Inc.
1122 S. W. Spokane St., Seattle, WA 98134
206—682-8655

WEST VIRGINIA

Pinnacle Pet Supply Co.
440 Central Ave., Oak Hill, WV 25901
304—469-9412

WISCONSIN

General Pet Supply, Inc.
3227 N. 31st St., Milwaukee, WI 53216
414—445-3111

Great Lakes Pet Supply
2111 E. Norse Ave., Cudahy, WI 53110
414—769-6011

Standard Leather & Pet Supplies Corp.
6030 N. 77th St., Milwaukee, WI 53218
414—466-0850

Appendix II: Product Inventory Check-list

AQUARIUM PRODUCTS

AQUARIUMS AND TANK ACCESSORIES
Profit 20-25%
Annual Turns 18
Aquariums
  All Glass
  All Plastic
  Betta
  Bowl
  Custom Built
  Regular (framed)
  Specialties
Profit 40 %
Annual Turns 12
Aquarium Stands
Cements and Sealers
Covers
Fixtures, aquarium display
Hoods
Lights
Nets, dip
Outlet, multiple electric
Reflectors
Tank divider

BREEDING PRODUCTS
Profit 48 %
Annual Turns 10
Breeding traps
Spawning materials
  Grass
  Mops
  Other

CLEANING EQUIPMENT
Profit 45 %
Annual Turns 7
Air operated
Battery operated
Electrically operated
Liquid
Manually operated
Other

FILTERS AND FILTERING MATERIALS/ACCESSORIES
Profit 50 %
Annual Turns 16
Filters
  Air operated
  Motor-driven
Profit 50 %
Annual Turns 10
Filter accessories
  Siphons
  Siphon starter
  Tubes
  Other
Profit 55 %
Annual Turns 24
Filtering materials
  Pre-filters
  Purifying mediums
Sterilizers, ultraviolet

DECORATIONS (TANK) INCLUDING PLANTS
Profit 50 %
Annual Turns 8
Air releasers
  Ceramic
  Metal
  Plastic
  Other
Bottom coverings
  Coral
  Glass
  Gravel
  Gravel guard
  Plastic
  Rocks
  Shells
  Other
Decorative backings
Inside
  Glass
  Plastic
  Rock
  Other
Outside
  Foil
  Lighted background
  Paint
  Paper
  Plastic
  Other
Decorative frames, outside
Foregrounds
Ornaments
  Ceramic
  Ceramic, lighted
  Lights, underwater
  Metal
  Optical fibers
  Plastic
  Wood
  Other
Plants
  Floating
  Pre-potted
Plant accessories
  Anchors
  Stays
  Tongs & Snips
  Tool Kits

FEEDERS & ACCESSORIES
Profit 45 %
Annual Turns 7
Feeders
  Electrical
  Mechanical
  Worm
Feeding rings
Feeding tongs

FOOD
Profit 50-55 %
Annual Turns 20
Compressed
Dried
Freeze-dried
Frozen
Insect eggs
Liquid
Paste
Plant
Other

HEALTH AIDS FISH & PLANT
Profit 45-50 %
Annual Turns 7
Plant cleaners
Snail control
Tranquilizers
Treatments/Preventives
  Fish
  Plant
Treatment/Preventive kits
Vitamins
  Fish
  Plant
Other

HEATERS & HEAT CONTROLS
Profit 45 %
Annual Turns 8
Heaters
  Non-submersible
  Submersible
Thermostats
Thermostat/Heater Combination
Thermometers
Other

POOLS & ACCESSORIES
Profit 48 %
Annual Turns 2
Algicides
Chlorine removers
Filters
Fountains
Fountain kits
Fountain lights
Fungicides
Pool liner
Pools, plastic
Pumps
Spray rings
Waterfalls
Waterfall kits
Other

PUMPS & ACCESSORIES
Profit 45 %
Annual Turns 14
Pumps
  Air-pressure type
  Air-vacuum type
Pump accessories
  Aerating connector
  Air stones
  Air tubing
  Air valves
  Check valves
  Connectors, T & Cross
  Gauges
  Lubricants
  Platforms for Air Pumps
  Pressure tanks
Pump kits

WATER CONDITIONERS & ACCESSORIES
Profit 45-50 %
Annual Turns 7
Algicides
Chlorine removers
Clarifiers
Hydrometers
Multipurpose
Neutralizers
Purifiers
Softeners
Test kits
  Hardness
  Metals
  pH
  Other

MISCELLANEOUS PRODUCTS, SERVICES
Profit 50 %
Annual Turns 3
Aquarium kits
Diagnostic services
Fish containers, individual
Fish mobiles
Greeting cards
Hatching kits
Hatching salt mix
Light timer

Records, care
Trophies
Other

SALTWATER PRODUCTS

Profit 50-55 %
Annual Turns 7
Aquariums
  All glass
  All Plastic
  Custom Built
  Regular (framed)
  Specialties
Aquarium kits
Conditioner, water
Decorations
  Backing
  Ceramic
  Coral
  Glass
  Plastic
  Pottery
  Rock
  Sand
  Shells
  Other
Diagnostic services
Filters
Filtering materials
Feeding stimulant
Food
  Compressed
  Dried
  Freeze-dried
  Frozen
  Insect Eggs
  Paste
  Plant
Gravel
Hydrometers
Lights
Medications
Nets
Neutralizers
Ozone generators
Plastic tubing
Pump accessories
  Air tubing
  Air valves
  Connectors, T & cross
Reflectors
Salts
Sealers
Slurp guns
Sterilizers
Testing kits
  Ammonia
  Chlorine
  Copper
  Nitrite
  pH
  Other
Treatments/Preventives
Vitamins
Other

TERRARIUM PRODUCTS

Profit 50 %
Annual Turns 10
Terrariums
  Glass
  Plastic
Terrarium stands
Bottom coverings
  Coral
  Glass
  Gravel
  Gravel guard
  Plastic
  Rocks
  Sand
  Shells
  Other
Ornaments
  Ceramic
  Ceramic, lighted
  Metal
  Optical fibers
  Plastic
  Wood
Plants
  Live
  Plastic
Miscellaneous
  Conversion kits
  Heaters
  Hoods
  Other

BIRD PRODUCTS

BREEDING & NESTING PRODUCTS
Profit 40 %
Annual Turns 3
Cages
  Metal
  Plastic
  Other
Incubators
Leg bands
Leg band cutters
Nest bowls (pigeon/dove)

Nest boxes
Nest eggs (dummy, pigeon/dove/canary)
Nests
  Hair
  Plastic
  Rattan
  Wire

CAGES & ACCESSORIES
Profit 40 %
Annual Turns 3
Bird baths
Bird showers
Cages
  Metal
  Plastic
Covers
Fronts
Litter, cage
Perches
Perch cleaners & scrapers
Springs
Stands, cage
Stands, parrot-like birds
Other

FEEDING PRODUCTS
Profit 45 %
Annual Turns 4
Cup holders
Feeders, cups
Self-feeder
Gravel
  Bulk
  Packaged
Gravel paper
Grit
Water Bottles

FOODS
Profit 40-45 %
Annual Turns 7
Food, bulk
Food, canned
Food, packaged
Treats
Other

GROOMING TOOLS
Profit 40 %
Annual Turns 3
Bill cutters
Claw scissors
Nail clippers
Nail files
Preening scissors

HEALTH AIDS
Profit 40-45 %
Annual Turns 5
Anti-plucking liquid (feathers)
Beak conditioner
Cuttlebone
Cuttlebone holders
Deodorizer, bird cage
Disinfectants
Insecticides
Minerals & vitamins
Mineral blocks & cubes
Purifier, water
Supplements
Treatments/Preventives
Vitamins

TOYS & EXERCISE EQUIPMENT
Profit 45-50 %
Annual Turns 5
Plastic
Wood

TRAINING DEVICES
Profit 40 %
Annual Turns 3
Records, Care & Training

MISCELLANEOUS PRODUCTS SERVICES
Profit 40 %
Annual Turns 3
Aviary fountains
Carriers, bird
Caskets
Chains
Diagnostic services
Nets
Shipping boxes
Trophies
Urns
Wall plaques
Other

WILD BIRD PRODUCTS

BATHS & FOUNTAINS
Profit 40 %
Annual Turns 2
Baths
Fountains, bath
Water warmer

FOODS & FEEDERS
Profit 40 %

Appendix II: Product Inventory Check-list

Annual Turns 6
Accessories
  Bee guard (hummingbird feeder)
  Squirrel guard
  Posts
Feeders
  Combination (with waterer)
  Hummingbird
  Kits
  Metal
  Plastic
  Post type
  Post type (with squirrel guard)
  Suet cake holders
  Wood
  Other
Profit 38 %
Annual Turns 9
Food
  Bulk seed
  Compressed
  Hummingbird
  Packaged mixtures
  Peanut Hearts
  Peanut suet
  Suet cakes
  Other
Health Aids
  Vitamins
  Vitamins & minerals

HOUSES

Profit 40 %
Annual Turns 4
House poles
Housing
  Kits
  Look in
  Plastic
  Wood

MISCELLANEOUS PRODUCTS/SERVICES

Profit 40 %
Annual Turns 2
Diagnostic services
Traps
Others

CAT PRODUCTS

BEDS & BEDDING

Profit 40 %
Annual Turns 6
Beds
  Metal
  Plastic
  Wicker
  Wire
  Wood
  Other
Covers
Cushions, mats, mattresses
  Heated
  Unheated
Pillows
Shavings
  Cedar
  Pine
  Other

CATNIP ITEMS

Profit 40 %
Annual Turns 7
Leaves
Oil
Spray

COLLARS, HARNESSES & LEADS

Profit 45-50 %
Annual Turns 6
Collars
  Chain
  Jeweled
  Leather
  Mylar
  Nylon
  Plastic
  Suede
  Velvet
  Other
Harnesses
Leads
  Chain
  Jeweled
  Leather
  Mylar
  Nylon
  Plastic
  Suede
  Velvet
  Other
Tie-outs
  Leads
  Stakes
  Trolleys
  Other

FEEDING PRODUCTS

Profit 45 %
Annual Turns 7
Dish (applies to single units only)
  Aluminum
  Ceramic
  Glass

Marble
Paper
Plastic
Plastic, weighted
Rubber
Stainless steel
Stoneware
Wall-bracketed
Other
Dining units (applies to units of multiple construction)
  Aluminum
  Ceramic
  Plastic
  Plastic, weighted
  Stainless steel
  Stoneware
  Wall-bracketed
Feeders
  Self
Nursing bottles
Nursing kits
Place mats
Waterers, self

FOODS, SUPPLEMENTS, TREATS

Profit 40 %
Annual Turns 8
Dry
Canned
Semi-moist
Special foods
  Cystitis
  Geriatric
  Milk replacer
  Nephritis
  Obesity
  Other
Supplements
  Fats & oils
  Minerals
  Mineral oil
  Protein
  Vitamins
  Treats

GROOMING AIDS

Profit 40 %
Annual Turns 5
Brushes
Clipper Disinfectant
Coat conditioners
Combs
Deodorants
Dryers
Nail clippers
Nail files
Nail scissors
Rinses
Shampoos

HEALTH AIDS

Profit 40 %
Annual Turns 7
Appetite control
Flea killers
  Collars
  Metal trap
  Powder
  Shampoo
  Soap
  Spray
  Tags
  Other
Tick Killers
  Collars
  Powder
  Shampoo
  Soap
  Spray
  Tags
Fungicides
Insecticides
Thermometers
Treatments/Preventives
  External
    Dentifrice
    Ear medications
    Eye solutions
    Skin treatments
  Internal
    Coat conditioner
    Constipation
    Cough
    Dehydration
    Deodorant
    Diarrhea (symptom)
    Digestion
    Fever (symptom)
    Flea control
    Hair balls
    Skin treatments
    Tranquilizers
    Worm treatments

HOUSES, CARRIERS & CRATES

Profit 40 %
Annual Turns 8
Cages
Carrying cases
Display crates
Doors
Houses
Shipping crates
Other

LITTER & LITTER ACCESSORIES

Profit 40 %
Annual Turns 10
Cat pan filler
  Alfalfa
  Cedar shavings
  Clay
  Diatom, earth
  Ground corn cobs
  Sand
  Sawdust
  Silica
  Other
Deodorizers
Pans
  Metal
  Paperboard
  Plastic
Litter spoons
Pan liner
Screens, litter
Screens, privacy
Other

REPELLENTS

Profit 40 %
Annual Turns 7
Anti-insect
Anti-mate
Indoor
Outdoor

SANITATION PRODUCTS

Profit 40 %
Annual Turns 4
Cleaners
Disinfectants
Pick-up tools

TOYS

Profit 50 %
Annual Turns 8
Catnip scented or filled
(L-Loose or C-Carded)
  Cork
  Fabric
  Fur
  Plastic
  Rawhide
  Rubber
  Vinyl
  Other
Without catnip
  Fabric
  Fur
  Plastic
  Rawhide
  Rubber
  Vinyl
Scratching posts, catnip scented
  Animated
  Multilevel
  Stationary
Scratching posts, unscented
  Animated
  Multilevel
  Stationary

MISCELLANEOUS PRODUCTS/SERVICES

Profit 45 %
Annual Turns 2
Bows
Burial markers
Car seats
Caskets
Diagnostic services
Display cases
Gift wrap
Heraldry
Identification
  Purses
  Tags
  Tubes
Jewelry
Lint remover
Signs
Stationery
Training devices
Trophies
Urns
Wall plaques
Other

DOG PRODUCTS

BEDS & BEDDING

Profit 40 %
Annual Turns 7
Beds
  Metal
  Plastic
  Wicker
  Wire
  Wood
  Other
Covers
Cushions, mats, mattresses
  Heated
  Unheated
Pillows
Shavings
  Cedar
  Pine
  Other

CHEW PRODUCTS

Profit 45-50 %
Annual Turns 10
Gelatin
Leather
Natural, sterilized
Nylon
Plastic
Rawhide
Rubber
Other

CLOTHES & JEWELRY

Profit 48 %
Annual Turns 3
Bath robes
Boots
Coats
  Adjustable
  Sized
  Custom tailored
  Lined coats
  Rain
Glasses, sun
Hats (caps & berets)
Identification
  Purses
  Tags
  Tubes
Jewelry (costume)
Pajamas
Ribbons & ornaments
Sanitary belts for females in season
  Regular
  With anti-mate deodorant
Sanitary pads
Sweaters
Other

COLLARS, LEADS, ALLIED ITEMS

Profit 45-50 %
Annual Turns 5
Collars
  Cable
  Fancy
  Choke
    Chain
    Leather
    Nylon
    Other
  Leather: round, flat, braided
  Mylar
  Nylon
  Plastic: round, flat, braided
  Studded
  Suede
  Training
  Vinyl
Couplers
  Chain
  Leather
  Nylon
  Other
Fence, chain snag
Harnesses, regular
  Leather
  Plastic
  Other
Harnesses, sled dog
  Leather
  Plastic
  Other
Leads (leashes)
  Fabric
  Leather
  Metal, bead
  Metal, chain
  Mylar
  Nylon
  Plastic
  Retractable
  Show
  Traffic
  Training
  Vinyl
  Other
Muzzles
  Leather
  Plastic
  Plastic-covered wire
  Wire
Padlocks
Tie-outs
  Leads
  Stakes
  Trolleys
  Other

FEEDING PRODUCTS

Profit 45 %
Annual Turns 7
Dishes (applies to single units only)
  Aluminum
  Aluminum, weighted
  Ceramic
  Glass
  Marble
  Plastic
  Plastic, weighted
  Rubber
  Stainless steel
  Stoneware
Dining units (applies to units of multiple construction)
  Aluminum
  Ceramic
  Plastic

Plastic, weighted
Stainless steel
Feeders
　Self
　Time-controlled
Place mats
Nursing bottles
Nursing kits
Waterers
　Self
Other

FOODS, SUPPLEMENTS, TREATS
Profit 40 %
Annual Turns 8
Dry (complete foods)
Canned
Special foods
　Geriatric
　Intestinal
　Kidney
　Milk replacer
　Obesity
　Puppy
　Other
Semi-moist
　Non-refrigerated
Supplements
　Fats (fatty acids)
　Fats & vitamins
　Minerals
　Protein
　Vitamins
　Vitamins & minerals
　Vit.-min.-protein
Treats

GROOMING & HANDLING PRODUCTS
Profit 40 %
Annual Turns 8
Aprons
Bath tubs
Brushes
Brushes, powered
Clippers & blades for trimming
　Electric
　Hand
Clipper attachments
Clipper cleaner
Clipper disinfectant
Clipper lubricant
Clipper sets
Clipper sharpeners
Coat conditioners
Colognes
Combs
　Flea
　Grooming, general
　Rake
　Stripping
　Other
Deodorants (not repellents)
Dryers
Dryer stand
Eye stain remover
Grooming gloves
　Bristle
　Wire
　Wire/bristle combo.
Grooming kit
Mat (tangle) splitters
Nail clippers
　Electric
　Manual
Nail files
Nail polish
Nail scissors
Posts, grooming
Scissors
　Ear & nose
　Thinning
　Trimming
Shampoos
Signs
Slings, grooming
Strippers
Tables, grooming
Tangle removers
Towels
Other

HEALTH AIDS
Profit 40 %
Annual Turns 8
Appetite control
Breath purifiers
Health care kits
Flea killers
　Collars
　Metal trap
　Powder
　Shampoo
　Soap
　Spray
　Tags
Tick killers
　Collars
　Powder
　Shampoo
　Soap
　Spray
　Tags
　Other
Fungicides
Insecticides
Thermometers
Treatments/Preventives
External
　Dentifrice
　Ear medications
　Eye solutions
　Foot pad conditioner
　Skin treatments
Internal
　Coat conditioner
　Constipation
　Cough
　Dehydration
　Deodorant
　Diarrhea (symptom)
　Digestion
　Fever (symptom)
　Flea control
　Skin treatments
　Tranquilizers
Worm treatments
　Adult
　Puppy
Water purifiers

HOUSING (PORTABLE) & STATIONARY
Profit 40 %
Annual Turns 4
Cages
　Single units
　Stacking
　Other
Carrying cases
Display crates
Doors
Gates
Houses
　Collapsible
　Insulated
　Regular
Pens, exercise
Shipping crates
Other

REPELLENTS
Profit 40 %
Annual Turns 7
Anti-attack
Anti-insect
Anti-mate
Indoor
Outdoor

SANITATION PRODUCTS
Profit 40 %
Annual Turns 4
Cleaners
Deodorizers
Digester, organic
Incinerators
Odor control
　For resale
　Shop use
Pick-up tools

TOYS
Profit 45-50 %

Annual Turns 8
Burlap
Latex
Plastic
Rubber
Vinyl
Other

TRAINING PRODUCTS
Profit 40 %
Annual Turns 4
Hardwood dumbbells
Housebreaking products
Hunting
　Scents
　Training kits
　Other
Records
　Pet care
　Pet training
Scent discrimination kit
Training glove
Training sleeve
Training sticks
Training suits (worn by trainer)
Whistles
　Audible
　Silent

MISCELLANEOUS
Profit 40 %
Annual Turns 2
Animal styled furniture
Bike baskets
Burial markers
Car safety belts
Car seats
Caskets
Decals
Diagnostic services
Display animals
Display cases
Greeting cards
Heraldry
Life preservers
Lint pickup
Paintings
Pedigree blanks
Pedigree service
Rack, clothes
Record books
　Breeding
　Grooming
Signs
Stationery
Tattoo kits
Trophies
Urns
Wall plaques
Whelping
　Boxes
　Cages
Other

GERBIL/HAMSTER PRODUCTS
Profit 45 %
Annual Turns 7
Absorbents, litter
　Alfalfa
　Clay
　Fiber
　Ground corn cobs
　Shavings
　Other
Brushes
Chew products
Coat spray
Deodorant, aerosol litter
Diagnostic services
Diet kit
Food, gerbil
Food, hamster
Profit 45 %
Annual Turns 7
Feeders
Housing
　Glass
　Metal
　Plastic
　Other
Leashes
Nesting material

Records, care & training
Supplements
Toys
Profit 40 %
Annual Turns 12
Treats
Treatments/Preventives
Vitamins
Vitamins & minerals
Profit 45 %
Annual Turns 7
Water bottles & fountains
Water bottle holders
Wheels
Other

GUINEA PIG/ RABBIT PRODUCTS
Profit 45 %
Annual Turns 7
Absorbents, litter
　Alfalfa
　Clay
　Fiber
　Ground corn cobs
　Shavings
　Other
Brushes
Chew products
Diagnostic services
Feeders
Profit 40 %
Annual Turns 12
Food
Profit 45 %
Annual Turns 7
Housing
　Glass
　Metal
　Plastic
　Other
Hutches
Records, care & training
Supplements
Tattoo kits
Vitamins
Vitamins & minerals
Waterers
Other

HERPTILE PRODUCTS
Profit 50 %
Annual Turns 1½
Aquarium converter
Cages
Chameleon cage
Diagnostic services
Food
Handling stick
Terrariums
Terrarium screen
Tongs & hooks
Treatments/Preventives
Vitamins
Vitamins & minerals
Other

OTHER PET PRODUCTS
Profit 40-45 %
Annual Turns 7-12
Absorbents, litter
Alfalfa
Clay
Fiber
Ground corn cobs
Shavings
Other
　Animal traps
　Ant products
　Brushes, pet
　Chew products
　Diagnostic services
　Houses, small animal
　Incubator
　Mice and rat food
　Mice and rat products
　Mink and chinchilla supplements

Appendix II: Product Inventory Check-list